Linux® Administration For Dummies®

Cheat Sheet

Essential Commands and Shortcuts

Command Option	What It Does
ArrowUp	Scrolls and edits the comma...
Shift+PgUp	Scrolls terminal output up.
Shift+PgDown	Scrolls terminal output down.
Ctrl+Alt++	Changes to the next X server resolution. (Of course, you need to have X Windows for this to work.)
Ctrl+Alt+BkSpc	Kills the current X Windows server. Again, you need to be running X Windows for this to work.
Ctrl+Alt+Del	Shuts down and reboots the system.
Ctrl+c	Kills the current process.
Ctrl+s	Stops the transfer to the terminal.
Ctrl+q	Resumes the transfer to the terminal.
Ctrl+z	Puts a current process into the background.
MiddleMouseButton	Pastes the text that is currently highlighted somewhere else.

Common Linux Commands

Command Option	What It Does
pwd	Displays the name of the current directory on the screen.
hostname	Displays the name of the machine on which you are working.
whoami	Displays your login name.
date	Displays the date your machine thinks it is.
who	Displays the users currently logged on the machine.
rwho –a	Shows all users logged on your network. The rwho service must be enabled for this command to run.
finger <user_name>	Shows information about a selected user account.
last	Shows listing of users last logged in on your system.
uptime	Shows amount of time since last reboot.
ps	Lists all processes.
uname –a	Displays all info on your host.
free	Displays number of kilobytes of free memory.
df –h	Prints disk info about all the file systems.
cat /proc/cpuinfo	Shows information on your host's CPU.
cat /proc/filesystems	Shows the types of file systems currently in use.
cat /etc/printcap	Shows the setup of printers.
Lsmod	Shows the kernel modules currently loaded. You can only run this as root.
set|more	Shows the current user environment.
echo $PATH	Shows the content of the environment variable PATH.
dmesg	Prints the boot messages. (It displays the file /var/log/dmesg.)

...For Dummies®: Bestselling Book Series for Beginners

Linux® Administration For Dummies®

Cheat Sheet

Basic Operational Commands

Command Option	What It Does
ls	Lists the content of the current directory.
cd <directory>	Changes directory. Using cd without the directory name takes you to your home directory.
cp <source> <destination>	Copies files.
mv <source> <destination>	Moves or renames files.
ln -s source destination	Creates a symbolic link.
rm	Removes files.
mkdir <directory_name>	Makes a new directory.
rmdir <directory>	Removes a directory. **Note:** If you have files in the directory, you'll need to use rm –r.
tar -xvf filename	Untars a tarball file.
find / -name "filename"	Finds the file filename on your file system starting from the root directory.
pine	A good text-mode mail reader. Another good standard one is elm.
talk <username>	Talks to another user currently logged on your host.
telnet <machine_name>	Connects to another machine using the Telnet protocol.
rlogin <machine_name>	Connects to another machine.
rsh <machine_name>	Yet another way to connect to a remote machine.
ftp <machine_name>	Ftps another machine.
xinit	Starts a bare X Windows server (without a Windows manager).
startx	Starts an X Windows server and the default Windows manager
xterm	Runs a simple X Windows terminal. Typing **exit** closes it.
xboing	An X Windows game.
netscape	Runs Netscape (requires a separate Netscape installation if you're not using Red Hat Linux).
netscape -display host:0.0	Runs Netscape on the current machine and directs the output to machine named host display 0 screen 0. (An X Windows command only.)
shutdown -h now	Shuts down the system to a halt. Must be root.
halt	
reboot	

...For Dummies®: Bestselling Book Series for Beginners

LINUX®
Administration
FOR
DUMMIES®

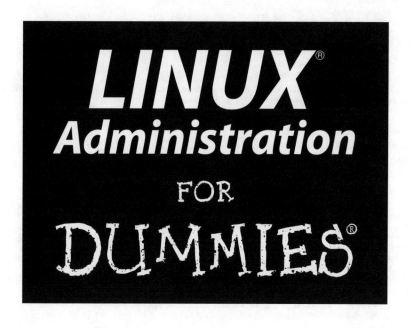

LINUX® Administration FOR DUMMIES®

by Michael Bellomo

IDG Books Worldwide, Inc.
An International Data Group Company

Foster City, CA ◆ Chicago, IL ◆ Indianapolis, IN ◆ New York, NY

Linux® Administration For Dummies®

Published by
IDG Books Worldwide, Inc.
An International Data Group Company
919 E. Hillsdale Blvd.
Suite 400
Foster City, CA 94404
www.idgbooks.com (IDG Books Worldwide Web site)
www.dummies.com (Dummies Press Web site)

Library of Congress Catalog Card No.: 99-66120

ISBN: 0-7645-0589-0

Printed in the United States of America

10 9 8 7 6 5 4 3 2

1B/RQ/QZ/ZZ/IN

Distributed in the United States by IDG Books Worldwide, Inc.

Distributed by CDG Books Canada Inc. for Canada; by Transworld Publishers Limited in the United Kingdom; by IDG Norge Books for Norway; by IDG Sweden Books for Sweden; by IDG Books Australia Publishing Corporation Pty. Ltd. for Australia and New Zealand; by TransQuest Publishers Pte Ltd. for Singapore, Malaysia, Thailand, Indonesia, and Hong Kong; by Gotop Information Inc. for Taiwan; by ICG Muse, Inc. for Japan; by Intersoft for South Africa; by Eyrolles for France; by International Thomson Publishing for Germany, Austria and Switzerland; by Distribuidora Cuspide for Argentina; by LR International for Brazil; by Galileo Libros for Chile; by Ediciones ZETA S.C.R. Ltda. for Peru; by WS Computer Publishing Corporation, Inc., for the Philippines; by Contemporanea de Ediciones for Venezuela; by Express Computer Distributors for the Caribbean and West Indies; by Micronesia Media Distributor, Inc. for Micronesia; by Chips Computadoras S.A. de C.V. for Mexico; by Editorial Norma de Panama S.A. for Panama; by American Bookshops for Finland.

For general information on IDG Books Worldwide's books in the U.S., please call our Consumer Customer Service department at 800-762-2974. For reseller information, including discounts and premium sales, please call our Reseller Customer Service department at 800-434-3422.

For information on where to purchase IDG Books Worldwide's books outside the U.S., please contact our International Sales department at 317-596-5530 or fax 317-596-5692.

For consumer information on foreign language translations, please contact our Customer Service department at 1-800-434-3422, fax 317-596-5692, or e-mail rights@idgbooks.com.

For information on licensing foreign or domestic rights, please phone +1-650-655-3109.

For sales inquiries and special prices for bulk quantities, please contact our Sales department at 650-655-3200 or write to the address above.

For information on using IDG Books Worldwide's books in the classroom or for ordering examination copies, please contact our Educational Sales department at 800-434-2086 or fax 317-596-5499.

For press review copies, author interviews, or other publicity information, please contact our Public Relations department at 650-655-3000 or fax 650-655-3299.

For authorization to photocopy items for corporate, personal, or educational use, please contact Copyright Clearance Center, 222 Rosewood Drive, Danvers, MA 01923, or fax 978-750-4470.

About the Author

Michael Bellomo received a degree in law from the University of California, Hastings College of the Law in San Francisco. Despite this awful start, he moved into the technical field and became certified in UNIX System Administration for the University of California, Santa Cruz. Currently, Michael is a Linux Network Manager. He recently contributed to IDG Books' *Linux For Dummies,* 2nd Edition.

ABOUT IDG BOOKS WORLDWIDE

Welcome to the world of IDG Books Worldwide.

IDG Books Worldwide, Inc., is a subsidiary of International Data Group, the world's largest publisher of computer-related information and the leading global provider of information services on information technology. IDG was founded more than 30 years ago by Patrick J. McGovern and now employs more than 9,000 people worldwide. IDG publishes more than 290 computer publications in over 75 countries. More than 90 million people read one or more IDG publications each month.

Launched in 1990, IDG Books Worldwide is today the #1 publisher of best-selling computer books in the United States. We are proud to have received eight awards from the Computer Press Association in recognition of editorial excellence and three from Computer Currents' First Annual Readers' Choice Awards. Our best-selling ...For Dummies® series has more than 50 million copies in print with translations in 31 languages. IDG Books Worldwide, through a joint venture with IDG's Hi-Tech Beijing, became the first U.S. publisher to publish a computer book in the People's Republic of China. In record time, IDG Books Worldwide has become the first choice for millions of readers around the world who want to learn how to better manage their businesses.

Our mission is simple: Every one of our books is designed to bring extra value and skill-building instructions to the reader. Our books are written by experts who understand and care about our readers. The knowledge base of our editorial staff comes from years of experience in publishing, education, and journalism — experience we use to produce books to carry us into the new millennium. In short, we care about books, so we attract the best people. We devote special attention to details such as audience, interior design, use of icons, and illustrations. And because we use an efficient process of authoring, editing, and desktop publishing our books electronically, we can spend more time ensuring superior content and less time on the technicalities of making books.

You can count on our commitment to deliver high-quality books at competitive prices on topics you want to read about. At IDG Books Worldwide, we continue in the IDG tradition of delivering quality for more than 30 years. You'll find no better book on a subject than one from IDG Books Worldwide.

John Kilcullen
Chairman and CEO
IDG Books Worldwide, Inc.

Steven Berkowitz
President and Publisher
IDG Books Worldwide, Inc.

Eighth Annual
Computer Press
Awards ≥1992

Ninth Annual
Computer Press
Awards ≥1993

WINNER
Tenth Annual
Computer Press
Awards ≥1994

WINNER
Eleventh Annual
Computer Press
Awards ≥1995

IDG is the world's leading IT media, research and exposition company. Founded in 1964, IDG had 1997 revenues of $2.05 billion and has more than 9,000 employees worldwide. IDG offers the widest range of media options that reach IT buyers in 75 countries representing 95% of worldwide IT spending. IDG's diverse product and services portfolio spans six key areas including print publishing, online publishing, expositions and conferences, market research, education and training, and global marketing services. More than 90 million people read one or more of IDG's 290 magazines and newspapers, including IDG's leading global brands — Computerworld, PC World, Network World, Macworld and the Channel World family of publications. IDG Books Worldwide is one of the fastest-growing computer book publishers in the world, with more than 700 titles in 36 languages. The "...For Dummies®" series alone has more than 50 million copies in print. IDG offers online users the largest network of technology-specific Web sites around the world through IDG.net (http://www.idg.net), which comprises more than 225 targeted Web sites in 55 countries worldwide. International Data Corporation (IDC) is the world's largest provider of information technology data, analysis and consulting, with research centers in over 41 countries and more than 400 research analysts worldwide. IDG World Expo is a leading producer of more than 168 globally branded conferences and expositions in 35 countries including E3 (Electronic Entertainment Expo), Macworld Expo, ComNet, Windows World Expo, ICE (Internet Commerce Expo), Agenda, DEMO, and Spotlight. IDG's training subsidiary, ExecuTrain, is the world's largest computer training company, with more than 230 locations worldwide and 785 training courses. IDG Marketing Services helps industry-leading IT companies build international brand recognition by developing global integrated marketing programs via IDG's print, online and exposition products worldwide. Further information about the company can be found at www.idg.com. 1/24/99

Dedication

To my friends.

Author's Acknowledgments

Thanks to Linus, for creating this. My family has been consistently supportive; I'm coming home! Thanks also to the staff of IDG Books.

Publisher's Acknowledgments

We're proud of this book; please register your comments through our IDG Books Worldwide Online Registration Form located at http://my2cents.dummies.com.

Some of the people who helped bring this book to market include the following:

Acquisitions, Editorial, and Media Development

Project Editor: Pat O'Brien

Acquisitions Editor: Joyce Pepple

Copy Editors: Barry Childs-Helton, Stephanie Koutek, James Russell

Technical Editor: Mir S. Islam

Media Development Editor: Marita Ellixson

Associate Permissions Editor: Carmen Krikorian

Media Development Coordinator: Megan Roney

Editorial Manager: Rev Mengle

Media Development Manager: Heather Heath Dismore

Editorial Assistant: Jamila Pree

Production

Project Coordinator: Maridee V. Ennis

Layout and Graphics: Amy M. Adrian, Brian Drumm, Angela F. Hunckler, Kate Jenkins, Barry Offringa, Douglas L. Rollison, Brent Savage, Janet Seib, Michael A. Sullivan, Brian Torwelle, Maggie Ubertini, Mary Jo Weis

Proofreaders: Vickie Broyles, Betty Kish, Nancy Price, Marianne Santy, Ethel Winslow

Indexer: Becky Hornyak

General and Administrative

IDG Books Worldwide, Inc.: John Kilcullen, CEO; Steven Berkowitz, President and Publisher

IDG Books Technology Publishing Group: Richard Swadley, Senior Vice President and Publisher; Walter Bruce III, Vice President and Associate Publisher; Steven Sayre, Associate Publisher; Joseph Wikert, Associate Publisher; Mary Bednarek, Branded Product Development Director; Mary Corder, Editorial Director

IDG Books Consumer Publishing Group: Roland Elgey, Senior Vice President and Publisher; Kathleen A. Welton, Vice President and Publisher; Kevin Thornton, Acquisitions Manager; Kristin A. Cocks, Editorial Director

IDG Books Internet Publishing Group: Brenda McLaughlin, Senior Vice President and Publisher; Diane Graves Steele, Vice President and Associate Publisher; Sofia Marchant, Online Marketing Manager

IDG Books Production for Dummies Press: Michael R. Britton, Vice President of Production; Debbie Stailey, Associate Director of Production; Cindy L. Phipps, Manager of Project Coordination, Production Proofreading, and Indexing; Tony Augsburger, Manager of Prepress, Reprints, and Systems; Laura Carpenter, Production Control Manager; Shelley Lea, Supervisor of Graphics and Design; Debbie J. Gates, Production Systems Specialist; Robert Springer, Supervisor of Proofreading; Kathie Schutte, Production Supervisor

Dummies Packaging and Book Design: Patty Page, Manager, Promotions Marketing

◆

The publisher would like to give special thanks to Patrick J. McGovern, without whom this book would not have been possible.

◆

Contents at a Glance

Cartoons at a Glance

By Rich Tennant

page 343

page 7

page 299

page 57

page 97

page 241

page 141

page 171

page 325

page 269

Fax: 978-546-7747 • E-mail: the5wave@tiac.net

Table of Contents

Introduction

. . . .

*M*ost books on administering Linux systems assume that you've already gotten your Ph.D. in Obscure Computer Sciences and worked your way into your present job by fixing things on the Mir space station. If that describes you, then congratulations — you should do well writing papers on Linux-mania at MIT.

More commonly, a Linux administrator is someone unfortunate enough to have been in the wrong place at the wrong time. With little or no warning, presto! You're the new person in charge of the Linux network. You have users with problems, lots of problems, and you need to know what to do, yesterday if not sooner.

If you fall into this category, take a deep breath. You've come to the right book.

About This Book

Linux Administration For Dummies is designed to be a quick, easy to understand reference book to help guide you through and solve the most common problems you'll face as a Linux Administrator. Why quick? Because you need your answers fast when you're on the spot. Why easy? Because if you can't understand "why" you're doing something on Linux, you're just one step above typing commands in randomly, which is a dangerous recipe.

And besides, Linux is fast, fun, and the wave of the future. Or at least the slice of the future that doesn't belong to Bill Gates. The topics you'll find in this book include

- Linux utilities an administrator should know how to use
- Starting, Stopping, Mounting systems
- Managing users and user accounts
- Setting up networked devices such as Linux boxes and printers
- Troubleshooting your network

If you have a specific question or problem, turn to the specific chapter that mentions it. You don't have to read the entire book if you're out of time before your power lunch.

Who Should Read This Book

Of course, I already said that this is a book for those who are Linux Administrators, whether of their own free will or not. However, you'll find that you get the most out of this book if you have the following:

- ✔ You have a Linux operating system already installed. This book assumes that you're inheriting a running Linux system. Or a limping system, anyway.

- ✔ You're familiar with the basic components of a computer system. That is, you know your way around a keyboard, you know how to turn the CPU on and off, and you can figure out when your screen is off and when it's running a screen saver.

- ✔ It helps if you know some basic Linux commands, such as how to change directories, find your location, and what a PATH is. If you don't, you shouldn't panic. We'll go over some of the basic commands and begin to add a few that you may not know.

Incidentally, if you still are learning how to install Linux, check out IDG's companion book, *Linux For Dummies*.

Conventions Used in This Book

What would a technical book be without conventions? A convention is a shorthand form of specific information. It's kept constant throughout the book, so you won't be spending valuable time flipping back and forth through the book or scratching your head figuring out what to type.

Typing commands

Commands in the text are shown like this. Commands not in the text, but set off on lines by themselves look like this:

```
[wally@linuxnet wally]#echo $PATH
/usr/bin
```

Type that's in boldface means that it's something you should type in. Non-bold text is text that your computer automatically displays on the screen. So, in the example above, you typed "echo $PATH" and pressed return. Your Linux system displayed /usr/bin on the screen.

Let's get a little more complicated. Take a deep breath, we'll explain everything. Check out the following line:

```
[root@linuxnet /root]# passwd <name>
```

Notice how *<name>* is in bold and italics? That means you should replace *<name>* with a name. Here, you'd put in your own name that you use to log on to your Linux network. And no, you don't need telepathy to have figured that out. I'll explicitly tell you what you should type, right in the chapter text.

Here's the Linux command syntax we'll be using throughout the book:

- Text not surrounded by [ ], { }, or < > must be typed as shown.
- Text inside brackets [] is optional.
- Text inside angle brackets < > need to be replaced with appropriate text.
- An ellipsis (...) means "and so on" or repeats the preceding command line as needed.

Keystrokes with less hassle

Multiple Keystrokes are shown with a plus sign (+) between the keys. For example, Ctrl+Alt+Delete means you need to press the Control, Alt, and Delete keys all at the same time. And no, you don't have to use one hand to do this unless you really feel ambitious.

Finally, you may see commands labeled as follows:

```
<ESC>
```

```
<ALT>
```

```
<DEL>
```

How This Book Is Organized

If you expect this book to be organized along the same lines as the other ...For Dummies books you've encountered, you'd be right.

If you're among the vast majority of Linux administrators who have been press-ganged into supporting a Linux environment against your will, you'll probably be best off with reading the first three parts to start off with so you'll have the basic Linux commands and Linux structure under your belt.

Of course, if you can "ps" and "grep" with the best techno-jockeys out there, then you don't have to read this book in any order. If you have a problem adding a user account, say, simply jump to the right section of the book and tackle it head on.

Part I: Linux at a Glance

In Part One, you'll get a "refresher course" over what Linux is, why you should be using it, and what you can do with it.

Part II: Taking Charge of Your World

In Part 2, you'll find out what it's like being the "alpha geek" on the block. In other words, you'll learn to stop being a Linux user and start becoming a Linux administrator.

My advice is to avoid Kryptonite if at all possible after this chapter.

Part III: Administering Network Communications

In Part 3 you'll learn about your basic protocols. You'll find out how to copy files without getting your fingers coated in printer ink, and how to connect your computers to each other without duct tape.

Part IV: Administering Office Networks

In Part 4, you'll learn how to handle your client base, otherwise known as your "users" or "user groups." You'll learn how to add or delete users from the Linux system.

Or at least restrict them from the system if they've been bad, which is part of the fun of being a Linux administrator. You'll also learn about how to work with networked printers and other resources that are commonly shared on a Linux network.

Part V: Network File and Machine Sharing

As a powerful network tool, Linux helps you manage all of your network equipment. Part 5 explains how.

Part VI: Electronic Mail, News, and Web Browsing

In Part 6, you'll learn how to effectively work with the various e-mail programs that Linux can use.

Part VII: Network Security

In Part 7, you'll learn about building good security on your system. You'll also learn about how to "lock down" special files you don't want people to tamper with, and how to effectively block outside intruders from strolling onto your system and causing damage.

Part VIII: Linux Disasters and Recovery Techniques

In Part 8, you'll learn basic techniques on how to prepare for system crashes. If I wanted to be foolishly optimistic, I could tell you that Linux never crashes, but alas, we live in a less than perfect world.

Part IX: The Part of Tens

Part of the Dummies tradition is to have a "Part of Tens" chapter, which allows you to get a neat shopping list of answers to important Linux issues.

Part X: Appendixes

In Part 10, you'll find a series of lists you can skim through to find useful nuggets of information.

Icons in This Book

Finally, if you haven't had the opportunity to use a ...For Dummies book before, you'll see humorous pictures sprinkled throughout the text. They're in here to give you a "heads up" on certain types of information.

This means that the information you're reading can be found, often with more detail, in another ...For Dummies book.

The information talked about here is on the CD-ROM included with this book.

Don't forget this information — it's important.

Nerd stuff. You'll like this if you wear a pocket protector and enjoy solving calculus problems for real entertainment.

Shortcuts, timesavers, and generally useful information that I've uncovered from general experience from working with Linux machines.

Watch out! This is a strong warning that you'd better pay attention to the information that's coming up.

Where to Go from Here

Unless you have a burning issue — and I mean burning, as in smoke coming out of a hard drive — start with a review of the basic concepts of Linux. Get familiar with what Linux can do and how it does it, and the rest will fall into place.

Ready? Carpe Linuxum!

"Seize the Linux Network!"

Part I
Linux at a Glance

The 5th Wave — By Rich Tennant

"Bill Gates dreams...

* Yes, he sleeps with his glasses on.

JUSTICE DEPT.

"THAT'S RIGHT, MS. BINGAMAN, HE'S COLLECTING A ROYALTY FROM EVERYONE ON EARTH, AND THERE'S NOTHING WE CAN DO ABOUT IT."

In this part . . .

If you're reading this book, you could already be evolving into a mysterious and powerful creature — a Linux administrator. You may have become one by accident (a bizarre twist of fate mentioned in the Introduction). Of course, not all Linux administrators are pressed into service like surprised draftees. You *could* be a Linux enthusiast who has volunteered (O brave soul!) to run the network. Or you might already *be* a Linux administrator whose system has gradually expanded.

The main assumption this book makes is that you've had some UNIX or Linux background in the recent past. So we're not going to spend this entire section on Linux installation tips. Instead, we go over the basic strengths of Linux, which give you real insight into why Linux came to be. (But wait, there's more! You also learn how exactly to pronounce the word *Linux* so you'll sound more erudite in company meetings.)

Part I also reviews the basic commands you probably know already if you're a regular Linux user — but with a twist. Instead of just running commands straight off, you'll be hot-rodding the same commands with all-new options designed to give you the information that any self-respecting administration wizard needs.

Finally, this first part introduces you to those helpful, behind-the-scenes programs called "daemons." You get a look at the vital role they play, learn how to configure them and get them running, and (a little later on) learn how to keep 'em strong and healthy by making sure your Linux network is in the right "system state."

Chapter 1

What Linux Is (And How to Say It)

*E*very great story has a beginning, and *Linux Administration For Dummies* is no different. In this chapter, you'll find out where Linux came from, why it came to be, and why it looks like the Linux operating system has a healthy future in store.

Linux: The Choice of a GNU Generation

As a budget-minded undergraduate student at the University of Helsinki in 1991, Linus Torvalds and a team of programmers created Linux in response to the high cost and high maintenance of the operating systems they had available. The resulting product took less computer muscle to run. Also, since they had invested their own brainpower to create an all-new operating system, it had the incidental benefit of being *free,* which is about as low-cost as you can get.

The organic operating system

Which company developed and supports Linux? Not a one!

Confused? Don't be. Linux stands out from all other forms of UNIX — and remains cheaper — because of this unusual origin. After creating Linux, the farsighted Linus Torvalds decided to make all of the Linux kernel's code freely available. To this day, Linux is called a *freely distributed* operating system. In practical terms, that means you can get Linux free (or nearly so) from lots of sources:

Okay, just how *do* I pronounce Linux?

Some people pronounce Linux *"Lynn*-necks" while others say "*Line*-ucks." I personally like the second variation because it reminds me of one of the characters in the comic strip *Peanuts* — Linus, the fellow with the unhealthy fixation on his security blanket.

There isn't a standard pronunciation, but creator Linus Torvalds took a moment to record how he

says it. To hear him, download `english.au` (or `swedish.au`) from `ftp://ftp.funet. fi/pub/Linux/PEOPLE/Linus/Silly Sounds/`

Whichever way you decide to pronounce it should be okay, since I haven't spotted any Linux police enforcing one version over the other.

> ✔ Over the Internet
>
> ✔ Packaged on software bundles
>
> ✔ CD-ROMs from software publishers, such as Red Hat or Caldera

But why go too far afield? There's a freely installable copy of Linux on the CD-ROM included with *Linux For Dummies,* 2nd Edition.

Also, since the Linux source code is so readily available, Linux has been called the most "organic" of all the operating systems because it can — and does — grow and adapt: Any user who knows how can change the code around and create new features for Linux.

So if you come up with a new, more efficient way to, say, search for files under Linux, you don't have to write to a software company and ask them to add it. You just add it to your Linux system, distribute it, and if it catches on, your feature becomes part of the permanent Linux "landscape."

Kernels, the stuff that Linux is made of . . .

What makes Red Hat Linux different from Caldera's brand of Linux, or from Solaris or HP-UX? Three things:

> ✔ Depending on which "brand" you buy, you'll be dealing with different forms of user support and a slightly different interface.
>
> ✔ At the surface level, there are small differences between commands, command arguments, and user interfaces.
>
> ✔ Deeper down, it's the *kernel* that makes the difference.

UNIX — Linux's big brother

Linux and UNIX are often mentioned in the same sentence, if not the same breath. You will also hear Linux being compared to Solaris, HPUX and maybe even SCO. Without bothering to pronounce those last two, let's clear up the confusion a little.

✔ UNIX is the basic operating system that underlies all these systems. It's known for its stability, speed, and lack of a GUI (Graphical User Interface).

✔ Solaris, HP-UX, and Linux are all specialized "brands" of UNIX.

When Sun Microsystems developed its own version of UNIX, it called the new creature "Solaris" so you'd know which company you'd bought your operating system from. Hewlett-Packard's version is called "HP-UX." By purchasing one brand over another, you would choose a version of UNIX that had slightly different commands and user interfaces, made to the specs of a particular company. Also, if you needed classes or customer support, you'd go back to Sun Microsystems or Hewlett-Packard to get what you needed.

The kernel is the "core" of the operating system, containing all the code that the commands access and use. Think of the kernel as a software equivalent to the microchip that runs your computer. How that component is designed makes a big difference — not only in how your machine processes data and routes messages, but also in how fast it does its job.

Linuxgruven: The Linux Phenomenon

Linux is definitely on the march in the computer world. Regarded as more flexible than UNIX, more reliable than Windows, and a heck of a lot cheaper than both, it has encouraged companies such as Corel, Oracle, and IBM to develop products using Linux.

Although Linux initially remained within the academic world, it rapidly spread into the business and government spheres. It's used in computing environments to cut costs and improve performance while retaining high reliability.

The acceptance in the worldwide user community has been even more impressive. In 1991, the total number of Linux users could have all fit on a Greyhound bus, with a few seats to spare. As of 1999, Linux has an estimated 10 million active users. Not bad for an operating system that has no parent company, marketing department, or advertising budget!

Linux is often found as part of a file server system, a desktop workstation, or as a Web server. Cash-strapped institutions (or college students who want to save more money for the deep-dish pizza) can slash their computing budgets to almost zero, since

- Linux can run on the most outdated machines (well, okay, not on primitive artifacts that predate the 386, but let's be *reasonable*).
- One Linux CD can be used — legally — to install Linux on every machine in a network.

The Linux Decision

You'll have a fair to large number of people using your Linux network, pushing it to its limits. You might encounter any number of the following issues:

- Hooking up network printers
- Network failures between Linux boxes
- How to select secure passwords
- Setting up a web browser in Linux
- Sucessfully running an NFS server to distribute files across your network

These are all issues that you can resolve by applying the material you'll be learning about in this book.

What the Linux phenomenon means to you is that this upstart operating system has enough practical advantages for enough people that it's here to stay, one way or another. It means you'll have a fair to large number of people using your Linux network, pushing it to its limits, toying with its controls, and (of course) crashing it.

Chapter 2

Why You Won't See Icons, Pictures, and Folders

In This Chapter

▶ Unsticking your expectations — why Linux isn't "gooey" (GUI)

▶ Finding where you are and getting around without clicking a mouse

▶ Storing, moving, and deleting files without folders or trash cans

▶ Opening X Windows to get your gotta-have-a-window fix

The first thing you'll see on the screen of a machine running Linux is . . . nothing. Your screen will be almost blank. This is because Linux, like other members of the UNIX family, doesn't use a GUI.

Linux: Less Gooey, More Filling

A *GUI* or *Graphical User Interface* is pronounced *gooey* by those Linux administrators in the know. On a machine that runs Microsoft Windows, Windows NT, OS/2, or the Macintosh operating system, GUIs are the primary interface between the user and the system. To make things sound homier and more inviting, the marketing types call GUIs the computer *desktop*.

If you're using a GUI-based system, you'll probably be familiar with clicking on little pictures to open programs, deleting things by putting them in a picture of a trash can, and moving files around by clicking and dragging. To hardcore Linux people, this is pure fluff.

As you click and drag a file across a desktop, the GUI is drawing the pictures as they move, calculating where to move the cursor as it slides across the desktop, and probably digging into the sound files to notify you when you've completed an important task.

All of this takes up valuable CPU cycles, essentially making your computer waste its brainpower drawing pretty pictures when it could be doing valuable work. Linux doesn't display pictures, and it's pretty terse; when you do something right, it rarely congratulates you. When you do something wrong, it sometimes will tell you — in as few words as possible, and with few hints on what you did wrong.

Knowing that Linux is terse is what makes true Linux administrators the rugged individualists they are. You don't get many second chances in the Linux world; you must take responsibility for what you do — and try to get it right the first time. For example, when removing a file, you won't be asked *Are you sure you want to delete this?* If you remove something, it's *gone* to the big byte pile in silicon heaven.

Interacting with Linux without Pictures

Here's a bit of forgotten computer wisdom: A GUI isn't the "real" operating system. It's simply a visual aid — an overlay of on-screen pictures that tell the user what's going on in the computer (say, a file deletion) in cartoon-like images of real-world actions ("manila folders" going into a "trash can"). The computer doesn't really *need* a GUI to do useful work; neither does a user who knows what's really going on in the machine.

Laconic Linux — the operating system with the attitude

Why is Linux so closemouthed? Many new Linux users, having grown up in the coddled, friendly world of Microsoft or Macintosh, are frustrated by the lack of positive or negative feedback. Believe it or not, there is a reason — and explaining it to people who are having a nervous breakdown trying to find the Recycle Bin will help calm everyone's nerves.

Linux was developed from UNIX — which was, in turn, developed at a time when computers didn't even use a cathode ray tube (what we now call a computer monitor) to display data. Instead, commands and results were printed out directly to paper on high-speed teletype machines. (Think back to episodes of *Mission*

Impossible or the espionage movies of the '60s and early '70s.)

Unlike the unlimited supply of photons that your computer monitor generates for pictures, paper and ink are always in limited supply (unless you have a storage closet the size of a blimp hangar). So UNIX was designed to be as short-winded as possible — to save paper. Which also (coincidentally) saves computer resources.

If your audience doesn't believe you, show them the contents of the `/dev` directory on your Linux box. You'll find files that handle the input of data called `tty` — an abbreviation for *teletype machine!*

Instead of interacting with Linux through a GUI, you'll be working with it via the *shell.* The shell is a command-line interface that passes instructions to the kernel. Think of it as the program that serves as a go-between so you can communicate efficiently with the operating system. When you log in to a Linux system — even when you start a window (called an *xterm*) — you're using a shell.

Still confused? Stand by for an example.

Shells aren't just for mollusks anymore

Interacting with a shell is almost as easy as falling off the pier. Let's say you log in to machine `linuxbox` as Wally the Wonder User, whose username is `Wally` and whose secret password (decoder ring optional) is `1drusr`. No problem:

1. You enter **Wally** at the login prompt and press Enter.

2. When Linux asks you for the password, you enter **1drusr** and press Enter.

   Linux protects your password by discreetly pretending you've typed in asterisks, and then thinks for a second *(Let's see — do I know a* `Wally` *whose password is* `1drusr`*?).* If your password is good, Linux then lets you log in to the system.

If you've logged in successfully as `Wally` with the correct password, the screen looks like this:

```
Login: Wally
Password: ******

[wally@linuxbox]$
```

The simple, blank *command line* after the $ is what you'll be using to execute commands, edit scripts, and perform administration tasks. That's all there is to your shell — a $ command prompt to tell you that you're using the *Bourne shell* — one of several kinds of shells Linux can use.

Wanna see shells? See C-Shells . . .

(Sho to shpeak.) Shells all look the same at first; There isn't much to see except the command prompt. But don't let their simple look fool you; each type of shell offers its own range of special features to the user.

When you create user accounts as a Linux administrator, you get to specify which shell does the automatic go-between chores for your users. Describing each type of shell in detail would take a whole lot longer than a walk on the beach. For now, consider a basic comparison: The most basic kind of shell (with the fewest utilities) is the Bourne shell. The most common kind is called the C-Shell — often a good choice because it has a large number of user utilities.

Incidentally, the Bourne shell is named after its inventor, Stephen Bourne. There's also an improved version of his shell, called the Bourne Again shell (no, I'm not kidding).

Managing Files

As a Linux administrator, you're required to organize and manage files on a hard drive. If you've grown up with Windows machines and Macintoshes, command-line file management takes a bit of thinking. In this section, you'll see how to find and arrange files with Linux — all from the command prompt.

Where am I?

In the Windows world, it's easy to know where you're located by seeing which "window" you're in. With a GUI-free Linux system, many beginning users are mystified how to keep track of their position in the system. (Are they in their home directory, the binary directory, or somewhere else? It all looks the same.)

What shells to use, and when

You can use any shell you want in Linux without significant handicaps. However, traditionally, there are certain shells that Linux administrators like to allocate for specific tasks. This isn't a hard and fast rule, but you might want to consider the following:

✔ **Bourne** - Traditionally, this is the shell that most administrators write their Linux "scripts" in to automate system tasks because it's found on all Linux systems by default.

If you want to make 100 percent sure that you're running in Bourne shell, simply type **sh** at the command prompt.

✔ **C-Shell** – This shell has a number of user-friendly utilities that can come in handy, such as the "source" command, which forces the shell to adopt changes you make in your Linux environment without restarting the machine. To ensure you're using C-Shell, type **csh** at the command prompt.

✔ **Korn** – The Korn shell is an extension of the Bourne shell, but it has a few extra utilities which are a boon to C programmers. Korn handles arrays, searches, and memory allocation slightly better than Bourne. To ensure you're using Korn shell, type **ksh** at the command prompt.

If you want to view a file in the /etc directory, it doesn't do you much good when you're in the /var directory and don't know it. Luckily, figuring out where you are in Linux is pretty simple. Use the **pwd** command. Pwd acts like a compass, always telling you exactly where you are. For example:

Let's say you use the **pwd** command:

[wally@linuxbox]$ pwd

You'll get back something like this:

```
[wally@linuxbox]$ /usr/home/wally
```

Linux is telling you that you're in the "wally" directory. Linux lists the entire "path" of your location for you. Instead of just telling you you're in "wally," it's also telling you that "wally" is under the "home" directory, and the "home" directory is itself under the "usr" directory.

By default, when you log in to a Linux machine, you always start in the same place: your *home directory*. The home directory can be set up anywhere on your Linux system (as you learn in the chapter on user administration). However, on most Linux systems, the user home directories are located in the /home area, because

   ✔ It's easy to remember (usr sounds like 'user')

   ✔ Putting user directories in one central area is easier to adminster

Listing files

You can list the files in your home directory using the **ls** command:

```
[wally@linuxbox]$ ls
[wally@linuxbox]$ test doctorate_thesis letter-to-mom
          printscript
```

You'll notice that unlike Windows or Macintosh, you won't get a nicely sorted list with pictures to clue you in to what the files are. You don't even get the benefit of an extension on the file (like test.*exe* to tell you it's an executable, or a printscript.*doc* to indicate it's a document).

Another aside to Windows folks: Linux allows you to string multiple words together to create a file name, so long as the words aren't separated by a space. So the following could be a valid file name under Linux!

```
the_quick_brownfox_jumped_over_thelazydog.txt
```

By and large, ls by itself is too brief a command to give you back useful information. I recommend that you use **ls –la** to get a good look at things:

```
[wally@linuxbox]$ ls -la
[wally@linuxbox]$    drwr__r__ /test
        rw_r__r__ .cshrc
        rw_rw_rw_ doctorate_thesis
        rw_rw_rw_ letter-to-mom
    rwxrwxrwx printscript*
```

By default, the "ls" command lists files in the shortest form possible. More importantly, the "ls" command will not show you files that have been "hidden" for system or security purposes. The -la option specifies that you want -l and -a: respectively, the *long form* of your list entries (more info that way) and *all* of them. When you arrange your list this way, you get some important clues. For example, you can tell that /test is actually a directory (it's got that telltale slash in front of it), and that printscript* is a program (or *script* in Linux-speak) because the word is followed by an asterisk.

Notice that there's a new file called .cshrc. This is a normally-hidden file we're seeing because you used the -a (let-me-see-'em-*all*) option of ls. When you edit a user's account, this hidden file is where the changes you make actually take effect.

Let's say you want to see what's in the /usr directory. Use the **cd**, or change directory command, and then do a long list (**ls –l**) to see what's inside. The following input and output shows two files are in the usr directory.:

```
[wally@linuxbox]$ cd usr
[wally@linuxbox]$ ls -l
[wally@linuxbox]$    rw_r__r__ mystuff
                     rw_r__r__ mystuff_2
```

Again, this shows how different the Linux and Windows-GUI worlds can be.

✔ With a GUI, you can tell where you are by observing which folders (or which windows) happen to be open, and which title bars appear in color.

✔ In Linux, you'll either have to *remember* where you are or rely on pwd to tell you. (Not as hard as it sounds, once you know your way around.)

If you forget where you are, use the **pwd** command to determine your location.

By the way, no matter where you are in the Linux file system, typing **cd** will return you to your home directory. So it's literally impossible to get "lost" in Linux.

Saving files without a folder

Saving or deleting files in Linux is a matter of typing simple commands, as opposed to clicking the mouse or "pressing" an on-screen Save button. On the plus side, you don't have to be *in* a particular program in order to save a file. The versatile shell interface that Linux uses allows you to save any document from the command line.

For example, you'll most likely be using the vi text editor to edit files. To save, press Esc to go to Command Mode, type **:wq**, and then press Enter.

You'll be introduced socially to the vi editor in Chapter 3.

Moving files without a mouse

There's no clicking and dragging in Linux, which is a real plus if you're among the many people who lack the dexterity to move miniscule graphics around until they overlap some tiny disk icon.

Linux uses the mv (or *move*) command for this purpose. Let's say you're in your home directory, /usr/home/wally, and you want to mv the file mystuff to the /etc directory. Type **mv**, the filename, the location you plan to put the file, and press Enter.

```
[wally@linuxbox]$ mv mystuff  /etc
[wally@linuxbox]$
```

Notice that Linux didn't tell you "File moved," or "Transfer complete," or "Gee, you're good"? That's Linux for you — never a wasted word. If you want to make sure the move took place, use the **ls** command in your home directory and the test directory.

Renaming files

Another useful tool for renaming files is the mv command. Say you want to change the file mystuff to be called the file mystuff_notyours. Use the **mv** command, type in the names (first the old, and then a space, followed by the new name), and press Enter. Here's what it looks like:

```
[wally@linuxbox]$ mv mystuff mystuff_notyours
[wally@linuxbox]$
```

Doing an **ls** on this directory would show one change — the file mystuff would be gone, but the file mystuff_notyours would be newly created. Of course, the contents of the file haven't changed by a single byte.

Deleting files without a trash can or recycle bin

To delete files in Linux, type **rm** (remove), followed by a space and the file-name, and then press Enter. It looks like this:

```
[wally@linuxbox]$ rm mystuff_notyours
[wally@linuxbox]$
```

Watch out when you use the rm command! It works like a death ray, not a trash can.

- ✔ Unlike Windows, Linux doesn't store your file in a Recycle Bin (which doesn't really delete the file unless you "empty" the bin). If you remove something, it's gone for good.

- ✔ Because Linux does what you tell it to, *don't* use rm with wildcard characters. If you do, Linux will delete every single thing from the directory in which you ran the rm command.

  If you commit this faux pas in a root directory, you'll have no recourse but to reinstall the entire Linux operating system. For openers. (Let's not even talk about lost data. . . .)

X Windows — When You Gotta Get a Window Fix

Many people simply feel more comfortable seeing some kind of graphic on the screen. An MIT computer project called Athena developed a terminal-emulator system known as *X Windows* to meet this crying need.

A *terminal-emulator program* is a great impostor: It "pretends" to be a particular type of computer system so convincingly that it fools the computer it's running on.

People are harder to fool than computers; for most, terminal emulators are a limited compromise between greater convenience and diminished performance. X Windows does have a few nifty features that straight-up Linux doesn't have — for example, a scroll bar and a task-manager bar.

X Windows is more of a tool than an actual GUI; it doesn't really change the basic nature of Linux: You'll still have to type all commands in through the shell.

Chapter 3

Linux Commands for Administrators

• •

In This Chapter

▶ Listing your files any way you want 'em — by name, time, size . . .

▶ Creating files on your own (let there be life!)

▶ Copying files without a Xerox machine

▶ Finding the needles in the haystack — Locations and find command

▶ Not wincing when Simon says, "It's time to learn about permissioning!"

▶ Stopping programs/scripts at touch of a (virtual) button

▶ Process searching without a magnifying glass

▶ Stopping processes, again at the touch of a button

▶ Going with the flow — tinkering with pipes and redirecting output

• •

*L*inux Administration For Dummies brazenly makes as few assumptions about you, the reader, as possible. Even if you've had some UNIX or Linux background, we'll cover some basic review material as a steppingstone to some more advanced commands, extensions, and variations. (The typical user might not care about them — but you, as Linux administrator, will find them very helpful indeed.)

Yet More Ways to List Your Files

In Chapter 2, you learned about the ls command, used to list your files. What you may not have realized is that while you ran the command the way a user might — to list files in your home directory — you used the command options that mark you as an administrator.

Command options, flags, and extensions

A *command option* is the mark you place after a given command to either expand or focus the command so it does what you want with more precision. In Linux, command options follow the command, and they're almost always set off by a space and a dash. Look at the following example.

```
ls -la
```

▸ ls is the command, to list files.

▸ The command option is -la, which tells Linux to execute the list command in a way that shows all of the files, and in the long form.

If you wish, you can enter the command as ls -l -a but that gets confusing. And besides, unless you're training for the Olympic freestyle typing event, why waste the extra .0002 calories it takes to type the extra letters?

You may hear people call command options by other names, such as *flags* or *extensions*. They're all the same thing to the Linux system. I prefer that you call them *command options;* to a Windows user, "extension" means the .exe or .txt letters that extend off a filename when a machine is running Microsoft's favorite product.

Where there are many options for a command that you'll find useful, we'll be listing them in a separate table for easy reference. With the ls command, there are many other extensions that are less commonly used but can still be of use as shown in Table 3-1.

Table 3-1	Other ls Command Options You May Find Useful
Command Option	**What It Does**
-c	Lists files by creation time (newest first)
-C	Lists file in column form
-d	Lists a directory's name, not its contents
-m	Merge the list of files into a series of names, separated by commas
-r	Lists files in reverse order
-t	Lists files according to modification time (newest first)

The wildest of the untamed wildcards

As a Linux administrator, you'll have to sift through more information and files than you can shake a keyboard at. You'll need to use what's called a *wildcard* to select the exact kind of file or files you want to see.

Wildcards are symbols that Linux treats just like you'd treat a wild card in a game of poker: the symbol literally can mean anything. There are several symbols that Linux uses as wildcards, but for simplicity's sake, you really only need one. It's the asterisk symbol, or *. In Linux, * is literally interpreted as meaning *one or more of anything else*. Because it's so flexible, you can use the asterisk at the beginning, the end, or even the middle of a wildcard command. You'll see how it works if you check out the next examples.

Let's say you have the following files in your directory:

```
Bigfile
Bagfile
Bogfile
Bigger-file
Bigger-file_than_you_can_imagine
Linux_commands
Linux_4_Dummies_file
Linux4U
Junque_4me
Usefulstuff_4me
```

Typing an ls command will list all of these files by default. However, you can have more control over what you list.

- Putting the asterisk at the *beginning* finds filenames that match the *end* of the search string.

  For example, let's say you want to see the files that end with _4me. You can do so by putting a wildcard in your command, like this:

  ```
  ls -la *_4me
  ```

- Putting the asterisk at the *end* finds filenames that match the *beginning* of the search string.

  To find all files that begin with the word "Linux", you can use:

  ```
  ls -la Linux*
  ```

- Putting the asterisk in the *middle* of the search string finds files that match *both ends* of the search string. Using the following command will give you "Bigfile", "Bagfile," and "Bogfile":

  ```
  ls -la B*gfile
  ```

Got to be out of town? Try remote listing

A common misconception is that before you can list the contents of a directory, you have to navigate to that directory first. This notion may be habitual, but it just isn't true. Instead of wasting time changing to the directory you're interested in, you can enter the directory's *path* into the command line and save a few more keystrokes.

For example, let's say you're in your home directory, and you want to list the contents of the `/etc/stuff/long/way_away` directory. If you use:

```
Linuxbox% ls /etc/stuff/long/way_
away
```

"Ls" is the command, while the "path" to that directory is the entire sequence of directories you'd have to go through to get there: "`/etc/stuff/long/way_away`"

```
[wally@linuxbox]$ ls -la
    /etc/stuff/long/way_away
[wally@linuxbox]$     -rw-rw-
    rw- Ayoufoundme
        -rw-rw-rw- far_file
        -rwxrwxrwx far_script*
```

It's Aliiiive! Creating and Editing Files in Linux

The simplest method of creating a file is the `touch` command, which I suspect was inspired by Michaelangelo's painting of God creating Man. While your accomplishment might be a tad smaller, you should feel no less satisfying. Use the command as follows:

[wally@linuxbox]$ touch <filename>

Of course, the fact that you created it doesn't mean much in itself. Like a box of extra dark, semisweet Godiva chocolates, the package doesn't mean as much as the contents. You'll need to know how to use a text editor. While Linux does have several built-in editors that could accomplish this task, you only should review the most common, useful one — the `vi` editor.

Vi's a coder! It's a word processor! It slices, dices, and even makes julienne fries!

Without a doubt, vi is the most powerful utility in Linux — and it's the most important one to know. It's the Swiss army knife of the Linux world, because it literally can do everything — provided you know how to use it.

You may think that Microsoft Word, Framemaker, or WordPerfect may be flexible, because they can do résumés, letters, and posters. But using any of these programs, can you create scripts that monitor your system for errors? Can you edit files that control your background and control panels? Can you edit the files that change user accounts across the entire network? Probably not.

Vi was designed to be one of the first text processors, and because it was so useful, it did double duty as a coding program. So when you edit or create your own scripts, vi is what you'll be using.

Vi is most commonly started by simply typing **vi** at the command line. If you're creating a file, you can start vi with the filename you plan to save — an operation that looks like this:

```
[wally@linuxbox]$ vi <filename>
```

As an administrator, you'll be less tied to the tasks of creating files — and correspondingly more interested in editing the ones that already exist.

For example, let's say you want to edit the .motd (message of the day) file, which contains the message that pops up every time a user logs in to the system. This file is located in the /etc directory. As with the ls command, you don't have to be in the same directory to edit a file that exists in some other place. Once you **vi** the file, the editor displays the file's current contents.

```
[wally@linuxbox]$ vi /etc/.motd
~   Welcome to Wally's Wonderful World of Linux.
~    There are no system upgrades scheduled today.
~    Have a great day, user!
```

The vi editor has two modes:

- Text Mode

  In Text Mode, you can type away to your heart's content. But until you jump into Command Mode, you can't save what you've inserted. To switch to Text mode from Command Mode, press "a" or "i" (to "Add" or "Insert" text).

- Command Mode

  In Command Mode; you can execute commands such as search, replace, quit, and save. The catch: You can't edit any text. To switch to Command Mode from Text Mode, simply press the "Esc" key.

Moving around a document in vi is tricky. In most cases, your number keys won't be mapped to use the arrows that are printed above the 4, 8, 6, and 2 on your keyboard's number pad. Instead, consult Table 3-2 for a quick translation.

Table 3-2	Movin' and Shakin' in vi
Command	**What It Does**
j	Moves 1 line up
k	Moves 1 line down
h	Moves one character to the left
l	Moves one character to the right
Ctrl+f	Scrolls down 1 full screen
Ctrl+b	Scrolls up 1 full screen
/	Searches for the following word
n	Searches for the next instance of a word

The easiest way to go from Command to Text Mode is to move the cursor to where you want to insert text, and type the letter **i** to begin inserting text. In fact, you have a few more options to help you jump to Text Mode. They're coming right up in Table 3-3.

Table 3-3	Commands for Inserting and Deleting in Text Mode
Command	**What It Does**
i	Begins inserting text before the cursor
a	Begins inserting text after the cursor
A	Begins inserting text at the end of the current line
x	Deletes 1 character
dd	Deletes 1 line of text

In this example, suppose you want to delete the line There are no system upgrades scheduled today and change it to The system will be upgraded at 2pm today. Using the cursor commands in Table 3-3, move to the beginning of the line that starts with There. At this point, you can delete the text one character at a time, by hitting the **x** key 51 times. Of course, if you're not trying to cultivate calluses, typing in **dd** will delete the line more efficiently.

There's no need to type the i command right now; by using x or (preferably) dd, you kicked yourself into Text Mode. Type in your new message.

To save your changes, first get back to Command Mode. You can always get to Command Mode by pressing Esc.

Whoops! I didn't want to do THAT!

Making typing errors is a grand tradition in vi, since you may forget if you're in Text or Command Mode. If you make a mistake, the most valuable command to know is Esc+u. Pressing Esc puts you in Command Mode, and pressing **u** undoes your last command.

To save the file, do the following:

1. **Decide what you're going to call this file.**

   Here, let's call the file "Sample_text."

2. **Press "Esc" to ensure you're in Command mode.**

3. **Type a colon.**

   A colon will appear at the bottom left of the screen. This colon isn't in your document text; it's just a saving and quitting prompt.

4. **Type a lower-case "w" and a lower-case "q." Don't insert a space between the two letters.**

   This tells the vi editor you want to "write" and "quit vi."

5. **Press Enter. Your document is saved.**

   Since you've quit vi, you'll be back at your familiar Linux command prompt.

It seems basic, but a lot of people forget to use the w command and simply quit, dropping out of a file and forgetting to save what they did. Your changes won't take hold unless you save your file!

Of course, you may want to avoid saving what you just did, especially if you made a major error and you don't want the error saved. In that case, do the following:

1. **Press Esc to get to Command Mode.**

2. **Type a colon, followed by a lowercase "q" and an exclamation point. Don't include spaces.**

   The "q" followed by the "!" forces vi to quit ASAP, without saving any of your changes.

3. **Press enter to execute this command.**

Copying Files without a Xerox Machine

If you're a typical Linux user, you're probably familiar with *cp*, the copy command. You can use cp to make a backup copy of a file you're going to edit, in the following format:

```
[wally@linuxbox]$ cp <filename> <new file's filename>
```

Keep in mind that Linux won't make up a name for you automatically. So if you're making a copy of the file Uniquestuff and you're planning to keep the copy in the same directory, you'd better type the command so it looks like the following:

[wally@linuxbox]$ cp Uniquestuff Uniquestuff_backup

Here, you've instructed Linux to use "cp," the "copy" command to make a copy of the "Uniquestuff" file. You've also instructed Linux to save the copy as the file Uniquestuff_backup.

Being an administrator, you're going to be a bit more sophisticated. As you may have guessed, you can apply the lessons you've just learned about wild-carding to the cp command — and again, you don't have to be in the directory you're copying from — nor even in the one you're copying to! As an example, let's say you plan to copy the files Wally, Wally_Prime, and Wallyworld from the /etc directory to the /dev directory.

You can easily do this without changing directories (or having to hassle with three separate copy commands) by issuing the following elegant command:

[wally@linuxbox]$ cp /etc/Wally* /etc/dev

Since the * wildcard means *one or more of anything,* this command copies all the files in the /etc directory that begin with Wally to the /dev location. Shazam.

There's one more trick you should know about cp. As an administrator, you'll need to copy files from one machine to the next. For this task, your best bet is to use cp's big brother, *rcp* — (as in Remote Copying). Use this command in the following manner:

rcp <remote machine>:<filename> <location of copied file>

Let's say you're copying the file Suit from a remote machine called Zoot onto your current machine, into the /etc/clothing/rack directory. You'd use the following command:

```
rcp Zoot:Suit /etc/clothing/rack
```

A word to the wise: rcp is *not* a substitute for FTP, the file transfer protocol. The rcp command is much more limited; it can't transfer files between completely different networks.

If you need to go through a hub, router, or bridge, you'll probably be better off using FTP. If (on the other hand) you're running a small system in which all the Linux machines are on one network, rcp will be more useful for you.

Where Files Live, Why They Live There, and How to Find Them

In Linux, certain types of files live in assigned directories for ease of use, or just to add a little order to the chaos that is often abroad in the world of Linux. This feature of Linux brings us back to its rep as the most "organic" of operating systems — with good reason: The directory structure for Linux has often been compared to the branches of a tree.

At the structure's base, the one directory that can lead you to all others is the (appropriately named) *root* directory. Linux identifies the root directory on-screen as the / directory. There are no directories above it. If you use **cd /** to change directories so you can get to root, you won't be able to go to a higher directory by typing **cd /../** because there *isn't* a higher directory; root is as high as you can go.

When not to root for the home team

From time to time, your users may tell you some variation on this theme: "I put my file in my root directory, and now I can't find it!" Confusion rears its head: Does Joe User mean the root directory for the entire system (/) or the "root" directory (/home/user) where he initially logged in to his account?

Consistency of terminology can save you a lot of frazzled nerve endings here. When *you're* talking about the system's root directory, call it that. But also recognize that when your users call a directory "root," often they *mean* their individual *home directories*.

The user's home directory is likely the last place the file showed up, if only because most users won't have the security permissions to create, delete, or copy files to the system's actual root directory. Which is as it should be.

If you run the ls -l command on the system's root directory, you'll probably see a dozen or more directories listed. Many of these may have been created by privileged users (or prior administrators) before you came on the scene. Any Linux system, however, has certain directories and subdirectories that you should be aware of — because they contain files or markers to areas that directly affect your job as the administrator.

/bin	The bin (or binary) directory contains the majority of executable files (programs, scripts, commands, and so on) that Linux uses. The ls and cd commands are located here, along with many other utilities discussed in later chapters.
/boot	Although not this one isn't found on all Linux systems, if you do have this directory, the kernel and other files used during system boot-up are kept in here.
/etc	The *ett-see* directory contains most of the files used in networking, NFS, and mail. You'll also edit files used in network services or mounting disks in this area.
/tmp	The *temp* directory is a small reserved area, that some times may reside under the /usr directory. You can use /tmp to store log files, but the system normally grabs this space as for *sswap-files,* (or virtual memory), to speed up its performance.
/usr	The *user* directory contains many subdirectories used for binaries not stored in bin. It also is the usual location of user's home directories.
/usr/bin	Stores more commands used by Linux.
/usr/sbin	Stores yet even more commands used by Linux.
/var	The *var* directory holds administrative files, such as system log files, which are used by various background Linux utilities.
/var/spool –	The *spool* directory is a temporary storage space set aside for files waiting to be accepted by the network printer or sent out on the network by the UUCP or FTP processes.

Why three /usr directories? Again, remember that when Linux was being developed, disk space wasn't as cheap or plentiful as it is today. Commands were stored on three separate disk areas because one disk just couldn't hold them all.

Off the beaten path

Now that you know Linux stores its binaries in at least three separate locations, how does it know which directory to go to when it starts a program?

The answer is that it follows the $PATH system variable in the account of the user who starts the program. A system variable is a value that can be set inside the .cshrc file of any user's account. System variables usually sport a dollar sign in front of them, to denote that the value isn't fixed — you can change it at will.

The $PATH variable is the most important of all of these variables because

> ✔ It tells Linux where to go for commands.
>
> ✔ It specifies which directories Linux should search first to find the command.

You can display your $PATH variable as follows, using the **echo** command:

```
echo $PATH
You'll get a response from Linux that looks something like
          this:
/bin /usr/bin /usr/sbin
```

Let's say you want Linux to perform the command ls, which resides in the /usr/sbin directory. Linux will first look into the /bin directory. Nope, ls isn't there. It then looks into /usr/bin. No such luck. Finally, it looks into /usr/sbin. Bingo! It executes the command.

If Linux can't find the ls command anywhere, it complains to you that the command isn't available. So if you're adding a new program and Linux can't find it, check your $PATH variable and make sure you **mv** it to one of the locations specified in the path.

The find command, the silicon bloodhound

If you need to find a file, consult the handy list of directories just given to get an idea where it might lie. For example, if you need to find a text file that a user just wrote, it's probably in the /usr area, which is where most systems store the home directories.

Running the find command

If you don't have more than a general idea of where to look, try using the find command. Although find has so many command options that another chapter could be expended on the subject, here's the most useful form of the command:

```
find . -name <filename>
```

Writing the `find` command this way tells it to search the current directory, and then start searching all the directories below the current one. Once the command finds a name that matches your file, it prints out your quarry for you. From there on, it's a cinch to **vi**, **ls**, or **cp** the file to your heart's content.

Where find only finds you system heartburn

Nothing about computers (or operating systems) is perfect; commands are no exception. The `find` command has two major limitations:

- ✔ It can't use wildcards properly. Doing a search for `Linux*` won't find `Linux_file`, `Linux_fool`, or `Linux_foul`. That's because you're searching *only* for `Linux*`. You're better off searching for an exact filename.

- ✔ It's a *resource-intensive* command (one that puts big demands on your system), particularly when you run it in a major directory. Remember, if you run it from the `root` directory (and remember: / means the same as `root`), you're effectively searching the *entire* Linux network. Tall order. Doing so can slow down the whole system, for all users. So it's best to narrow your search to a subdirectory, or do your search during off-peak usage hours.

Simon Says . . . It's Time to Learn about Permissioning

In Linux, the permissions allocated to a file determines the way in which someone can use it. Depending on how a file's permissions are set, the casual user might be able to read it, make changes to it, or execute it as a program. Or, for security purposes, the user may be blocked from doing any of these things.

Writing permission commands

By now, if you've used an `ls -l` command, you've probably noticed the non-sensical string on characters that precede each file. For example, performing an **ls –l** command on the file `Linux_file` gives you this critter:

```
-rwxrw-r— Linux_file
```

I've been asked before if those letters were some encoded version of the file-name, the machine ID, and even if the letters represented the file's Price Code. Nothing so interesting, I'm afraid, for the casual user. However, in your role as administrator, this information is priceless.

The string of characters in front of `Linux_file` refer to the *permissioning* assigned to it. (Relax. All that buzzword means is "a set of network permissions." But it's an awkward enough term that Murphy's Law practically guarantees you'll hear it again.)

There are three things you can do with a Linux file:

✔ You can *read* a file. Reading, designated by the letter r, allows you to look at a file.

✔ You can *write* to a file. Writing, or w, allows you to actually make changes to the file with the vi editor.

✔ You can *execute* a file. Executing a file is not as gory as it sounds — all it means is that you can run this file as a script. So if it helps you, when you hear *execute*, think *run*.

The permissioning string is easier to look at if you break it into its four component parts. Let's look at how `Linux_file`'s string would look if we separated its fields with spaces:

```
-    rwx   rw-   r-
```

The first field is only 1 character long, and the rest are 3 characters long. Here's how to read the fields:

-	The first, 1 character field is blank, so this is a regular, hum-drum file. If Linux_file were a directory, this would have a d here.
rwx	The first 3-letter field shows the permissions the user has over this file. Since it's rwx, this user can read it, write it, or execute it.
rw-	The second field shows permissions for the user's group. Anyone in the group can read or edit this file, so it's probably not too important. If a file is private or shouldn't be touched, it should be unwritable (and possibly unreadable) to all others.
r-	The final field shows permissions for all users on the Linux system. Anyone can read this file, but they can't edit or execute it.

Three more examples should help you make sure you can identify the various combinations you might see on your system:

```
drwxrwxrwx        PublicDirectory2.2
```

The d in the first field shows this is a directory. Also, the user, user's group, and in fact anyone on the Linux system can read, write, or execute this file. Most likely this is a directory with very low-level stuff in it, since anyone could — intentionally or not — delete it and all the contents in it!

```
-rw-rw——        department_forms
```

This is a regular file which lets only the user and the user's group access the file. Notice that the general Linux public can't even read, let alone write to this file? Most likely, this is sensitive department specific information.

```
-rw——-        pvtmail
```

Only the user can read or write to this file. Probably private stuff. Permissioning a file this way amounts to hanging a DO NOT DISTURB sign on the door.

Changing file permissions to suit your mood

To change the permissions on a file, first you must own it. As administrator, you'll effectively own permissions on *all* files on the Linux network (it's *good* to be king — sometimes, at least), but that's for the next chapter.

Assuming that you own the file, you'll use the chmod command to change the permissioning. The chmod syntax works as follows:

```
chmod <permissions> filename
```

The easiest way to change permissions on a file is to specify which of the fields you want to change (user, group, or other) and which permissions you want to bestow on the lucky file (read, write, or execute). In order to select the field to change, use the first letter as an abbreviation: U for user, g for group, and o for other users.

I also like to use the + sign to add the permission and the – sign to remove it.

Let's put this into action.

The directory `PublicDirectory2.2` is having problems because users are randomly deleting it when you need the directory to distribute important information. The permission scheme was set to

```
drwxrwxrwx        PublicDirectory2.2
```

You want to change this situation so that while everyone can read it, no one except you (the owner of the file) or your group can write to it. You'll use the following command to deprive the other users of permission to write to it:

```
chmod o-w PublicDirectory2.2
```

Doing an ls –l on the file will now show

```
drwxrwxr-x        PublicDirectory2.2
```

Suppose you accidentally revoked your own privilege to read the file, by using

```
chmod u-r PublicDirectory2.2
```

You would add the permission back as follows:

```
chmod u+r PublicDirectory2.2
```

As a general rule, it's best to make sure that any files the users shouldn't be playing with (like your system files or `/usr/bin` binaries) aren't writable by anyone but yourself. Fair's fair, but business is business.

Changing file ownership without signing a deed, claim, or will

Another task you may need to perform as an administrator is to change the ownership of files from one user to another. You may also need to change the ownership of a file to belong to a specific group on your Linux network. Both tasks use a command similar to `chmod` — namely, `chown` (for *change ownership*). You can use `chmod` as follows:

```
chown <new ownship name> <filename>
```

Wally the Wonder User has just left for another company and would like to transfer ownership of his file `Mailbag` to Lance Linuxdude. Lance's username is `llance`, so you'd perform the following command:

```
chown llance Mailbag
```

To make matters interesting, Wally's file has to be maintained in his absence by the accounting group. To change the group that owns the file, use the **chgrp** command — you guessed it, it stands for *change group*. (Aren't Linux naming conventions tricky?) Use chgrp as follows:

```
chgrp <new group name> <filename>
```

To complete the transfer to accounting, perform:

```
chgrp accounting Mailbag
```

And remember, if you want to double-check your work — as any good administrator should — use the **ls –l** command.

Starting Programs at the Touch of a Button — Well, a Few Buttons . . .

You execute scripts in Linux simply by typing the script's name in and pressing Enter. The shell then runs the script until it's finished.

A file can be executed only if it is explicitly permissioned as an executable file. If there are no x marks in the permissioning strip, then it's just a regular file.

As a rule, it's best to execute a script in the *background* by adding a space and an ampersand (&) sign to it, and then pressing Enter. Executing the script kleendisk in the background would look like this:

```
[wally@linuxbox]$ kleendisk &
```

You want to do this handy maneuver because scripts can take a chunk of time (from seconds to hours) to run. In the interest of maximum productivity, you'll want to leave your command shell free to do other things while you're waiting for the script to run.

Help! I can't execute this script!

If you typed **kleendisk &** and nothing happened, you've got a couple of possibilities:

✔ Do an **ls –l** to find out whether it's executable. If it isn't, use **chmod** to make it executable.

✔ If the script is executable already, then it probably isn't in your $PATH. Check by using **pwd** to determine the script's location. Use **echo** on your $PATH and compare — if the script you're looking for isn't in your $PATH, then the computer isn't looking in the script's proper directory.

At this point, you have three choices.

✔ Add the directory to your $PATH variable.

✔ **Cp** the script into a directory in your $PATH variable, such as /usr/bin.

✔ If you don't plan to run this script regularly, you can just indicate to the operating system that this once, you want to ignore the $PATH variable and execute a script in the local directory you're in.

You can do this (brave soul) by simply adding ./ before the script's name and pressing Enter.

Process Searching without a Magnifying Glass

Besides starting programs and scripts, you'll also need to monitor and stop them. You'll do this by using the ps, or *process search* command. If you run ps on your system at any given time, you'll find a dozen or several hundred processes running on your Linux network — depending on the size of the network, number of users, and time of day.

The ps command can use several command options. These include the set you can find in Table 3-4.

Get with the *program* or read the *script*— what's the difference?

Program and *script* are terms that can be used interchangeably. Both refer to a sequence of commands that someone has written for the computer to use. (The commands themselves are called *code*.)

The only difference I've been able to uncover between the terms is kind of colloquial — in effect, a *script* is something you can put together in a few minutes, using the vi editor. A *program* is generally the name given to a more complex script — or series of scripts — requiring more computer resources to run.

Here's a rule to go by: If you can vi the file, it's a *script*. If it's in machine language, comes in a brightly colored cardboard box, or is labeled "Microsoft," it's a *program*.

Table 3-4	Some ps Command Options You May Find Useful
Command Option	**What It Does**
-a	Lists all processes, including system processes.
-e	Lists all processes, such as -a.
-f	Lists processes with Full information.
-j	Lists just the group ID and the Session ID.
-l	Lists processes in *long form*, as with the -f option.

Try using **ps** on your Linux network right now. The output will look some-thing like this:

```
root    752      1  0  Apr 28  ?              0:00 /usr/sbin/inetd
root   1105   1098  0  Apr 28  ?              0:00 /usr/sbin/nfsd
              4
root    802      1  0  Apr 28  ?             0:00 sendmail:
              accepting connections
root   1678    752  0 10:27:37 ttyp1    0:00 telnetd
root   1092      1  0  Apr 28  ?          0:00
              /usr/sbin/rpc.mountd
root   1029      1  0  Apr 28  ?              0:00 /usr/sbin/cron
root   1053   1052  0  Apr 28  ?          0:00
              /opt/audio/bin/Aserver
wally1752   1707  5 14:12:02 pts/0    0:00 ps -aef
wally1754   1707  5 14:12:02 pts/0    0:00 printscript20
wally1755   1707  5 14:12:02 pts/0    0:00 print-allreports
```

To sift through this mountain of data, it's best to use the ps command with the | grep command. The | symbol is a pipe, and grep is a second command, allowing you to search for names or patterns. This combo is one of the most potent you'll find in Linux, and you'll be doing it a lot. Use it as follows:

```
ps | grep <filename>
```

If you want to isolate the print scripts running in the example above, use it as follows:

```
ps | grep print
```

You'll get the following output.

```
wally1754   1707  5 14:12:02 pts/0    0:00 printscript20
wally1755   1707  5 14:12:02 pts/0    0:00 print-allreports
```

The most important part of this output is the PID, or process ID number. The process ID number is always the first number to the right of the name of the user who executed the script. In this example, `printscript20` has a PID of `1754`, while `1755` is the PID of `print-allreports`. The PID is most useful when you're about to *kill* a process.

Killing is a rough and tumble way to express stopping a given program or script. I can only guess where this command originated. Probably the wide-open, wild Linux territories were more lawless way back when than they are nowadays.

A fistful of processes: kill 'em to stop 'em

Scripts Will Normally Stop Running When They've Completed Their Assigned Tasks. However, Stranger Things Than Walking-Dead Scripts Have Happened In The World Of Linux, So You May Need To Kill Those Vampire Processes As Follows:

```
Kill <Option, If Any> <Process Id Number>
```

It came from the Silicon Lagoon: The process that refused to die

Once in a long while, a process may refuse to die quietly. Instead it keeps on running after it's outlived its usefulness. Continuing in the macabre state of mind that gave us command *executions* and *killing* processes, Linux calls these creepy creatures *zombie processes*.

Killing these processes involves a sterner `kill` command. Luckily, `kill` has a number of options available for you to use as shown in Table 3-5.

Table 3-5	Kill Command Options You May Find Useful
Command Option	*What It Does*
`-1`	Hangup Signal.
The most gentle form of `kill`, because it allocates extra time beyond the default setting of "kill" for the program to finish exiting.	
`-3`	Quit (default setting of the `kill` command)
"Quit" allows the program killed time to finish its last task before exiting.	

(continued)

Table 3-5 (continued)

Command Option	What It Does
-4	Exit due to Illegal Instruction
This form of kill forces a program to terminate in the middle of performing an action. It's only used within complex programs by software developers.	
-5	Exit Due to Trace/Breakpoint Trap
This is similar to kill –4, only for a different kind of programming bug. Also like kill –4, you probably won't be using it unless you do serious coding.	
-9	Exit immediately and don't wait to clean up.

Of these, the strongest is kill -9. This command forces programs to exit immediately, without question — very risky at absolute best. Such extreme measures should be used rarely, if at all. Otherwise you could cause serious problems if the program you killed was in the middle of doing something vital, such as reallocating disk space.

Linux Plumbing — Pipes and Redirects

Linux may not have drains to clog up and gutters to clean, but it does have plenty of *pipes* for you to use.

A *pipe*, represented by the | symbol, is one of two ways you can redirect data flowing between commands. The pipe is the more commonly used of the two, and it's primarily used to send the results of one command to another command. You just learned one way this is done, to funnel data from the **ps** command to the grep command so you can search for processes by name.

```
ps | grep <filename>
```

The second method is used when directing data from a command into a static file. Luckily it's not too difficult to remember; it's the *arrow* or *greater-than* key. Using it is also easy:

```
<Command> > <File to store output of command>
```

Let's say you want to list your files and review the list later when you have time to pore over it. (And if you *do* find yourself enjoying poring over these things, then I suggest you get out of the house and go see a movie with friends or something. Right away.)

You'd create a file called `filereview` or something similar. Redirect the output of your ls command to it as follows:

```
ls -l > filereview
```

`Filereview` now has the information from the ls –l stored inside, for you to view or edit with the vi editor.

Let's say you want to create a file called "filereview." Redirect the output of your ls command to it with the following steps:

1. **Type the ls –l command at the command prompt.** *Don't execute the command yet; don't press Enter.* **The command prompt should look like this:**

```
Linuxbox% ls -l
```

2. **Add a space, then press the greater than sign ">" to tell Linux to redirect output into whichever file follows the arrow.** *Don't execute the command yet; don't press Enter.* **The command prompt should look like this:**

```
Linuxbox% ls -l >
```

3. **Add the file name "filereview."** *Don't execute the command yet; don't press Enter.* **The command prompt should look like this:**

```
Linuxbox% ls -l > filereview
```

4. **Now press Enter!**

You can view the results as filereview with the vi editor.

Chapter 4

Daemons — the Programs That Make Linux Go

● ●

In This Chapter

▶ What Linux Daemons are, and why that helps you

▶ System Startup States — The Daemon Invocation

▶ Network Daemons that Run Under Linux

▶ `lpd`, the Linux Printer Daemon

▶ `cron`, the daemon that runs 'round the clock

● ●

*I*n this chapter, you learn about the processes that run behind the scenes, keeping the Linux system running as you send your e-mails, print your files, and chastise your users for spilling sticky soft drinks on your file server. You learn which of these processes, called *daemons* are the important ones to look for when something doesn't operate the way it should. And you learn how to use one of the most powerful daemons of all to automate your system-administration tasks.

Daemons: The Gremlins on Your Side

Daemons are small, lightweight processes that run in the background on your Linux system. You never have to consciously invoke them — they spring into being automatically, depending on the condition of the Linux system. For example, certain daemons start life as soon as you boot your Linux network — and run continuously until you shut the system off. Should a daemon of this sort go on strike before you exit the program, you'll certainly notice it — and so will your users.

Other daemons are not so ever-present. Some come to life only when you invoke a specific command — for example, starting certain types of network connections, sending jobs to a printer, or copying files from one machine to the next.

The mysterious, mystical origin of the "daemon"

Before you start blaming my spell-checker for failing to protest when I typed *daemon* for this chapter, you should know that the term is actually correct. (I suppose the word *demon* could have been used, provided religious arguments weren't so easy to start, but let's not even go there.) *Daemon* (pronounced *day*-mun) gives the term a more classical, exotic feel.

Yes, I know the whole business of calling background processes "daemons" sounds more than a bit mystical. In fact I suspect that some early Linux and UNIX developers may have played a few too many late-night sessions of Dungeons and Dragons. Which is one reason (aside from raw admiration, of course) that Linux experts are often referred to as "wizards."

Myself, I like the term "techno-mage" (and so does TV science-fiction writer Michael Straczinski). After all — as Arthur C. Clarke once pointed out — "Any sufficiently advanced technology is indistinguishable from magic." And you, by reading this book, are on the way to joining the wizard's guild.

I like to think of daemons as helpful little creatures that hide out of sight until you look for them. People who worked in assembly-line plants had a name for the destructive version of such creatures (*gremlins* — whose joy was to disrupt machinery). Just thank your lucky stars that instead of gremlins, Linux has daemons — they're on *your* side, and their joy is to make your life easier for a change.

There are two general rules you can count on when you go looking for daemons:

✔ Just about every service offered by the Linux network has a daemon associated with it. There are daemons for printing, daemons for connecting, and daemons for handing out information like informational pamphlets.

✔ Their names tend to end in the letter d (as in `telnetd`). The *d* stands for (you guessed it) *daemon*. (Duh!)

Linux System States: Daemon Spawning Grounds

Daemons come into being to run and provide services of all kinds to your system. Since these services are dependent on the *state* of your Linux machine, it's important to know how to tell the state of your system, and how to alter these states. Otherwise, your daemons simply won't exist — to continue with the demonic analogy, they won't "spawn" — and your Linux machine will be as inert as a mass of steel, wire, and coffee-stained plastic.

Running from the run level

If you ask any Linux administrator what state the system is in, he or she will probably answer promptly, "Confusion!"

But when talking about *system states* in Linux, you're looking at more than the general condition or atmosphere of well being on your system. A Linux system's *state* means the actual level of functionality that applies to the entire networked system. These states are also called *run levels* (perhaps to distinguish them from other kinds of state — such as, say, anticipation, chaos, or New Jersey).

The *run level* of your system determines what kinds of automatic system scripts are run, and which services are running. If no services are running, no daemons have been spawned. Table 4-1 provides a handy list of run levels on a Linux system. They even come with numbers.

Table 4-1	Types of Run Levels on a Linux System	
Run Level	*Level of Functionality*	*Daemons Running?*
0	System is Halted	No
1	Single-User Mode	Nope
2	Multiuser, no NFS	A few
3	Multiuser, NFS (default)	Lots
4	Not Used	Zilcho
5	X11 console mode	Some
6	Reboot	Are you kidding? Nada, compadre.

Run Level 1

Run Level 1 is called *single user mode* because none of the services and the daemons that run the services are started. In this mode, your Linux system is confined to one box, the CPU that your monitor is attached to. If you have a Windows PC at home, this is the PC's natural state, unless your family has your computers all hooked up via cabling to the server in the basement and the printer in the kids' bedroom.

Since no one except the administrator account is allowed access, it's as if all the network lines have been snapped. No one can get in, get out, or go about their business. Although this sounds like an awful state of affairs, it's actually very useful to perform administrative tasks. So long as you do this after hours (or have a stout lock on your office door to prevent angry users from breaking in), you can work on the system with 100 percent confidence that no one will muddle with what you're modifying.

Run Level 3 — where your system should be

Run Level 3 is the usual default state of the Linux system. Run Level 3 is the state that your Linux system is shooting for when you reboot the system, which is when the daemons are spawned.

Your default state may be Run Level 2 if you don't share networked resources such as files or printers.

When your Linux system boots up, it runs a process called `init` *to initialize* the system. The first thing `init` does on startup is to run the `/etc/rc.d/rc.sysinit` script. `rc.sysinit` checks each file system for integrity and consistency. It also activates the swap partitions, which allow your system to perform at maximum speed.

Since these functions are needed on every run level, this check is performed regardless of whether your system shares out files, sits on a network, or stands alone without network connectivity. `init` next calls the appropriate file to kick off the services needed to reach the default run level of the machine.

The /etc/rc.d directory contains six more directories, each pertaining to a different run level the system can attain. Sensibly, these are numbered rc.0 through rc.6. Each of these subdirectories contains a number of scripts that begin with K or S, depending on whether the script *S*tarts daemons or *K*ills them.

In a rare moment of organizational skill, the Linux and UNIX developers decided to number the scripts in the order they are run. So if you're booting the system up the Run Level 3, `/etc/rc.d/S104` will run before `/etc/rc.d/S216` does. Kill scripts perform the opposite function, shutting down processes that don't belong in a particular run level, or smoothly shut down services when the system is being brought down gently (as in, *not* with `halt`).

Other run levels

Run Level 1 is actually a state your machine stays in, but in case of heavy-duty emergency, it can be used to stop the machine so the computer-doctor can perform critical work on the system. You *can* kick your Linux box into

Run Level 1 by typing **halt** at the command line. But you'd better have an *extremely* good reason for doing so, or you'll have a lot of angry users on your hands.

Friends don't let friends type halt. Knocking your system into Run Level 1 in this manner is the equivalent of pulling the plug out of the back of your machine. Your computer won't like this, and will find a way to get back at you, by not saving files that were being worked on, or ending up with corrupt file systems.

Unless you truly enjoy installing your Linux system — multiple times — don't use this command unless things are truly out of control. (I'm talking things like the Linux system belching smoke and fire from the network ports.)

Run Level 4 isn't used by your Linux system, nor by anyone else I can think of. Why not? Probably for the same reason that 3-track tapes never caught on — some mysterious principle that nature will let us know when it's good and ready.

Run Level 5 is used on occasion, but unless you run an X11 console it won't do you any good. (If you don't know what an X11 console is, then you probably don't have one. In which case, don't worry about it.)

Run Level 6 is hardly a state at all — as soon as you switch the system to this state, it shuts everything down and begins the reboot process. Unless something is badly wrong, Linux will spend no longer than 60 seconds in this state — at which point the startup scripts begin to run, putting the system into a new state. If you're from the Windows world, Run Level 6 is the equivalent of hitting Ctrl+Alt+Delete to restart your Windows system.

Changing system states: tel-init on the mountain . . .

Linux is nothing if not flexible; if you want to change system states the same way you change gears in your car, you can. The telinit command can change the run level of your system by activating the appropriate scripts in the /etc/rc.d area without rebooting the entire system.

To use this command, simply type **telinit**. The only command options available to telinit are the numbers of the run levels available to you (0 through 6). Luckily, *only* the administrator can run this command. It's particularly useful when you want to bring the system *gently* to Run Level 1 so you can troubleshoot problems.

Network Daemons that Run under Linux

Network daemons include any and all processes that run when making use of a Linux network service. The majority are one-shot daemons; they come into being when the service is invoked, then disappear off the radar screen when the service is canceled or completed.

- ✔ telnetd is such a one-shot daemon. When you telnet, or remotely connect to another machine, the telnet daemon is spawned. We probe the mysteries of the telnet session in a later chapter; for now, be aware that since it involves an active machine that can talk on the network, it's not going to run under Run Level 1.

- ✔ ftpd is another of this kind of daemon. The ftp service that this daemon oversees involved transferring files from one machine to a remote location, or vice versa. Again, this isn't the sort of thing that works on a machine set to Run Level 1, the single-user mode.

You can look for either of these daemons by using the **ps –aef | grep** command described in Chapter 3.

Don't panic if you don't see these daemons. It could mean that no one's using their respective services right now, so they haven't been spawned. Of course, feel free to panic if either the telnet or the ftp service doesn't work at all. This means the daemons aren't running properly, and it's time for the administrator (guess who?) to troubleshoot the problem.

The permanent daemon residents: inetd and nfsd

The two most important daemons that run more or less continuously on your system are inetd and nfsd. True, nfsd won't be around if you're in Run Level 2, but over 90 percent of Linux systems use some form of NFS, so you're better off knowing what to look for.

NFS stands for Network File System, and it's a convenient way of sharing out the files needed by multiple users (or Linux machines) on your network. NFS is a subject that deserves its own chapter — in fact, whole books are justly devoted to the subject — but all you need to know (right at the moment) is that NFS is the purest form of the client-server networking method.

Say what? Nothing to do with attorneys and waiters. In a client-server setup:

✔ One machine acts as the NFS *server,* handing out the exported files or file systems

✔ The other machines act as *clients,* taking data from the server when needed

Both servers and clients need the services provided by the nfsd daemon to run properly.

So if you're having problems with a client receiving files that should be from an NFS-mounted file system, do a ps and check for the nfsd daemon.

If you have the same trouble on all your clients, check the server itself — odds are pretty unlikely that every single one of these daemons would die at the same time, unless there's a power outage. (And if there has in fact been a power outage, the nfsd daemon is the least of your problems!)

The inetd *daemon* (also called by the more intimidating title "inetd meta-daemon") is used to start programs automatically. The "start" signal is a user's request. Depending on the port the request comes in on, the daemon will start up a telnet, ftp, or other one-shot daemon. How does inetd know how to do this? Its job is to act as the master daemon-spawner by watching the request ports.

Since inetd has such a tricky and demanding role to play in the Linux world, it has not one but *two* files devoted to its configuration, /etc/services and /etc/inetd.conf. If either file is missing, corrupted, or mismanaged, inetd won't run — and you'll be back to reinstalling your system. So although you can learn about these two Very Important Files in some detail here, it's best not to practice your vi editing skills on them. But you knew that.

Your friendly /etc/services file

The /etc/services file lists the TCP/IP port number associated with every service the Linux system invokes. It also lists any additional information about that port, such as an existing alias.

If you **vi** the /etc/services file (carefully), you'll see entries that look something like this:

```
ftp         11/tcp
telnet      12/tcp
smtp        13/tcp              mail
name        14/tcp              nameserver
time        15/tcp              timeserver
whois       20/tcp
gopher      88/tcp              #port for 'gopher' server
```

Here's how to read the entries in each line of the `services` file:

✔ The first entry in each line is the *name of the service* that can be invoked.

✔ Next, the *port number* and the *protocol* used with that port is listed.

✔ Finally, there's a note on any *aliases* or *comments* to tell you what the port is used for.

From this file, you can tell that if you try to use the `telnet` service, your request comes in on port 12. `inetd` is watching this port. Next it kicks off the `telnet` daemon (`telnetd`) to get the service going, and then goes back to its business — watching all the ports listed in the file.

Techie terms sometimes mutate into new meanings. For example, a Linux *port* is different from the receptacles at the back of your Linux box (like a serial port or a parallel printer port) that accept physical plugs and cables. For openers, a Linux port isn't really physical; it's a "location" in your computer's logical structure: The term "port" a way of saying that and exchange of information is happening along a particular logical route, somewhat like the way an exchange of electricity happens along the physical cables in your computer system.

✔ In the software sense, a *port* is like a selected rendezvous where two programs agree to meet and exchange information.

✔ Such a rendezvous is a "logical" location; it has no physical form, so the only way to tell the programs exactly where to go is to give each program the same number and file, and tell them both to make the exchange there. All daemons, scripts, and programs are programmed to look in certain files (such as `/etc/services`) to find the number of the logical location where they're supposed to meet and exchange information.

To provide a final real-world analogy, a `telnetd` daemon understands the information in `telnetd tcp/50` as clearly as you or I would understand the instruction, "Meet me at 7:00 p.m. at the Stagger Inn Hotel and I'll give you the report you want."

Watching those ports with /etc/inetd.conf

`inetd` knows what ports to monitor by taking the port information contained in the `/etc/services` listings and applying it as specified in the `/etc/inetd.conf` file.

If you **vi** the /etc/inetd.conf file — again, *be careful not to change that file* — you'll see something similar to this:

```
# Standard Services
ftp       stream  tcp  nowait  root  /usr/sbin/tcpd  in.ftp
telnet    stream  tcp  nowait  root  /usr/sbin/tcpd  in.tel-
          netd
gopher    stream  tcp  nowait  root  /usr/sbin/tcpd  gn
```

Here's how to read the file:

- ✔ The services listed (ftp, telnet, gopher) are from the entries in the /etc/services file.

- ✔ The term stream specifies the type of information packets to be processed by the protocol listed in the next field (for the port connection).

  stream is the packet method used by the TCP protocol; dgram is used for UDP.

- ✔ The option nowait tells the inetd daemon to not loiter around until a connection is made. This setting sends the daemon back to watching ports ASAP, with no coffee breaks allowed. Of course, if nowait is selected, then only one instance of a program will run at a time.

- ✔ The next setting tells the system what user it should run as (by default, it's root, the administrator account).

- ✔ Next up is the path to the program.

- ✔ Capping it off is the name of the program the system is to look for.

If you ever want to add a service to your Linux system and are reasonably sure you know what you are doing, make sure to edit this file — as well as the /etc/services file — with the **vi** editor. So long as you fill out each entry in a new line and select a port number that hasn't been used, you won't run into trouble.

lpd, the Daemon That Runs Your Linux Print Shop

One thing you'll notice about print services in Linux, right off the bat, is that they're all named after variations on a theme: LP- something.

Legend has it that this nomenclature is from the old term *Local Printer,* but I've never been able to confirm it. Also, the name doesn't exactly make sense since you use lp to print from any printer on the network, not just your local one.

Keeping with the naming convention (as well as that old origin myth), the Local Printing Daemon is called lpd. The lpd daemon is an odd sort of hybrid between the daemons which remain resident and the ones that just exist for the length of a job. lpd itself lasts as long as your Linux network is running, but it spawns duplicates of itself — one to handle each print job. Once all jobs are completed, the extra daemons automagically vanish back to where they came from.

Like the inetd daemon, lpd has a configuration file. lpd watches over the printer ports like inetd watches the network ones. When lpd spots an incoming print job, it immediately consults the /etc/printcap file and then spawns a new lpd daemon to take care of the job.

This new daemon directs the print job request to one of the device files in the /dev directory. If the device is hooked up through the older serial ports, the file is sent to the devices named after the old teletype machines, /dev/ttys0, /dev/ttys1, and so on. Newer kinds of printers may be attached by a parallel cable. If so, lpd directs the file to the devices labeled /dev/lp0, /dev/lp1, and so forth.

Port assignments are made when you configure the print services. The changes are made in the extremely complicated and messy /etc/printcap file. The file is so complex and hard to read; it's best never to edit it with the vi editor.

If you really need to edit the /etc/printcap file, use the printer-configuration tools that came with your Linux system. Consult the handy "Printer Configuration" sections of *Linux For Dummies* for this info.

Unfortunately, working with the lpd daemon has taught me to be cautious about recommending its reliability. Every now and then, lpd has astounded me with its random ability to lie down and die. Worse, there are times that it *doesn't* die, but instead decides to have a snit and go on strike for no apparent reason.

When lpd freezes up or runs without doing anything, it's best to treat it as a *zombie process* — not usefully alive, just undead — and take an electronic axe to it. (Killing old lpds was known at my work as "Doing the zombie stomp.")

Use **ps** to determine its PID and use **kill –9**. Of course, this kills whatever print job it was trying to execute, but it's better to lose one job than to lose an entire afternoon's work. Such trade-offs do happen.

To restart the print daemon, simply type in the entire command line:

```
/usr/sbin/lpd
```

Is your print daemon lying down on the job?

First, do a **ps** to make sure the lpd process is actually running. If it is, your best bet is to send a test file to your default printer. You can do this by running the following preinstalled command:

```
lptest | lpr
```

This test should print ASCII text from your default printer (as configured in the /etc/printcap file). You can check the status of print daemons — and of users sending print jobs — by using the following command:

```
lpc status
```

You should also test to make sure that the printer is using the right port by sending a file directly to a specified port. If the ports are configured wrong, then the print daemon is watching the wrong port and will miss any print requests coming in — causing more headaches for you. You can test printers on serial ports as in the following example:

```
lptest > /dev/ttys1
```

This will force the command lptest to use the specific device, in this case the ports configured to connect print job information to this serial device. To check parallel port devices, use the following command:

```
lptest > /dev/lp1
```

If your Linux system has an X Windows system with a Printer Manager tool, you can test and reconfigure your print daemon (and the print devices) by using the GUI provided. If you're a Linux purist, this may be distasteful, but if you're not a Linux guru yet, it may shave a few precious minutes off the response time to a perplexing print problem.

cron — the 'Round-the-Clock Daemon

crond (the cron utility daemon) reads your crontab file regularly and executes commands stored in the crontab at the times specified in the file. cron doesn't really have a command line to execute it, nor does it have command options. It always runs in the background via the cron daemon, crond.

cron is all Greek to me

Ready for another taste of mythology? The `cron` process, appropriately enough, is named after the Greek god of ongoing time, Cronos (otherwise known as Chronos, who kindly lent his name to a whole line of fancy wristwatches).

`cron` is a very useful utility to work with because it's how you automate system-administration tasks. You can have the `crond` daemon erase all log files in a certain directory every day at 11:00. You can have it copy errors into a file for easy viewing every Tuesday afternoon. You can even make it print out a copy of its status to you whenever you feel lonely and in need of something to do on a Saturday night. To do these marvelous things, all you need do is make sure `crond` is running (details, details), and edit the `crontab` file appropriately.

The first part is almost too easy: `cron` starts when the Linux system boots up; the `crond` checks for the `crontab` file to see whether there's anything it should be aware of. The `crond` even runs when your Linux network is in Run State 2, the non-NFS, multiple-user mode. (To be doubly safe, do a **ps** to make sure it's happily running in the background.)

The file that the `cron` daemon actually reads is called the `crontab`, which is located in the `/var/spool/cron/crontabs` directory. Each user should have a `crontab` file in this location, sorted by user account name — like so:

```
/var/spool/cron/root
/var/spool/cron/samspade
/var/spool/cron/wally
```

To provide the commands for `cron` to follow, edit your `crontab` file. Keep in mind that *unless you're the administrator,* you can't edit anyone's `cron` file except yours. If you are that august individual, you can edit the `crontab` file with this command:

```
crontab -e
```

You can use **crontab** with the **edit** command option to open your `crontab` file in the `vi` editor. It's best to put in a separate line explaining what job your command is going to perform; that way, if you need to edit it, you won't be dependent entirely on long-term memory. This enlightening process is called *adding a comment.* (Whoa. How technical can you get?)

You can add as many comments as you like to a file. The Linux operating system won't read them, so long as you include a **#** or *hash mark* at the start of the line. Let's say you want `cron` to copy the file `/etc/mine/log` every Monday, Wednesday, and Friday at 2 p.m. You want `cron` to put the information into a file called `whazzup` in the `/usr/home/wally` directory.

Start with the comment. After typing **crontab –e**, use the **vi** editor to add the following line:

```
# Copy file /etc/mine/log on M-W-F, 2pm & put it in
         /usr/home/wally/whazzup
```

Next, input the cron *time fields* in the crontab entry. The format used by cron in the crontab file is six fields long (see Table 4-2 for what each field means):

```
Minute    Hour    Day of the Month    Month    Day of Week
          Command
```

Table 4-2	Crontab Fields and What They Mean
Field	*How To Set It*
Minute	Specify this field from 0 to 59 *only*. Really. Setting this field to 90 won't run the job every hour and a half; cron just won't understand it and will refuse to run.
Hour	Specify this from 0 to 23. Yes, I did say *23* — . cron doesn't have a setting for a.m. or p.m. Instead, cron follows strict military time (as does Linux in general, *sir*).
Day of the Month	Specify this from 1 to 31.
Month	Specify this from 1 to 12, or by the first three letters of the month (such as **jan, feb, mar**).
Day Of Week	Specify this from 0 to 6, (0 = Sunday). As with the month field, you can use the first three letters of the day (**mon, tue, wed**).
Command	Specify the command you want run here — you can use multiple commands as long as they interact with one another via a pipe or a redirect.

For all the fields except Command, you can use the all-purpose wildcard you learned about in Chapter 3, the asterisk (*). Since * means *one or however many more,* using it indicates that you want the command run every time the time cycle is complete. Let's look at some possibilities for setting up different cron cycles for performing the command ps.

If you want to run the ps command at 1:30 p.m., Monday, January 30, voilá:

```
30    13    30    jan    mon    ps
```

To run this command every Monday in January at 1:30 p.m., your specs look like this:

```
30      13      *     jan    *     ps
```

To run this command every hour on the hour, every day of every month, here's what it looks like ("Volga Boatman" soundtrack optional):

```
00      *       *     *      *     ps
```

Since in our example, you need to run two commands that are connected by a *redirect*, you'll have to put together the following command line with the command options explored so brilliantly in Chapter 3.

```
# Copy file /etc/mine/log on M-W-F, 2pm & put it in
          /usr/home/wally/whazzup

cp /etc/mine/log /usr/home/wally/whazzup
```

Refer to the examples just given to fill in the remaining five fields, determining which times you want to run the cp command. Your end result should look a lot like this:

```
00      14      *     *      mon, wed, fri cp /etc/mine/log
                    /usr/home/wally/whazzup
```

When you're done, save and exit from vi with the command **:wq**. You can check out your handiwork without using vi:

```
crontab -l
```

Your result should bear a striking resemblance to this one:

```
# Copy file /etc/mine/log on M-W-F, 2pm & put it in
          /usr/home/wally/whazzup
```

When you separate different fields in the crontab file, use spaces or tabs, not commas. If you've putting in multiple entries into one crontab field, always use commas, or you'll get results you didn't plan on. For example, in the first two fields (minute and hour) you may be unpleasantly surprised if you meant to run the cron job on the hour and at 15 past the hour so you put in

```
00      15
```

instead of

```
00,15
```

The second set of numbers does the job; the first set, lacking a comma, runs the job only once per day — at 3:00 p.m. sharp!

Part II
Taking Charge of Your World

Fault-Tolerant Rickshaw

In this part . . .

*I*t's not enough to be an administrator in name only. Part II is about power . . . real power . . . lots of power . . . ahahahaha! (Oops. Sorry.) Here's where you get a briefing on your mission as the Head Knocker, the Big Kahuna, the Alpha User of your Linux network — by exercising your control of the `root` account. What's more, you learn how to use your capability to become the "superuser" to advance the cause of truth, justice, and network security.

Part II also gets into the vital topic of managing a user community on a Linux network. It's a sweeping vista — from the nuts and bolts of adding a new user's account (or shutting off access to the system if someone leaves your company or becomes a security risk) to the ticklish art of keeping your user community happy, productive, and relatively peaceful.

You also learn about the Network File System, perhaps the most powerful way yet devised to distribute entire Linux file systems across your network. You learn how to start, stop, mount, and unmount directories and devices — until your Linux network is as configurable as a brand-new Lego set.

And finally, you start to branch out beyond your initial administration machine and onto the network. You start learning the use of the `ping` and `spray` commands to determine whether your net(work) has a few holes worn in it and what you can do about it if you find some. Have some heroic fun (cape and boots optional).

Chapter 5

"Root"ing Around: Becoming the Master User

*I*n this chapter, you learn about the root account. You'll be spending 90 percent of your work time as root to do your job of starting, stopping, and configuring your Linux system. That's because the root account allows you to become, in essence, the god of your Linux world.

To begin with, it's best to find out why such amazing powers were bestowed upon one small, relatively insignificant user account.

Linux Is Open, but the Window Is Shut Tight

The first question that crops up may be, "Why is only one account allowed to do the administration? That sounds like one person gets to be a control freak!"

Well, not to put it too bluntly, that's about the size of it. One — and only one — account on a Linux system gets to be omnipotent. This is the all-powerful root *account,* sometimes called the *superuser account.* Like a more mundane, regular-Joe kind of account, the root account has its own home directory, its own $PATH, and its own password.

It's a bird, it's a plane, it's . . . Superuser!

Did you notice that I said "Only one *account* gets to be root?" I didn't say "Only one *person* gets to be root." That's because anyone who knows the password to enter the root account can become root! This is often the case when you have three or four administrators who might work different days. All these administrators must know the password in case they suddenly have to do (gasp!) *administrative* work on their shifts.

Administrator, beware: Any user who discovers a terminal left open by the root account (or overhears the password can cause major havoc). Through malice or ignorance, such a sorcerer's apprentice can bring your network to its knees.

Linux has only one administrator account because Linux was developed, like its big brother UNIX, as an *open system* intended for shared use by multiple users. Microsoft Windows was developed, in contrast, as a *closed system*. Unless you're running Windows NT, it's comparatively difficult to remotely log in to another Windows machine from your own. Even with NT, by default most users' files are completely inaccessible to you.

"Great," you might think, "That's good for my privacy." True, but it's not so good when you're holding forms, databases, or information that everyone in your department or company needs. By definition, a closed system is composed of isolated machines that need tender loving care (and maybe a sledgehammer or two) to open up and share files over a network.

Linux is the complete opposite. From the first versions of Linux, if you worked on one Linux box in San Francisco, you could easily make a hop, skip, and a jump to run a process on a remote machine in Toledo, list directories on another Linux box in Dallas, and print out your results on a machine in Walla Walla, Washington.

Use the previous paragraph for imaginative purposes only; flying to Walla Walla to retrieve a printout may not be cost-effective (gee . . . ya think?).

Until recently, you couldn't display more than a couple of remote telnet sessions on your Windows computer — and what you could have those remote machines *do* was pretty limited. One reason for this limitation is that Windows uses a GUI, and all those pictures make the interface very slow and difficult to transport over a Telnet session. Linux lacks a GUI and so never had this hang-up. You could open up as many sessions as you liked and run a veritable symphony of machines to your heart's content.

The flip side of this situation is that *anyone* with the proper passwords could log in to your Linux network from around the world — and bring things to a crashing halt on a whim (potentially, at least).

In essence, the Linux root account is the first, most basic security tool you can use to prevent users from damaging the Linux system inadvertently.

For example, **cd** to the root directory. This is where the root account begins. List the files there; you'll see all the directories that handle important information, such as /etc, /usr, /dev, and so on. Do an **ls –l** and you see an interesting pattern: All these directories are owned by the root account. That means if I'm Wally the Wonder User and I decide I'm feeling out of sorts today because you (the cruel administrator) didn't give me more disk space, I can't just rm the /usr directory to make room! As a typical user, I'll have to cd through the directories until I get to my home area (such as /etc/user/home/wally) before I find the directories and files I already own — which I can delete away to my heart's content — and nobody's files get zapped but mine.

Keep in mind that 99.9 percent of all damage done to a Linux system is *not* malevolent at all. It's usually caused by people making natural mistakes, typing errors, and by blundering into places they shouldn't be. Linux, by its very nature, is not an electronic totalitarian system.

The whole idea of an open system is, specifically, to allow large groups of people to share data while working on a project. Or to allow them to modify information in another area when they have news to report. Or to let someone print out a report in another building so it's ready to pick up when they blast in the door hellbent for a meeting.

Perhaps the biggest function that root serves is to crack open (or slam) doors that lead to certain files or directories, depending on whether the information needs to get out or needs to remain private. Which is why the root account can chmod, chown, or chgrp any file on the system.

You, the superuser, are in charge of making sure that the department memos on the /usr/public/docs directory stays readable and writable by all, while the /usr/home/mail directories remain private to all but their owners.

Root privileges: Use the Force, Luke . . .

A noted physicist once said that duct tape was like the Force in *Star Wars*:

- ✔ It has a light side.
- ✔ It has a dark side.
- ✔ It holds the universe together.

I can't think of a better way to describe the root account's powers in Linux.

The `root` account has one special property that extends to no other account. That is, the usual file permissions and security measures set up to prevent damage and secure privacy *do not apply* to `root`.

Being `root` allows you to bypass the very Linux security mechanisms that are put in place to discourage users from tampering with what they shouldn't. A good number of the files that handle administration simply won't allow users to see, touch, or edit them without `root` permission.

However, you *can* be tempted by the dark side of the `root` force. (Rumor has it that Darth Vader started out as a Linux administrator who went bad.) For example, as `root`, it's your job to make sure the mail accounts stay private. But there's nothing stopping you from waltzing in, changing the permissions so you can read a person's mail, and leaving without a trace.

Also, because you're swinging a heavier set of privileges, you have to tread more lightly as the `root` account. Shutting down a process — or even rebooting a single machine — as `root` can have much more of a ripple effect than it would if one user decided to log off a system. Your shutdown command can literally shut the rest of the place down!

Don't get too paranoid about this. What I'm trying to tell you is that as `root`, you have more responsibility, so you should never rush into things. No matter how bad a situation seems, rest assured that you can make things a *lot* worse by pulling plugs and shutting down processes at random.

So as one vastly experienced system administrator once told me when I was starting out, "Stay cool. Uncool dudes get stomped on."

Changing to Superuser without the Glass Phone Booth

You don't need to duck into a telephone booth to change into Superuser. (Come to think of it, why did Superman use a telephone booth to change? You could still see through the glass . . .) Instead, you have two different options available to tap into your godlike powers.

- ✔ Direct login
- ✔ "Morphing" from another login

Direct login

You can simply log in to your system directly as root. On your Linux terminal, when asked for your username, simply type **root**. When asked for your password, enter in the password that you've selected for root. Normally, when you become root, the prompt will look slightly different. Where Wally the Wonder User's account might look like this —

```
[wally@linuxbox]$
```

root's screen normally doesn't have a name displayed. (Hey, as root, you're too *cool* to display a name.) While you're working as root, your prompt will almost always be a simple, understated hash mark:

```
#
```

If root is so wonderful, you may ask, then why have your own account? Why not just log in to the Linux system as root each time? Thereby hangs a tale.

On my system, I prefer to have a user account (michael@linuxbox.com) as well as my root account, and I suggest you do the same. Why?

✔ Reducing the amount of time you spend as root when you're not actively administering the system also reduces the chance of your making a mistake that takes down the system.

When you become root you should be more mentally focused on the task at hand, not traipsing through your email.

✔ If someone e-mails you, he or she might feel pretty silly addressing you as part of a tree, as in Hey, root, old buddy! Let's meet for dinner after work.

Moral: Keep business and pleasure separate; give 'em different accounts.

Morphing from another login

Another way to become root is to use the su command. The su command stands for — you guessed it — superuser!

In fact, you can use su to become *anyone* on the system.

Morphing from another account

su allows you to morph into anyone's account on the system, even if that person is already logged in on another machine — or even the same machine! For example, let's say that you were already logged in as root. Typing the *identify* command, **id**, at the prompt would confirm who you are:

```
# id
# root <gid 0>
```

You have the power to become any user on the system (any user's account, that is). Let's assume that for some legitimate reason you want to become user Wally. Using the command structure su <username>, you type in the change:

```
# su wally
Password: <Wally's Password>
[wally@linuxbox]$
```

Morphing into the Superuser from any user account is even easier. Let's say you're logged in as user Averagejoe. Use **id** and the **su** command as before — but when you su, you don't have to put in a username. Unless you specify a username, su automatically assumes you mean to become root. Here's how your commands and outputs will look.

```
[Averagejoe@linuxbox]$ id
[Averagejoe@linuxbox]$ Averagejoe <GID 4>
[Averagejoe@linuxbox]$ su
#
# id
# root <GID 0>
```

Monitoring access

Using the su method of becoming root is intrinsically better because it's more secure. (Or to be more accurate, it lends itself to system security more easily, because it allows you to note and track down anyone who's using the su command improperly.)

Each time you use the su command, it's noted in a log file that's automatically kept by your Linux system as part of its system accounting. The file is located in the *system logs directory,* namely, /var/log/messages. **vi** this file and you see the current example noted appropriately:

```
July 1  14:00:10  linuxbox  su: Averagejoe on /dev/ttyp1
```

In English, the entry tells you, "On July 1, at ten seconds past two in the afternoon, user Averagejoe successfully became the root user on machine linuxbox." A log like this may not necessarily help you stop people from becoming root, but it can help you track down who's doing what on a system.

On a system with multiple system administrators, each of whom use root to maintain the network, /var/log/messages will clue you in to who did the "maintenance" that might now be causing problems! Let's see an example of how this capability might work.

Let's say that on the morning of December 1, you notice that the Message of the Day that greets you when you log on has been changed to "An Ode to Linux Hackers." The .motd, (for Message of the Day) file can only be edited by the root account. Thus, to paraphrase Hamlet, something has passed its expiration date in Denmark.

You **vi** the /var/log/messages file. There you see these entries for the last few days:

```
November 21  15:20:56  legitmachine  su: innocent1 on
             /dev/ttyp1
November 28  12:10:10  alibi  su: adminguy on /dev/ttyp3
November 29  02:30:00  suspectbox  su: Loki on /dev/ttyp2
December   1  08:11:20  linuxbox  su: wally on /dev/ttyp1
```

The December 1 login is you, of course. On the afternoon of November 21, user innocent1 logged in from the Linux box legitmachine. Around noon on November 28, user adminguy logged in from machine alibi. Both adminguy and innocent1 are Linux administrators on different shifts, so everything checks out in the log so far.

But on November 29, at the suspiciously late hour of 2:30 in the morning, a user named Loki logged in from machine suspectbox. When you do a quick check of your records, you find that Loki isn't a member of your admin staff.

Do you immediately locate Loki, shut down his account, and beat him with bunch of wet noodles? No. Remember that Loki is a user account, not the person himself. What if Loki had simply left the computer lab with his account still up and running? Anyone could have used his account to commit Linux heresies at will. A better strategy is to question user Loki about his account, and then determine the real problem.

The problem, of course, is that someone who shouldn't have known the root system password *got* it. We'll be covering password protection more in a later chapter. And if you're of the disciplinarian mindset, you'll be glad to know that you also learn how to discipline user Loki if it turns out that he *was* the one who caused the trouble.

The multiple-su hazard

One of the worst ways you can let system security slip into the wrong keyboards is by flagrant use of the su command. Too many of these stacked on top of one another can cause you to forget who and what you are, leading to disaster. Here's how this can happen in the course of a normal, but very busy day:

You're logged in to linuxbox as root; the hash mark shows up as usual:

```
#
```

You need to check your mail, so (let's say) you su to become your humble alter ego, mild-mannered Linux reporter Kent Clark (username: kclark):

```
# su kclark
Password: ******
[kclark@linuxbox]$
```

While checking mail, Wally the Wonder User asks where to find his .cshrc file. You oblige by quickly su'ing to his account to show him:

```
[kclark@linuxbox]$ su wally
Password: ******
[wally@linuxbox]$
```

Wally leaves but user Averagejoe stops by and asks whether he's vi'ed a file correctly. To check without leaving your console, you su to the Averagejoe account:

```
[wally@linuxbox]$ su Averagejoe
Password: ******
[Averagejoe@linuxbox]$
```

Stop for a minute. After a busy day, are you going to remember what you started out as? Maybe, maybe not. How deep are you here? Let's say that Averagejoe walks by the console after hours and sees his name on the screen. He exits out of the account (which is his, after all), and then sees Wally's account. Hey, neat! He quickly reads all of Wally's private mail, then exits so he won't be caught.

He sees kclark, and realizes he's in the root administrator's account. Averagejoe is on a roll here, so he reads all of your mail, deletes a few files for fun, then exits again so no one knows he's around.

And now he's in the root account. Oh, the humanity!

Starting and Stopping the System with the Root Account

Second only to the power of changing file permissions is the root account's power to be the only one that can properly start or shut down the Linux system.

True, any *person* can shut down the Linux system improperly, by flicking the right switch, yanking the right plug, or setting fire to the right building. But these aren't ways that will bring the system up problem-free — and they can't be done from a user *account*.

Also, no user account can properly configure a Linux system to boot up in the right manner. Only the `root` account can configure the system to come up righteously — so all Linux users on the network can work effectively.

If you come from a UNIX background, particularly of the Sun-Solaris vein of the UNIX world, your past experience may lead you astray. Beware of booting the Linux system, booting off your Linux CD-ROM, or attempting to boot off the network from a mounted server. These tricks work well under UNIX — *but* I've never heard of anyone trying this in Linux without the process turning into a moderate-to-major disaster.

Automatic reboot

If, like 90 percent of all Linux administrators, you've inherited your system from someone else, the startup should be automatic. Linux is smart enough to know how to boot up automatically should the power fail; let the system come back online and then go in as `root`. Make sure all the files you want mounted are actually mounted, that the printers are working, and so on.

If you do suffer a power outage, immediately go around the office and start turning off as many machines as possible. Yes, I know that if the power is already off, it doesn't seem as if this would change anything. But what you're doing is *preparing the system to come back on*. Remember, a network of machines comes back to life slowly when you add one, two, or five extra machines that get plugged in one at a time. If you have, say, *fifty* machines and they all come back at the same time as the power, you have an enormous power surge that could knock the system for a loop and blow out a fuse. Which puts you out of commission even when the power is back in the building! To avoid this disaster, turn those machines off and then *gradually* bring the system back online, one machine at a time.

Incidentally, some users may get the idea that they'll lose all their work if you turn their machines off. Explain to them very firmly that they already lost all their work when the power went out! If that doesn't work, make sure they know they'd better be ready to explain to their manager why their actions resulted in a blown fuse and further loss of productivity as you waited for the electrician to show up.

Booting from disk

If your installation of Linux is a relatively recent one, you have an extra fall-back position: the boot disk. Current Red Hat Linux installations either come with a premade boot disk, or the installation CD-ROM asks, during the course of the install, whether you want to make a boot disk.

The CD-ROM that comes with *Linux For Dummies* should prompt you to create a boot disk. See that book's installation chapters for help with creating the disk.

Always accept an offer to create a boot disk. If (for some unknown reason) the system doesn't come *all the way* back up, your best bet is to shut the system back down. Next, insert the boot disk, and reboot the machine. The box — particularly if you're running Linux on a PC — will sense the disk in the drive and boot from it, allowing the system to come back up. Follow your normal checkup procedures to ensure that the system is whole and functional.

LILO, LILO, it's off to work we go . . .

Another way you might use to start your Linux system is LILO (which stands for Linux Loader). LILO is what you'll probably use if you have multiple operating systems loaded on your system. For example, if you're running your Linux system off a box which happens to be a PC running the universally loved/loathed Microsoft Windows, you have to specify whether you want the system to come up running Linux or Windows.

You may have heard computer folk use the term dual-boot. This is the situation we're talking about here. When you have a machine which can boot one of two available operating systems, it's called a dual-boot system. If you want to get really wild you go for a triple-boot system with three operating systems, but your computer might start suffering from a multiple-personality disorder.

Dual-boot can be a very confusing term because you're still only booting one operating system. Unfortunately, we're stuck with it for the moment.

When you're installing your Linux system, you'll be prompted to install LILO if your machine is running a different operating system. From then on, LILO is one of the easiest utilities to deal with in Linux because it's all automatic, and you only deal with it once — at system boot time.

When you flip the power switch on your box to on, your machine will go through its typical warm-up whines, groans, and whistles to give you the LILO boot: prompt. Press the Tab key to see the operating systems you can choose from. Type the name of the operating system you want to use — and of course, you'll pick Linux, right? Linux will then boot, bringing you to the familiar login: prompt.

What can go wrong at boot-up and how to fix it

On occasion you may find that at boot-up, the system might give you an error message, or the system reaches a point where it refuses to do anything else.

This is called *hanging* by Linux gurus, and it's what you're going to feel like doing to yourself if you can't get things back in order.

Here's a bevy of common reasons for a hanging system and how to fix them:

Driver Loading Errors:

If Linux complains about this area, you're looking at one of the easier problems so long as you have a grounding cable and a screwdriver.

Basically, you're looking at a hardware problem. If Linux is complaining about a piece of hardware that's external to the system (that is, attached by a cord), go check the cord to make sure it's plugged in and the connection is tight. And you thought being a Linux administrator was tough, right?

For an internal piece of hardware, you need to shut the system down, switch it off, and remove the nonessential cards from the system, such as the Ethernet card, serial network card, and sound card. Start the system up again. If one of these cards was badly damaged, the whole motherboard can go on strike.

A couple things about dealing with Linux, or any computer hardware.

- ✔ Never assume that something *isn't* powered. You may be in for the shock of your life.

- ✔ When you're told to check a cord, don't settle for a visual examination. The cord may be in the socket, but the metal connectors inside are just a little too far apart to touch. Make sure the connection is tight.

- ✔ Invest in a good grounding cable, and wear static wrist guards if you plan to work on the inside of a machine. Nothing ruins memory or network cards better than static. Neither power surges, solar flares, nor giant meteors hitting Earth — nothing!

Startup Script Errors:

Remember that on boot-up, the system reads the start-up scripts in the /etc/rc.d directory. These are the scripts that Start or Kill the processes that run during the start-up procedures.

If one of these scripts get corrupted, the system will hang on that very script procedure. This is the clue you'll need.

Follow these steps to fix the corrupted script:

1. **Reboot the system in single-user mode using your emergency boot floppy disk.**

2. **cd to the /etc/rc.d directory and look through the scripts until you find the one that contains the instructions that caused the holdup.**

3. **Reinstall the backup script from your floppy or your CD-ROM.**

It's best to copy your /etc/rc.d directory to another directory, or on your emergency boot floppy in case this happens. If you do this, you don't even have to hunt for the specific script. Just **rm** the entire directory and replace it with your backup copy.

System Only Starts Up In Run Level 1:

This problem is associated with incorrectly set run-level instructions. You solve the problem with two steps.

1. **Fix the immediate problem by changing to Run Level 3 with the telinit command discussed in Chapter 4.**

2. **vi the /etc/inittab file, which is where the run level is set. Change the run-level setting to 3.**

The next time you boot, the system should come up in Run Level 3.

Automatic Fsck Failure:

On bootup, Linux automatically runs the fsck command. Although fsck looks vaguely obscene, it's a helpful utility that checks the file systems on your Linux box. If it fails, you're automatically dumped into Run Level 1. Run fsck manually by typing **fsck**. This utility will prompt you whenever it finds an error by asking Would you like to fix this error? My advice: always answer **yes**.

You can automate this by setting the answer to fsck's query to always yes. Use the following command:

```
fsck -y
```

Installation Media Error:

Probably the most common of the bootup errors, this happens when you first try to boot from a floppy or CD-ROM. Check the CD or the disk for scratches. Make sure that it's been kept away from magnets, high temperatures, and spilled sodas.

If you determine that this is your problem, either get a new download of the Linux installation from the web or contact the vendor directly. Most of the Linux vendors in the field can help you quickly.

Shutting down the system: Hitting the BRB (Big Red Button)

Hitting the BRB (Big Red Button) is Linux-speak for simply reaching over to the off switch and giving it a flick. If you can help it, just don't do this.

Linux caches its disk writes in memory. Disk writes are a technical term for the process that Linux goes through for running commands, saving data, and general system functions. Shutting off the power without proper safeguards corrupts data, which leads to reboot problems, users losing important files, and all sorts of nasty stuff.

Halt is one step above pulling the plug on your Linux box (or hitting the BRB), but if you really need to get the system down fast, you can make it safe by using the `sync` command. `sync` makes the system finish its current disk writes and prevents corruption. Oddly enough, you sometimes need to run sync multiple times to get this effect. You're best off shutting the system down with halt by typing sync and pressing return. Repeat three times and then type **halt**, as follows:

```
# sync
# sync
# sync
# halt
```

Another, even faster method is available to those with less time and more finger dexterity. Known as the Three-Fingered Salute or the Vulcan Nerve Pinch of the computer world, the following command will also shut down a Linux system with a minimum of fuss while avoiding corruption: Press Ctrl+Alt+Del.

A final option for shutting down the system is the sensibly named `shutdown` command. When not in a hurry, this is the method you should be using. `shutdown` works quickly if needed, but only when you specify it in the command options as follows:

```
shutdown now
```

The command options for shutdown are the most varied, which makes shutdown the command of choice for nonemergency situations.

Table 5-1 lists many other extensions that are less commonly used but can still be of use.

Table 5-1	Command Options You May Find Useful
Command Option	**What It Does**
-c	Cancels a running shutdown command.
-h	Halts the system after shutdown.
-r	Reboots the system after shutdown.
-time	Selects the amount of time before the shutdown, in +minutes. If you're in a hurry, you can just type **now** instead of **-time +0**.
-message	Sends a message out to all Linux users on the system that the system is going down.

A good example of the polite way to shut down the system — with no chance of file corruption — might look like this:

```
Shutdown -r -time +5 -message "Attention all users: The
        system is coming down in five minutes. Please save
        all work and log off the system to avoid losing
        your data."
```

 Of course, if you want to make doubly sure that you won't have irate users demanding that you keep the system up just a *little* longer, you'll need to notify them a day in advance. You can do this by **su**'ing to the root account and using the **vi** editor on the /etc/.motd file. Explain the situation and when the shutdown will occur and save the file. From then on, anyone who logs in will be notified automatically of the upcoming event.

When the time comes to pass, run the shutdown command with a reminder message to log off the system. shutdown is really a friendly front end to the telinit command. Although shutdown executes the same command to change the run-level state, using it with telinit in this manner is guaranteed to keep you in the user community's good graces.

Chapter 6

Managing Users: Like Herding Cats but More Difficult

. . . .

In This Chapter

▶ Marshaling the files you need for user account administration

▶ Adding users to your Linux network

▶ Deleting users when appropriate

▶ Disabling users — how and when to do this

▶ Managing user groups, herding cats, and other miracles

▶ Dealing with nontechnical issues in the real-world workplace

. . . .

*I*n this portion of the book, you get a look at how to manage the users who actually put your Linux system to use. Most basic of these operations is manipulating user accounts — adding, deleting, and disabling users. You'll also see how to manage your users by corralling them into manageable groups called — wait for it — *user groups*.

Many Linux books talk about users being your "customer base." The reasoning goes that you should think of users as "customers" utilizing your service, so you should treat everyone nicely. All sugar and spice, right? Well, I'm not advocating that you treat people improperly, but you'll probably recall (with some unease) the first traditional rule of customer service: "The customer is always right."

That doesn't quite make it in the Linux world. If someone claims to have lost a file and swears they saved it to the root directory, you can pretty well bet they're wrong (unless you've granted other accounts access to write to where only the root account should be).

I'd like you to consider thinking of your users as part of your *user community*. Your Linux user community is like a small town.

✔ You're Sheriff Andy, the smartest person in town.

✔ Users, your community residents, will leave you alone unless they need a favor or call to report a problem.

✔ If you can't agree to some of their requests, then you'll have to say "no" — and help them feel okay about it.

✔ It's up to you to discipline your users if they cross the line so you can protect everyone's safety and privacy.

And the beauty of this model is that you're not elected, so you don't have to make any campaign promises you can't keep!

Admission to the Linux Show: Adding New Users

The most basic task of a Linux administrator is adding new users to your world. You have control over every aspect of the new addition to the family. You'll have to determine each new user's home directory, the shell they use by default, and their initial password.

Some people may ask, "Why have user accounts at all? Just have two accounts — `root` for the administrator, and `guest` for everyone else. Linux is an open system, after all."

True, this is possible under Linux. As Chapter 5 reveals, a user account is just a construct. Anyone who has the password to the account can use it — so one account can be used by one person, three people, or ten people, all at the same time.

This is very rarely done. Aside from the chaos that would probably result from such a free-for-all, user accounts serve some practical purposes beyond providing Linux administrators some well-earned job security:

✔ User accounts allow the Linux system a say to distinguish systematically between users for identification and logging purposes.

✔ User accounts allow a system to focus the distribution of information to only those who need it.

✔ User accounts provide a built-in layer of security: the password for each user.

Adding users — the files you need

The most important file to know about when adding users is the /etc/passwd file. The modest-seeming /etc/passwd is more than it appears to be. Besides providing a list of all user accounts and passwords, it also determines three vital attributes for each user account:

- ✔ Shell
- ✔ Home directory
- ✔ User ID

Each and every account on the Linux system, including root, has an entry in this file. With large user communities, /etc/passwd can get pretty large.

To take a look at this file, **vi** it. If you do an **ls–l** on it, you'll notice that it's owned by the root account. On most systems, other accounts are allowed to read the file, but not write to it. If you're feeling really paranoid sometime and want to put the feeling to good use, you can **su** to root and **chmod** the passwd file to make it nonreadable to everyone except root.

Here's a sample of what your /etc/passwd file will probably look like:

```
root:EIUiuh654DSA:0:0:Root User:/:/bin/csh
averagejoe:128939JY:100:101:A.
        Joe:/usr/home/averagejoe:/bin/csh
dsmith:3487KJHU74:100:102:Dan
        Smith:/usr/home/dsmith:/bin/sh
kclark:MMHAAF37547:100:103:Kent
        Clark:/usr/home/kclark:/bin/csh
kiko:654KLQWER:105:108: Kara 'Kiko'
        Karlson:/usr/home/kiko:/bin/csh
loki:ZXCE302822:100:132:Loki, God of
        Mischief:/usr/home/loki:/bin/csh
nobody:OOWAJHQL2:105:122:Dummy
        Account:/usr/home/nobody:/bin/sh
stever:654IOHG6K:100:106:Steve
        Roberts:/usr/home/stever:/bin/bash
wally:TROI8761111:105:161: Wally the Wonder
        User:/usr/home/wally:/bin/sh
```

Sure, it looks like a jumble, but that's mostly due to the second field in the list, which is an encryption code. Each user's account has one *entry line*, which contains seven fields:

```
User Name: Password : UID : GID : Gecos : Home Directory :
        Default Shell
```

I can name that account in five letters . . .

A word about naming schemes. You *do* need one, if only to help keep things straight in your mind.

A naming scheme, also called a *naming convention*, is a pattern that you, the administrator, decides on to create user account names. It doesn't have to be complex, precise, or even have to make sense. It just has to be consistent. Most naming schemes on Linux networks follow the first-initial-last-name rule. So user Johnathan Jakes becomes jjakes, and Laura Ann Marie Hudson becomes lhudson. Another popular method is to use first name-plus-last-name-initial. Emma Maeberry becomes emmam and Boris Ludchowisky becomes borisl. You can assign people numbers, so Lars Richard Witherspoon-Pearson becomes user124. Or you can let people request their own user account names, so Michael Crane becomes Mike, Indiana Jones becomes Ark4me, and William Gates becomes UwillBmineRelse.

In my experience, this scheme can make you very popular but less efficient. In most Linux communities, you have a rough idea of who does what; account names based on personal names work just fine. If you know (for example) that Johnathan Jakes is a programmer who always seems to need more disk space, and you see an e-mail from jjakes, you'll probably start thinking about ways to solve his problem even before you answer it. Otherwise, if you haven't memorized every account name on the network, you could get e-mail from user THX1138 and have no clue to what it's about.

Here's how to read the lines of the passwd file:

✔ User Name is a unique name for the user account. It's important to distinguish this from the user's actual name precisely because the account information must be unique to each subject. For example, it's highly probable that with a large user community, you'll have two people named John Smith. You're obviously going to have problems with the Linux network if you assign them both the same account name.

Depending on the naming scheme you have set up, you could set up the two John Smiths as jsmith1 and jsmith2, as jsmith and johnS, or as johnsmith and bubba. In Linux, any of these ways can function in Linux just as well as the others. It's entirely up to you. Remember that the names don't even have to match the user's real name. In the passwd list just given, for example, notice that Kara Karlson didn't have to be kcarlson or kara, or anything in particular — kiko would work just as well — and so would bubba for the second John Smith.

✔ Password is a jumble of letters because it's an encrypted field. When you first enter a user's password or create a new account, Linux automatically encrypts the letters and/or numbers you put in. So, even if other users besides root get to the passwd account, no one's leaving with the actual passwords themselves.

✔ UID stands for *User Identification*. This is a unique number that Linux uses to identify the user account when running processes for the user in the kernel. Creating a new user account with a duplicate UID causes Linux more problems than a duplicate username, and can cause the system to crash.

Why both a user name and a UID? It's really a question of efficiency; when Linux is processing the user's requests and actions, it's easier for it to pass around a number rather than a byte string (which in the computer's language becomes a much longer string of numbers). So you can consider the UID as the identification that the computer uses. By contrast, you could call the user account name the identification the Linux administrator uses.

✔ GID stands for Group Identification. Linux uses this integer to set the user account's default group. You'll be learning about user groups a little later in this chapter, so sit tight. For now, be aware that multiple people can have the same GID, since more than one person can be in a group.

✔ Gecos has nothing to do with small lizards. That said, the acronym GECOS stands for General Electric's Comprehensive Operating System. Back in the late '70s, this field was added to provide compatibility with some of the services GE was offering through UNIX.

It's not used now, so it's not bringing anything good to life, not even small lizards.

✔ Home Directory is the user account's default home directory. When the user first logs in, this is where he or she starts out. The user's scripts, saved material, and user-specific shell information are all written to this location. Normally, most systems put the user community's home directories on /etc/home or /usr/home, but there's nothing to stop you from putting it on /var or /dev.

✔ Default Shell is the shell first activated by the user when that user logs in. The different shell types washed ashore in Chapter 3. /Bin/sh stands for Bourne Shell, /bin/csh means the user starts out with the C Shell, and Steve Roberts' /bin/bash stands for the Bourne-Again (really) Shell.

Special accounts

The example /etc/passwd file we used contains two accounts you'll probably see on your own Linux system:

```
root:EIUiuh654DSA:0:0:Root User:/:/bin/csh
nobody:OOWAJHQL2:105:122:Dummy
            Account:/usr/home/nobody:/bin/sh
```

✔ root is, of course, the Great and Powerful Root Account for the system. Its UID *and* GID are always zero (0).

Never duplicate the root *account.* Giving another account root's UID will confuse the system and possibly crash it; giving another account root's GID will give that account most of the same privileges that root commands.

✔ nobody is, as Gecos says, a *dummy* account. (And no, it has nothing to do with this publication's line of books.) This account is an example of one that may be set up with no user to assign it to.

These accounts are utilized by system daemons that need to access certain files as a user but cannot (or should not) access the files as root.

The most common example of a dummy account occurs when you have your system configured to retrieve news from an outside site. The news daemon needs a user account to log in. Of course, the outside site has its own root account with its own password, so it won't accept a login from another root. The dummy account is a nonthreatening alternative. Also, the news daemon may need a user directory to store the news files, which is done more easily with a dummy account.

As a rule, you won't need to bother with dummy accounts unless you've inherited a system that already has them in place. In that case, just be aware that you'll be wasting at least some of your time tracking down user nobody to get him to clean up his files.

/Etc/skel — roll the bones, roll the bones . . .

One more file you might need to be aware of is /etc/skel file — the basic "skeleton" of what a user account needs to function. Whenever you create a new user account, you'll need to copy the contents of this directory into the new user's home directory.

As time has gone on, Linux has made this task easier and easier. Nine out of ten times, you won't need to copy this directory. The new versions of Linux come with utilities that do this for you. If you have an older copy of Linux running on your network, don't worry. You'll be learning when and where you need to cp the contents of this directory.

Adding users

You have many ways you can add users to your Linux system.

Most versions of Red Hat Linux come with a Control Panel that allows you to add users with a few clicks of a mouse or a few taps of Tab on the keyboard.

Of the command-line methods for adding users to a Linux system, you're likeliest to get familiar with the adduser command.

The adduser command: the 90-percent solution

If you know how, you can add users directly through the command-line interface. Over 90 percent of Linux systems come with the user-administration command adduser, which makes your life a bit easier.

To run adduser, follow these steps:

1. **Log in as the** root **account, or** su **to it.**

2. **Type** adduser **at the command line, follow the prompts it gives you for information, and then press Enter after each entry to go the next prompt.**

It's best to accept the defaults when starting out. The default values are indicated in square brackets [ ]. You can always edit things later if you change your mind.

Here's how a sample adduser session might look:

```
# adduser
Adding a New User.  The username should not exceed 8
         characters in length.
Enter login name for new account (^C to quit): <account name>
Editing information for <account name>

Full Name: <User's Full Name>
GID [100]: <Press Return to Accept Default>

Checking for an available UID...
First unused UID is 107

UID [107]: <Press Return to Accept Default>
Home Directory [/usr/home/<account name>]: <Press Return to
         Accept Default>
Shell [/bin/csh]: <Press Return to Accept Default>
Password: <think of a password for the user, enter it>

Information for new user <account name>
Home Directory: /usr/home/<account name>
Shell: /bin/csh
Password: *******
UID: 107
GID: 100

Is this correct? [Y/N] <Y>
```

```
Adding login <account name> and making directory
          </home/account name>
Adding files from the /etc/skel directory...
```

After this session is complete, you can notify your new user(s) of their accounts. They'll be able to log in to the Linux system immediately.

What if my Linux machine has no adduser command?

Don't panic if you type **adduser** and nothing happens; 10 percent of Linux machines don't have the adduser command. You can still add users, it's just a few steps more.

Make sure you're logged in as root and that you're very careful when you use **vi** to edit these sensitive files.

1. vi **the** /etc/passwd **file.**
2. **Add a new line to the bottom of the text.**
3. **Copy another line, letter for letter, to the bottom of the text.**
4. **Replace the string of encrypted characters in the new user's password field with an asterisk.**
5. **Make the changes you need for the new user, such as the account name and the UID (both of which must be unique).**

   The new user's /etc/passwd entry might look like this:

```
Nu_uzer:*:108:100:New Kid On The
          Block:/usr/home/Nu_uzer:/bin/csh
```

6. **Save and exit this file.**
7. **Change directories to** /usr/home **and create the** /Nu_uzer **directory with the** mkdir **command.**
8. copy **over the contents of the** /etc/skel **directory to the newly created** /usr/home/Nu_uzer **directory.**
9. cd **to** /usr/home, **then** chown **the directory so that** Nu_uzer **owns his or her home directory.**
10. **Use the** passwd **command to set a password, like this.**

```
# passwd Nu_uzer
```

Linux will respond by asking for `Nu_uzer`'s password — twice, to avoid problems caused by typos.

`Nu_uzer` is good to go!

Deleting and Disabling: Drastic Doings, Determined Daily

It's useful to be able to block out system access for users who are away temporarily or permanently. Most Linux systems give you a couple of methods for halting or eliminating user accounts.

It's up to you to decide when to delete a user and when to disable one. There is no technical reason for you to decide one way or another. A user account doesn't normally take up so much space that it has any great impact on the system. Instead of shooting from the hip, review your current situation. When you're deciding, consider

- What you want to restrict
- What you want to save
- Whether the user will return

  For example, if Sally is taking a six-month trip to Tahiti or Bora Bora, she won't be signing up for your fan club if she comes back and finds all her work has been deleted.

  On the other hand, if an employee is leaving the company permanently, then you might consider deleting the account completely. This is particularly helpful if the departing party owns a user name that is popular or stands a good chance of being used again (like John Smith, a.k.a. `bubba`).

Before you delete a user, it's best to check with that person's department to see whether the account had possession of any files the department could use. In that case, you have got two tasks:

- Disable the account for the interim.
- Delete the account when you get word that all the usable data has been stripped from the user's directories.

Delete, or forever hold your peace

If you have the `useradd` utility, you can use the flip side of the command, the `userdel` utility. Not surprisingly, these utilities come in pairs; if you have one, you can bet a whole stack of blue silicon chips that you have the other.

Always use the `userdel` command with the `-r` option. The *r* stands for *recursive,* meaning that it will delete all of the user's directories *and* the files *inside* those directories. That's important; you don't want debris from former user accounts lying around where someone could (virtually) trip over it. The command string will look like this:

```
# userdel -r <username>
```

If you're among the poor souls who lack `useradd` — and hence also lack `userdel` — you again need to perform these tasks manually.

If you have to delete a user account by hand, make sure you're logged in as `root` and that you're very careful when you use **vi** to edit these sensitive files.

1. **Change directories to** `/usr/home` **and locate the user's home directory.**

2. **Use** rm **with the –r option, which allows you to delete the user's directory and anything contained within:**

   ```
   # rm -r <user's home directory>
   ```

3. **vi the** `/etc/passwd` **file, locate the line that contains the user's account, and move the cursor there.**

4. **Select the line that contains the account, make sure you're in Command Mode, and then use command option** dd **to delete the line.**

5. **Save your work and exit the** `/etc/passwd` **file.**

Whether you use `userdel` or excise the account manually, there are two things I recommend you do when you remove a user's account:

1. **Check to see that the account is well and truly gone by attempting to log in as the deleted user.**

   If you try to log in as a nonexistent account, the system should refuse you entry after it requests the user's password.

2. cd **to the** `root` **directory (that's /, not the ex-user's** home **directory) and perform the following command:**

   ```
   find / -user <username> -ls
   ```

This command goes looking for all files — from the `root` directory on down — associated with the user account name you've specified. Once this list is compiled, you can manipulate these files at will — copy, change ownership, or delete. Keep in mind that using the `find` command from the `root` directory requires a lot of computing power, so reduce everyone's annoyance factor and perform this check when there are few people on the system.

Disabling — why and when

You can disable a user's account without touching his or her files. Just follow these handy, cautious steps:

Make sure you're logged in as `root` and that you're very careful when you use **vi** to edit this sensitive file.

1. vi **the** `/etc/passwd` **file.**

2. **Move to the line containing the user's account information.**

3. **Using the cursor controls and the** x **key in Command Mode, delete the** `Password` **field in the account line.**

4. **Change to Insert Mode by typing** i **or** a, **and then put an asterisk in the** `Password` **field.**

   The account line should look like this:

   ```
   wally:*:105:161: Wally the Wonder
           User:/usr/home/wally:/bin/sh
   ```

   Until you use the **passwd** command as `root` to grant a new password for Wally the Wonder User, there's no way that Wally — or anyone else — can log in as account `wally`.

Whenever you edit the `/etc/passwd` file, *never* delete the encrypted `Password` field and leave it blank. Although you may think that you're blocking this user from logging on, you're doing the exact opposite. Leaving this field blank tells Linux that this user doesn't *need* a stinkin' password to get onto the system at all! This is a gaping security hole which should never have been opened. So use an asterisk — or don't touch the file.

All Right, Pair Up in Groups of Three

Your Linux system utilizes *user groups* to collect and share out data to specific combinations of people for efficiency.

For example, it's highly unlikely that accounting and engineering will have the same interest in accessing the same files. Instead, set permissions for accounting files that allow access by groups such as `accnt1`, `timesheets`, and `balance`; engineering documents should fall under groups like `buildit`, `calc-q-late` and `pkt_protector`.

Consider creating groups that reflect areas of *responsibility* in addition to specific types of documents.

Group creation and membership is set in the `/etc/groups` file. Except for GID zero (the `root` group), each user in a group has two qualities:

- ✔ The user must be a member of at least one group.
- ✔ The user can be a member in as many groups as he or she might like.

As with the `/etc/passwd` file, you set group identities in one line per group, like this:

```
Group Name : Password : GID : Members
```

Here's how to read the lines of the `groups` file:

- ✔ `Group Name` is similar to `User Name` in `/etc/passwd`; it provides a character string that allows both humans and Linux to identify the group.

- ✔ `Password` is an optional password used for this group, to allow non-group members to access the group with the `newgrp` command.

  This optional password is almost never used; you should limit the power to add people to groups to the `root` account alone.

- ✔ `GID` (Group ID) is similar to `UID`. Instead of a character string, a number is provided so Linux can identify the group more efficiently.

- ✔ `Members` means a list of user accounts that belong to this group.

  Since a person can have multiple user accounts on a Linux system, it's possible for one person to be on this list several times. Avoid that situation if you can; it can cause confusion.

Using the **vi** editor on the `/etc/groups` file, you can see something similar to this list:

```
root:*:0:
accounting:*:103:kiko, kclark
engrs:*:105:averagejoe, wally, kclark, loki
pkt_protector:*:110:stever, root, wally
techpubs:*:111:nobody, kclark
timesheets:*:112:
users:*:100: averagejoe, wally, kclark, loki, kiko, stever,
          dsmith
```

To add someone to a group, simply **vi** the /etc/groups file and add his or her user account name to the appropriate line. The next time that user logs in, they'll have access to all their old group files, plus the new group's files. Of course, to remove someone from a group, you'll still use **vi**. Go to the person's name, make sure you're in Command mode, and **x** it out.

To add a completely new group, **vi** the /etc/groups file and add another line, following much the same procedure. Notice that you don't necessarily need to add users to the group for the group to exist. In the example, group timesheets exists without causing problems, even though no one has been added. Similarly, deleting groups means you'll have to delete the entire line that describes the group.

Managing Users in the Real World

If you're not much of a people person, it's worth your time to make sure your human interactions go as smoothly as your software operations. I won't lecture you on the Golden Rule or explain ethics to you, as that should have been done from kindergarten on up. However, a couple of principles can help you get your job done and still keep you looking good to the world at large.

The Simplicity Principle

When explaining a process to a user, don't assume that they know what you do. Very often, they're only pressing keys, sending e-mail, and reading newsgroups dedicated to their favorite rock stars. So instead of giving them a full technical explanation, just say, "You tried to save the file to an area that didn't have enough space," or "I'll need to make sure your machine can talk to mine."

The Fair Warning Principle

If you're going to take the system down for repair or maintenance, be kind and let people know ahead of time using the Message of the Day and e-mail. You're best off if you warn people three or four days in advance. Too late, and people complain. Too early, and people forget,

The Principle of Reason

If someone is demanding something that you can't do, then don't just refuse. Make it clear that you're not saying that you won't do something, you just can't. Provide a clear reason, which can be as simple as "This would seriously inconvenience everyone else."

The Principle of Being root

If you're still being hounded, say no — and stick to it! Remember, you're the `root` account, and it is good to be `root`. If you don't do it, your supplicants have no recourse. Make it subtly clear that they'll be better off treating you with common courtesy. (Of course, a little two-way food bribery never hurt anyone, right?)

The Scotty Principle

Most importantly, use the time principle founded by Montgomery "I canna do it!" Scott, Chief Engineer of the Starship *Enterprise*. No matter how long you estimate a job will take, multiply the time needed by four. Not only does this give you some crush space if you run into problems, but if you finish early, you're a bona fide Miracle Worker.

Chapter 7

Are Your Users Connected?
Pinging the Net

· ·

In This Chapter

▶ Plugging into Ethernet and networking basics

▶ pinging the Net

▶ spraying the Net

▶ Testing, testing . . . the netstat command

▶ Getting network interface statistics — Doctor, Doctor, gimme the news!

· ·

*H*ang out at any cocktail party with a percentage of technical types milling about and you'll hear a few buzzwords thrown around — "Ethernet cards," "Ethernet cabling," "TCP/IP," and (of course) "the client-server relationship."

Not only will this chapter show you what this is all about, it'll also allow you to hold your own at these same parties when you hear these terms. At the very least, you'll be able to nod your head sagely and say, "Ah, yes, I'm quite familiar with that."

You learn about that prince among network testing tools, the ping command. This chapter will also teach you what kind of network framework software you should be using — or are already using — to get files to your user community.

Either No Net, or Ethernet: Basic Network Concepts

Ethernet emerged from the last two decades of chaotic system network design as the standard way to connect large numbers of networked computers. Developed in the early '70s as one of the first networks based on the broadcast model (about which more in a moment), it had the advantage of being incredibly cheap compared to the other methods available at the time.

Ethernet suffered from two main problems:

- ✔ **Signal strength** was an issue when hooking up computers that were physically more than 50 meters apart.

  This was solved with the introduction of signal devices called *repeaters,* and eventually the introduction of modern network paraphernalia such as bridges, switches, and routers.

- ✔ **Packet loss** remained a problem on Ethernet until the common use of the TCP/IP protocol.

With these two issues out of the way, Ethernet quickly dominated the networking world.

The broadcast model of Ethernet is fast replacing the older, *token-ring* format that was the mainstay of network computing in the '80s. With a token-ring network, an electronic packet called a *token* was passed around a network of machines like a discount subway pass. Only the machine that actually had the token at the exact time it sought to transmit a message could "talk" on the net. When it was done, it would pass the token on. This system got to be too cumbersome and prone to failure, so people began switching to the broadcast model.

On a *broadcast model,* every machine gets to talk (that is, send out message packets) all the time. If two machines send out a packet at the exact same time, a collision results, both machines go into reset mode and send the packet again after a random reset time. The buzzword *network bandwith* comes from this setup. If you have too much network traffic — from a hyper-talkative machine, for example — your collision rate gets too high and people start noticing the slowdown.

All these transactions I'm talking about take place at nearly the speed of light, so it's possible for many, many computers to talk on a network without "colliding."

As an administrator, you'll need to know what Ethernet technology is, and what parts of it you'll need to be familiar with on a physical and an application level. Ethernet connectivity, on the *physical* level, has two parts — the cabling and the Ethernet card inside each of your Linux boxes. The *application* part is easier (unless you consider typing strenuous work); it involves testing out the connection with Linux utilities like `ping` and `spray`.

The thickness of the net

Locating the first part of the Ethernet network is easy; reach around the back of your Linux box and find the cable sprouting off the back (not the one plugged into a power socket). In case you have multiple cables that fit this category, it's the cable that plugs into what looks like a phone jack on the back of your computer.

There are three kinds of cable you'll need to be aware of in the Linux/Ethernet universe:

- ✔ **Thicknet:** A thick, black or brown cable that looks like the kind of cable they use to lay transoceanic phone lines. No longer in use, this old type of 15-pin connector cable should be replaced if it's in your system. The only thing good about it is that it's very easy to spot — it's the only computer cable you can't cut through with anything less than a chainsaw.

- ✔ **Thinnet:** Also known as *coaxial cable* (or *co-ax* for short), thinnet works on a *series circuit* model. On a co-ax network, the cable is basically one long wire that attaches all the machines, which branches into each computer's Ethernet connection by adding *taps* (or *T connectors*) along the entire length of a wire. You'll see this very rarely, but you can spot it by looking for T-shaped connectors sprouting from the network cable.

  If you have thinnet, I recommend that you get rid of it immediately. Although it's very cheap, it has the potential to cause major headaches. Any break, anywhere along the line, causes the whole network to break down. One analogy should make this clear: the best known use of a series circuit is on old-fashioned Christmas tree lights. When one light goes out, a whole segment of them goes out — because they're all part of the same circuit. If you've ever spent hours fiddling with a string of flickering bulbs on your garage floor, trying to figure out which one is causing the problem, you know the torture you could face with thinnet.

- ✔ **10-BaseT:** This cable is the current standard of the Linux world. (It's also called *RJ-45* in the elite circles of cable experts. I don't know about you, but I'm certainly impressed.) 10-BaseT looks like a standard phone cable, and it's only moderately more expensive. It also doesn't go in for the series-circuit guessing game; if one machine suffers a broken wire, the rest of the network stays afloat.

  10-BaseT has the capability to run at either 10 Mbps (megabits per second) or 100 Mbps. The rule is that faster data rates are more expensive, but this type of cabling gives you the option of choosing a cable system based on price-versus-performance needs.

Pick a card, any card

The second portion of the Ethernet is the *Ethernet card,* or *network card.* Any computer on your Linux network needs an Ethernet card installed inside so your 10Base-T line can snick into that wall plug that looks like (*but isn't*) a phone jack.

If you don't know how to install the card, don't worry. Most vendors of Ethernet cards, such as 3Com, provide support and instructions on how to do so.

Once the card is installed, reboot the system so that the Linux kernel recognizes the new hardware. The /sbin/ifconfig program will register your card automatically. Red Hat Linux provides an excellent network configuration tool to set or alter these if you choose to do so.

As an ultimate fallback, if you have problems setting the network address (or you lack the Red Hat setup tools), you have one more drastic-but-effective solution. Save all your important files off the Linux box. Reboot the machine with the installation CD-ROM or boot disk and then reinstall Linux.

Since the kernel will detect the new Ethernet card, it will automatically prompt you for default addresses you can take or change. Once that's done, all you need to do is put your files back in place.

This *is* pretty drastic; you shouldn't do this with a major Linux server. (Then again, you can't have a Linux server unless it's already on the network, so if you're just now adding the card, by definition your box isn't a server yet!)

Using Diagnostic Tools

As the system administrator, you're often trying to sort out connection and communication problems. Linux is designed to make networking easy, so it's equipped with plenty of artillery to find problems and wipe them out.

Pinging the Net

The ping command is probably the most basic network-test tool around. ping stands for Packet Internet Groper and to my knowledge has nothing to do with submarine sonar operations.

ping is used to determine whether you have a working network connection between two machines and to ensure that the connection is working trouble-free. Once your Ethernet hardware is hooked up properly, simply use ping in the following manner as either root or a typical user account:

```
# ping <name of machine you want to talk to>
```

The machine you typed the command on is the *request machine;* all you have to do is wait for packets to make the round trip from your machine to the pinged machine and back. Let's say you need to determine if your new Linux box, Nova, can talk to the main server, Linuxbox. While on Nova, you type

```
# ping Linuxbox
```

Linuxbox hears the ping request and sends back a series of response packets. On Nova, the printout is put on-screen:

```
PING Linuxbox: 64 data bytes.
-- Linuxbox PING Statistics --
7 packets transmitted. 7 packets received. 0% packet loss
Round-trip (ms) min/avg/max = 10/20/30
```

If ping was unable to reach Linuxbox, it will either display an error message or it will hang and eventually time out, returning you to the command prompt.

Let's say that you just set up Nova and when you ping Linuxbox you get the following message:

```
# ping Linuxbox
ERROR: Unknown Host
```

Don't panic, or at least don't panic immediately. This is actually a halfway good sign. This error tells you that you're connected to the network in a nebulous fashion — your ping packets are leaving your machine and getting on to the network. However, it also tells you that you're not yet talking to the main server, Linuxbox, which is where you want to get some files.

You can sometimes correct this error by resorting to using the machine's IP address instead of the host name. The *IP address* is the machine's network address, normally stated in four fields of up to three numbers apiece, as in 130.34.57.29.

You learn more about this in the chapter on TCP/IP protocols, but for now you just need to be aware of the address. Linux uses this address in the same way it uses the User ID number instead of the user account name to run user processes; it's the way a machine handles data instead of the way we slow, bumbling humans use it. So if we determine that Linuxbox lives at IP address 130.34.57.29, you can ping it:

```
# ping 130.34.57.29
PING Linuxbox: 64 data bytes.
[ping output appears at this point]
-- Linuxbox PING Statistics --
7 packets transmitted, 7 packets received, 0% packet loss
Round-trip (ms) min/avg/max = 10/20/30
```

You should note that the ERROR: Unknown Host message is not always displayed when your Linux box can't find the host you're pinging. As a rule of thumb, any time you ping a remote box, try using the IP address if you can't locate it by host name.

Another question I often hear is, "How long should you wait for a `ping` response?" That depends on what you're `ping`ing. Normally, a `ping`ed box should respond within three seconds. But if you're `ping`ing a major server at the height of its network demands, then be generous and allow it to finish what it has on its plate before it gets back to you. A wait time of five to fifteen seconds is the upper limit of what's acceptable.

`Ping` is most useful as a source of information on whether the TCP/IP protocol is working properly, whether a remote machine can be accessed, whether the `ping`ed machine has a valid IP address, and whether the requesting machine knows the `ping`ed machine's host name.

However, most people overlook `ping`'s usefulness as a tool for judging the overall health of the network. Let's take a quick look at the last two lines in the reply from `Linuxbox` to `ping`'s network query:

```
7 packets transmitted, 7 packets received, 0% packet loss
Round-trip (ms) min/avg/max = 10/20/30
```

`Ping` is telling you that of the seven query packets that went out, seven response packets were received, completing the packet round trip successfully and establishing the electronic circuit. `Ping`, being a most helpful command, also tells you the percentage loss of the packets. Since you lost none, you had zero percentage loss, which is an excellent example of why we invented computers — to do the difficult math for us.

The round-trip statistics are more revealing. `Ping` measures response time between computers in milliseconds. In this case, your minimum response time was 10 milliseconds, the maximum 30, and the average 20 milliseconds.

Is this good? Bad? Should you worry if the average time jumps to 21 milliseconds? Hardly. As a rule, you shouldn't be concerned with minor fluctuations in the response time, since it's in milliseconds, a time-frame which we slow, lumbering humans don't notice all that often unless we're part of the Olympic track team or in the middle of a long, boring lecture.

If the lag time is noticeable by human standards, these statistics are most helpful in determining where the problem lies. Let's say that it's taking 20 or 30 seconds to get a `ping` reply back from `Linuxbox`. Look at the following statistic lines:

```
14 packets transmitted,14 packets received, 0% packet loss
Round-trip (ms) min/avg/max = 10/20/1000
```

No packets have been lost, but the minimum and maximum return times vary tremendously. Also, the average is very low. This could mean that only one or two packets are being held up. Since this isn't consistent, probably the server `Linuxbox` just got held up to service a big request and had to sneak a packet out to us when it could.

On the other hand, see the following report:

```
10 packets transmitted, 7 packets received, 30% packet loss
Round-trip (ms) min/avg/max = 10/20/30
```

A packet-loss rate of more than 5 percent should be investigated. Someone is either putting a tremendous amount of stress on the system, or you're running at a chronic overload. If you get this kind of reading constantly, consider some options:

✔ Purchase additional Linux servers.

✔ Spread out the load by assigning users to use different machines for different tasks.

✔ Purchase some 10-BaseT cable that runs at 100 Mbps.

Spray the Net for the sweetest-smelling network you can get

A second (less sophisticated) tool for testing basic network use is the spray command. Although spray doesn't exist on all versions of Linux and it can't do half of what ping can, it's useful in one area: network stress testing.

Spray sends out request packets the same way that ping does, and it works in a comparatively simple way — either of these commands:

```
# spray Linuxbox
```

```
# spray 130.34.57.29
```

You'll get back (as you might expect) a spray readout that can give you a good working idea of how the network traffic flow is going.

Where spray differs from ping is in how it handles packets. Where ping sends out one packet at a time (like a water-balloon launcher) and waits for a reply, spray goes all-out like a fire hose set on, well, *spray*. The command squirts a dozen packets at a machine all at once, testing whether it can play "catch" (or, if it can't keep up, "dodge ball").

Using spray on a newly installed server can give you a rough idea of how much traffic it can handle. Granted, this is a relatively backward way to determine how much bandwith you have. But if you've inherited a Linux system with little or no documentation on the network cabling or the Ethernet connectivity, then this approach may be your only choice.

When possible, perform a spray stress test *after* work hours. Multiple spray commands can also put stress on your machine, maybe enough to shut it down. It's rare, but if multiple spray commands overload a badly stressed system, they might cause it to crash — or at least go on strike until you hit the BRB (Big Red Button). Since this book is concerned with helping you *avoid* stress (what a concept), take my word and don't have a spray-fest in the middle of your busiest day at the office.

Testing, testing . . . the netstat command

In Linux, netstat is a sort of catch-call command that does a great job of summarizing network statistics and information. Although it usually isn't as machine-specific as ping or spray, it's better at giving you the "big picture" of your entire web of machines.

Netstat has a whole slew of options to choose from. However, your best bet for checking connectivity, especially from your main Linux server, is the -a option.

The -a option displays all the network *end-point data* — what machines are connected, using which protocols, and whether their connections are being actively served at the moment. Let's say that a user is trying to make a TCP connection from box pinto to server Linuxbox.

Log in to Linuxbox and perform **netstat -a**. You should get a result that looks like what follows:

```
# netstat -a
Active Internet connections
Proto  Recv-Q  Send-Q  Local Address  Foreign Address
          (state)
tcp     17         10              tpci.1001       mustang.1201
          ESTABL.
udp     1024       0              tpci.1002       nova.2501
          LISTENING
tcp     0          0              tpci.1005       colt.login
          ESTABL.
tcp     0          0              tpci.1006
          bronco.2477      ESTABL.
tcp     0          0              tpci.1008       equus.678
          CLOSED
tcp     0          0              tpci.1009       pinto.1222
          TIME_WAIT
```

This output tells us that there are six machines contacting or waiting to contact Linuxbox. The (state) column shows that mustang, colt, and bronco have made connections. Nova is listening, which is another form of connection where the connector is just waiting for packets to be sent. A glance at the Recv-Q column shows that machine Nova is getting just that.

The bottom line of the output shows that `pinto` is trying to connect, but that the connection has been put on hold. Now, unless `pinto` has blown up (is that tacky or what?), most likely this problem will solve itself when `Linuxbox` has fewer requests to handle. If `Linuxbox` continues to handle all other requests besides `pinto`'s, then `pinto` itself may have something wrong with it. Rather than hunt for which network daemon might be down, if there's nothing vital running on `pinto`, your best bet is to reboot the machine.

Network interface statistics: Doctor, doctor, gimme the news!

Of all the command options available to `netstat`, the `-i` option is by far the most important in determining the overall health of your Linux network. Where `ping`, `spray`, and `netstat -a` are like a stethoscope or a thermometer, `netstat -i` is more like a CAT scan. `netstat -i` determines the actual behavior of the network interface cards on your machine.

On a healthy Linux box, `netstat -i`'s output will look similar to this:

```
# netstat -i
Name   Mtu   Network  Address    Ipkts   Ierrs   Opkts
          Oerrs  Collis
lo0    8464  loopback localhost  400   0    400   0    0
lan0   1478  177.0       Nova              2399   0    243
          0    0
```

Here's how to read the column heads in this report.

- ✔ `Name` refers to the logical name assignment that your Linux box has given to the network card.

- ✔ The `lo0` is a *loopback* interface that the machine uses for its general feedback check. The outgoing connection is usually `lan0` or `le0`.

  `Ierrs` and `Oerrs` refer to the number of incoming traffic errors and outgoing traffic errors, respectively.

- ✔ `Collis` field reports how many packet collisions happen on the net.

Your `lo0` interface will rarely if ever cause a problem, since if it starts to error, it means the whole network card will refuse to work. Otherwise, whether you see high error numbers in `Ierrs`, `Oerrs`, or `Collis` determines what kind of problem you're facing.

Let's assume that you're having problems getting information on the machine `pinto` again. The `netstat -i` shows you what you need to know:

```
Name    Mtu    Network  Address    Ipkts    Ierrs    Opkts
               Oerrs    Collis
lo0     8464   loopback localhost   400      0       400    0     0
lan0    1478   177.0    Nova                         2399  2318
               243      0        2
```

Since the collision rate (Collis) is so low, you can rule out problems coming in from off the box. Also, since there are no errors in the outgoing traffic, no processes running on pinto are pinging or spraying improperly. Instead, the likely cause of the problem is the Internet service daemon (inetd). Your best bet here is to do a **ps** and find the daemon's process ID number. Killing the daemon and restarting it should cure the problem.

Suppose, on the other hand, you get the following output:

```
Name    Mtu    Network  Address    Ipkts    Ierrs    Opkts
               Oerrs    Collis
lo0     8464   loopback localhost   400      0       400    0     0
lan0    1478   177.0    Nova                         2399   0    243
               0        2003
```

This could signal a major network glitch. You'll see the same high number of collisions when attempting to use ping. You may need to expand your system's bandwidth by adding more servers and higher-speed cabling. Another course of action is to attempt to determine which machine is flooding the network with packets. In order to do so, you need to understand the nature of these TCP/IP packets we've been talking about. You'll also need to understand the properties of TCP versus UDP and the utilities that run with them. Stay with us.

Part III
Administering Network Communications

The 5th Wave   By Rich Tennant

The GENIE in the MACHINE

"YES, I'M NORMALLY LARGER AND MORE AWE-INSPIRING, BUT THIS IS ONLY A 4MB SYSTEM!"

In this part . . .

Part III covers the care and feeding of network communications in more detail. You learn exactly what the
TCP/IP protocol suite stands for, how it differs from the
older UDP protocol, and what each is good for. You get a
look at why TCP has become the mode of choice with network connectivity, even though it's more system-intensive
and a lot slower.

You also get some more of the practical lowdown on all
this network connectivity. You behold new realms of
power: transferring files, copying files, and getting
machines to do your bidding when you're not even in the
same room — or even the same continent. (This particular magic trick is covered in the section on the favorite
kids of the TCP/IP suite, UUCP and FTP.)

And as an added bonus, you'll be learning more TLAs
(Three-Letter Acronyms) than you can shake a mainframe
at. They're sure to be a hit at parties. (Just kidding. I think.)

Chapter 8

Your Basic Protocols:
TCP and UDP

*W*hen I ask newcomers to the Linux world what *protocol* means to them, and then ask the same question of experienced Linux administrators, I get very different answers:

- The experienced administrators start talking about computer connectivity, handshaking, and virtual circuits.

- The newcomers, on the other hand, mention things like black-tie diplomatic functions, military salutes, and which fork you're supposed to use for the lobster thermidor.

Interestingly enough, they're both right! A computer protocol is really no different from a diplomatic or formal dinner-party protocol, because they serve the same function. (Mind you, don't try serving your lobster thermidor with a TCP/IP packet or you're bound to get sauce on the rug.) Protocols exist in order to allow two different computers to follow a preset sequence of orders to communicate properly with each other.

Client-Server Architecture: The Network Computer Brought to You by Protocols

For the last few chapters, I've been touting Linux as the greatest thing since TV dinners and Top Ramen noodles. One of the attributes I've been going on about is how easy connectivity is between Linux machines. This is actually true — I haven't been pulling your leg — but this connectivity would grind to a halt if it weren't for protocols.

"But why do we need protocols if Linux is an open system?" I hear the more inquisitive readers asking. The reason is simple: Just because Linux is "open" doesn't mean it has no rules that need to be followed. For example, at first glance you might reason that if everyone in New York City ignored those pesky stoplights on each block, traffic would move much faster and more smoothly. In reality, the city as a whole is more efficient if everyone follows the exact same rules of the road, at least some of the time.

Having each computer follow the rules of the road via its protocols allows any machine, whether it's a PC, laptop, or Linux box, to talk to other machines without difficulty. Since it virtually guarantees connectivity, it allowed the creation of the *network computer model* (which is now put into practice as the *client-server model*).

If you've ever been intimidated by someone who starts talking about network architectures, don't be. A network architecture is just a drawing, sketch, painting, or doodle that shows exactly how you have your machines hooked up.

If you really are looking at an architecture doodle instead of a top-flight PowerPoint presentation with little computer icons, remember these basic conventions:

- ✔ Squares are normally computers.
- ✔ Lines connecting the squares show how machines connect and talk to each other.
- ✔ If you connect to the Web, you'll normally see a cloud that looks like the thought bubble that hangs over the head of a cartoon character who's thinking about something.

Client-Server: The wave of the future

Think of the client-server model as a really efficient restaurant. Let's say that the restaurant has fifty customers who are served from one central kitchen. If this were the old, stand-alone model, then each of the fifty people would have

No computer is an island: The Old Stand-Alone Model

Before the client-server model really became the standard for business and academia, most computer systems worked as *stand-alone* systems. The stand-alone system allowed everyone to have their own computer, hard drive, and printer.

Sound simple? Granted, there are some advantages to this method that were more pronounced in the early stages of the computer revolution, including:

Stand-alone systems are very *compartmentalized* — if one user's machine crashes, it doesn't affect anyone else.

At first glance the stand-alone system appears to be easier to administer — each user is responsible for their own system.

Stand-alones allow maximum privacy — no user's files can be shared with any other person unless one person is willing to walk down to the other person's office with a floppy disk in hand.

Each of the preceding assumptions is either wrong, or outdated.

✔ Linux — and, to be fair, Windows — are much more stable than operating systems a couple of decades back.

A client-server network can be designed to avoid single points of failure by having a backup server on stand-by.

✔ Stand-alone systems are actually harder to administrate, partly because each person keeps their files in different locations on their machine if they don't have to conform to a single model. And of course, if you're responsible for weekly backups, you'll have to wander around to each office and repeat the same backup procedures on each single machine.

✔ Companies today need to share data between individuals or departments more than ever before.

Security is a bigger problem on a stand-alone system than the client-server method because you have absolutely no control over a person's computer if he or she forgets to lock the keyboard or turn the console off when they leave it unattended.

to have an individual kitchen, gas stove, microwave, pots to cook with, and plates to serve the food on — diagram or no, you can see what a nightmare that would be.

With the client-server model, the clients — in this example, the customers — don't need to have separate setups. After all, they're only here to consume! The server side, in this case, is the restaurant, which shares its resources on demand as each customer orders and is served when the resource (be it piping hot food or data) becomes available.

Now let's add one more twist to this analogy. Here, let's say that this restaurant is a fine local eatery called Chéz Bubba's American-Style Steak House.

Chéz Bubba's menu is in English, and the servers speak only that language. How well can the servers at Chéz Bubba's serve someone who speaks only German? What if a given customer can read the menu only if it's written in the Cyrillic alphabet? Or what if a customer orders only vegetarian curry dishes?

Finally, what if a diner refused to place an order until all the appetizers, silverware, and napkins were piled in front of him in alphabetical order? Obviously, this gentleman's dinner protocol is so unusual, he'll be lucky to get served.

Just as if the protocols for different customers would cause problems, so would each computer run into difficulties if they all used their own methods of talking to the server. In order to avoid this, UDP and TCP quickly become the industry standard protocols to allow widely different computers to communicate on a more detailed level than just exchanging error messages.

UDP: The Prodigal Son of the Protocols

The UDP in the *UDP* protocol stands for User Datagram Protocol. UDP predates TCP (and is correspondingly used less frequently), but you should be aware of what it is and how it differs from TCP.

Think of UDP as that friend of yours who might forget your birthday, miss his anniversary, lose his keys, and not remember his own name. The plus side of this friend is that he travels in a private helicopter. This, in a nutshell, is the good-side-bad-side relationship Linux users have with the UDP protocol.

UDP is known in the technical world as the *connectionless* protocol. As with any other data transmission, when you send data via UDP, that data is broken into packets. With UDP, the average packet size is very small, meaning that each packet contains relatively little data. At the scale of the absurdly small — we're talking about electrons passing through your computer's circuits here — breaking data into packets is not resource-intensive. However, the transmission of the data can take up more of your computer's resources. So UDP takes advantage of this quirk and acts like a speed demon, shuffling hordes of small *datagram packets* to where they need to go.

For those who are truly nerdy but also in the know, UDP also stands for "U Don't `ping`." This is a quick mnemonic phrase to remind you that the `ping` command, discussed in Chapter 7, creates a TCP connection, not a UDP one.

This means that just because you broadcast a UDP packet doesn't necessarily mean that you'll be able to make a TCP connection with another machine. It also doesn't mean that you'll be able to `ping` it. Of course, the reverse situation is also true — just because you can `ping` a machine doesn't mean you'll be able to broadcast to it.

The one company where UDP will never gain employment is Federal Express. Why? Because with all the zip that UDP gives to your data, the one thing that UDP *cannot* do is guarantee your information will get to the right destination.

This is why UDP is called the connectionless protocol. UDP doesn't target a specific machine; it radiates data the way a lump of radioactive ore spits out gamma rays. So compared to TCP, which is like mailing a letter to a friend, UDP is like walking into a crowded cafeteria and shouting at the top of your lungs that you have (or need) some information.

Also, if packets are dropped or lost, UDP won't bother telling you about it. Compare that kind of customer service to the TCP-based `ping` command:

```
UDP: (Nada, zip, zilch information)
TCP (Ping): 10 packets transmitted, 7 packets received, 30%
            packet loss
```

This kind of low reliability limits the use of UDP to certain applications and functions. Not surprisingly, the applications that use UDP are ones that care less about dropping the odd data packet or two; they focus on getting as many packets out onto the network as possible.

The most common use of UDP on a Linux system is the NFS (Network File System) server. When starting up NFS, your Linux server will be actively looking for other machines. Remember the analogy that using UDP is like walking into a cafeteria and shouting? While it might not do much for your reputation as a polite person, if your message is like "If anyone can hear me, raise your hand!" this is a very efficient way to get maximum response.

TCP/IP: Welcome to the Virtual Circuit

The TCP/IP networking protocol is the current standard used by Linux and PC machines around the world. There are two main reasons for this:

- ✔ TCP/IP was developed as the first standardized set of computer protocols by ARPAnet (Advanced Research Projects Agency).

  ARPAnet needed standardized protocols for both compatibility and computer security, due to the fact that ARPA was primarily funded by military research projects.

- ✔ TCP/IP's design and open-system policy allows any kind of computer hardware to use it.

While it sacrifices some speed, TCP/IP is the overall best protocol to use because of its reliability.

The reliability of the TCP/IP system is literally built into the protocol's structure. Remember how we compared computer protocols to dinner protocol in a restaurant? Let's take the analogy a little further to clarify the TCP/IP advantage a little.

Imagine that you're back at that four-star example of roadside diners, Chéz Bubba's. The restaurant has been having a little trouble making sure the customers get their piping hot data (or lobster thermidor, as the case may be). Somehow, along the way the dish is getting dropped, lost, or sent to the wrong table.

To prevent this and increase reliability, Chéz Bubba decides to use the TCP/IP model. When a dish of food — a packet of information to a computer — is served to a customer, Chéz Bubba waits until the customer signals that they're done with the food, and sends the plate back to the kitchen. Although it's slower (because the kitchen servers have to wait for the diner to inhale their portion), the servers know exactly when to send the next serving because the return of the empty plate guarantees that there was a connection at both ends: kitchen server and customer.

That's why TCP/IP is called the *virtual circuit*. A real, physical circuit constructed of batteries and wires must have a complete connection, or the circuit is broken and no power flows through. A virtual circuit connection is the same way, except that electrical current is replaced with packets of information.

The slight sacrifice in speed is usually more than compensated by the importance of guaranteeing that data reached its destination. Because of this, the vast majority of communications that take place on a computer network — and almost 100 percent of Internet connections — are taking place thanks to TCP/IP.

The TCP/IP family tree

The full name for the TCP/IP protocol is a real mouthful. *TCP* stands for Transmission Control Protocol and *IP* stands for Internet Protocol. TCP can't work without its IP portion. In essence, the TCP portion provides the point-to-point reliability and the IP portion acts as the engine. Therefore, *TCP/IP* is the official acronym, but you'll often hear people say just TCP. Again, it's just easier to say.

Further complicating matters is that TCP/IP is not actually a single protocol. In fact, it's the name for an entire *family* of protocols that have the same basic structure but perform different tasks. This protocol family tree is called a *protocol suite,* probably because it sounds more professional to say, "FTP is in the TCP/IP suite" than "FTP is TCP/IP's second cousin on the father's side."

Since it's the actual way each protocol is used that makes the real difference in the Linux world, it's also the best way to examine each member of the

TCP/IP protocol suite. While you may not be manually installing or running these protocols, it's important that you know the names and the functions of each protocol.

Networking Protocols

These members of the TCP/IP protocol family provide Linux's most important network services. More than anything else, these network protocols allow Linux to become the true network computer: They form the basis for data connections between machines and enable them to share information.

- ✔ **TCP (Transmission Control Protocol):** The virtual circuit protocol that guarantees connections between two network points before data is transmitted.

- ✔ **RPC (Remote Procedure Call):** This allows applications run on remote machines to communicate with each other.

- ✔ **SMTP (Simple Mail Transfer Protocol):** The postman may always ring twice — but SMTP, the e-mail postman, won't give you your mail until it guarantees that it can deliver.

- ✔ **SNMP (Simple Network Management Protocol):** Ironically, the most important thing to note about SNMP is *not* to get it mixed up with SMTP. SNMP doesn't provide a popular a service like SMTP — ever hear of anyone refusing to get e-mail? However, you can use SNMP to determine the status of the TCP/IP configurations and software. SNMP is rarely used because you need to use a loopback network interface in order to utilize it.

- ✔ **NFS (Network File System):** NFS is more of a system than a protocol, but it falls in this category because of its vast usefulness. NFS allows you to *mount* remote directories on a given machine for users to access for information freely and without needless copying or redundancy.

- ✔ **NIS (Network Information System):** This system increases the efficiency with which you can administer and maintain user accounts, allowing you to update important information across entire networks and improve security by simplifying the process of updating system passwords.

Transport Protocols

This branch of the TCP/IP family tree is dedicated to actually moving packets, not directing them. Transport protocols act as the movers and shakers on your network.

- ✔ **IP (Internet Protocol):** This protocol is the one that actually puts the pedal to the metal and moves the datagram packet across the network. It would work like UDP, except the TCP portion that it's paired with ensures that the data is targeted, and that no more data will be sent until the first acknowledgment is received from the recipient machine.

✔ **ICMP (Internet Control Message Protocol):** I suppose you can think of this protocol as the Igor to IP's Dr. Frankenstein. Much like that notorious lab assistant, ICMP provides the IP protocol with status messages it can use, such as network errors and routing changes that could affect whether the TCP packet ever gets to where it needs to go.

✔ **RIP (Rest in Peace):** Just kidding! RIP really stands for *Routing Information Protocol.* This protocol works off of the data provided by the ICMP protocol (a.k.a. Igor) and deduces the most efficient routing method for your datagram packets.

Addressing Protocols

The protocols in this area serve the Networking protocols and also try to translate machine numbers into symbolic letter names that humans can use to find their way around the network. Essentially, this is where the Networking protocols get their bearings from.

✔ **ARP (Address Resolution Protocol):** Although it sounds like something a trained seal might say, ARP is the protocol that helps determine the unique numeric address for each machine on your network.

✔ **RARP (Reverse Address Resolution Protocol):** This protocol does the exact same job as ARP, but, as you might have guessed, RARP does it in the reverse manner from ARP.

✔ **DNS (Domain Name System):** This system does the same job that ARP and RARP do. However, DNS tries to do it for the benefit of the carbon-based life forms (humans) as well as the silicon ones (computers). DNS determines what a machine's alphanumeric name is and extrapolates the machine's numeric address.

✔ **BOOTP (Boot Protocol):** This protocol is very rarely seen anymore because the price of disk space has fallen as quickly as a lead-filled submarine. Back when disk space was at a premium, many networks contained *diskless clients* — machines that were little more than a screen and a keyboard that normally didn't have space to store boot information. When you rebooted a diskless client, BOOTP would communicate with the server, pulling boot information off that the client could use. Since Linux is so lightweight that all but the most stingy of networks should have enough space, you may never see this protocol used.

Gateway Protocols

Whenever you hear the term *gateway* in Linux, think networks and routers. Each of these protocol services assist the network communication by passing along routing and status information for the TCP and IP protocols, and by handling data transfers between different subnets on your network.

✔ **EGP (Exterior Gateway Protocol):** This protocol works with your router, switch, or bridge device to pass on data-transfer information between external networks.

✔ **IGP (Interior Gateway Protocol):** Similar to EGP, IGP is EGP's stay-at-home relative. IGP also works with devices that hand data from one network to another, but it works at transferring the routing information between internal networks only.

✔ **GGP (Gateway to Gateway Protocol):** A more complex and specialized version of this kind of protocol, GGP only works on a narrow subsection of data transfer. But GGP is popular — GGP transfers routing data for gateways on the Internet.

User Service Protocols

User Protocols are the most common ones you'll see — you may very well come into daily contact with these services. Not only are they useful for a user, but they're also basic to the work of a Linux administrator. Because they're so useful, you'll be learning about each of these protocols in more detail later in this book.

✔ **FTP (File Transfer Protocol):** A low-cost and efficient method of transferring data files between computers at a user's request. In fact, the demand for FTP'ed items may be so great on your network that you'll be using what you learn in Chapter 12 to set up your own FTP server.

✔ **TFTP (Trivial File Transfer Protocol):** People ask me if this is a special protocol to transfer Trivial Pursuit questions around over the network. Sad to say, this isn't the case. TFTP works the same way as FTP, but it actually uses a UDP-like formula. TFTP is faster, but you're not guaranteed the same level of reliability, which is why you'd better not copy around files using this unless the contents of the file truly *are* trivial.

✔ **Telnet (short for Telephone Network):** A daemon, and has its own protocol that works on the TCP/IP model, as does the `ping` command. Telnet allows you to remotely log in to machines that can literally be half a world away. It's an amazing thing being able to control machines on another continent with your own keyboard, so you'll find more on how to use Telnet in Chapter 11.

Installing, using, and updating protocols

Now for some good news, especially if you're into avoiding unnecessary labor. Just because we've gone over every TCP/IP protocol in the book doesn't mean you're going to have to install them.

In fact, every single one of the protocols in the above list *are already installed* in your Linux network. They come with the Linux installation already, no matter whether you got your copy of Linux via a Red Hat CD-ROM, a Caldera diskette, or a no-name variation off the Internet.

Terminals for dummies

Diskless clients are also called, in true geek-speak, *dumb terminals.* Contrary to popular belief, this term has nothing to do with the intelligence of the people using them. Dumb terminals are simply computers that literally can't do much without a server connection — including booting up and storing data.

The advantage to this system is that each dumb terminal is dirt cheap. The disadvantage is that you're often putting your eggs in one old, frayed basket — if 99 percent of your computing ability is tied up on your server — then that's exactly how much performance you lose if the server

decides to take a vacation in Tahiti without telling you.

The latest incarnation of dumb terminals recently cropped up from an unexpected direction: Oracle. The CEO at Oracle, Larry Ellison, announced broad support for the terminal idea, and repackaged with a slick new name to make it sound more palatable than dumb terminal — the *network computer.* If you think this name sounds like what Linux practically is already, you're right — which is why you see a lot more Linux stations around today than dumb terminals!

Similarly, you're not going to be kicking off protocols the same way you'll be starting up applications and executing commands. Unlike programs, protocols aren't in and of themselves binaries. They're only a means to an end, so you'll probably never have to touch them. The programs and utilities that you use do the starting and stopping of the protocols themselves, because that's what the program(s) are coded to do. For example, when you use the `ping` command, you're telling the `ping` utility to invoke the TCP/IP protocols and print the results out for you in a way that tells you the state of the network. You don't actually have to go in and type "Use TCP/IP" at all, which makes your job that much easier.

You also won't have to worry about upgrading your protocol suite set. To start out with, these protocols are universally known standards. TCP/IP is maintained by a standards body that is part of the Internet community. Any change made to the protocols will always be backward-compatible, because the Internet community has no interest in suddenly having a large percentage of its membership suddenly become unable to connect to the Internet.

When a new TCP/IP version is released and you want to get it for efficiency's sake, simply wait until your Linux vendor (Red Hat or Caldera, for example), releases a new version of Linux. The Linux CD-ROM is sure to have all the new standards, including the updated protocols. Of course, if you're pulling Linux in off the Web, you'll have to wait until the new version(s) of Linux are posted on the Linux Web sites.

Chapter 9

Internet Addresses, Masks, and Services

- -

- -

*I*n this chapter, I discuss that mysterious method of staking out location on the Internet — using the IP Address. You can also see what kind of hardware you need to stake your claim, how the IP address and the network mask work together in helping other computers locate your Linux box and, more importantly, how computers use the IP address to send data to and from that location.

You're also going to see how easy it is to set up and customize all the goodies and services that you learned about in Chapter 8. Rather than just blather about the TCP/IP protocol family, I *show* you how to put members of the whole clan to work for you.

Fishing in the Network Pond with Your Homemade Ethernet

If you were going to surf the World Wide Web, you wouldn't hit the cyber-beach without your surfboard, would you? Of course not. On a similar note, you'll be up an electronic creek without a paddle unless you have the right equipment in your Linux box.

If you want to grab your place on the great homestead of the electronic age —
the Internet — you'll need to get on a computer network. And if you want to
hook your Linux box up to a network, you need a special piece of hardware
called a *network card*.

Linux uses a special kind of network card called an *Ethernet card*. In Chapter 8
I discuss the growth of the Ethernet cabling industry — Ethernet is still the
standard of the Linux networking world. Some of the network cards used in
PCs may not be compatible with Ethernet, so you may have some work cut
out for you. Make sure you know where your tool kit is if you need to pry
open the backs of some of your PCs.

Watch out! Network cards and Ethernet cards aren't necessarily the same
thing, although a lot of people use the terms interchangeably. A network card
can be an Ethernet card, or it can be a totally different kind of card that gets a
PC onto an ISP (Internet service provider). But even if you can connect to
America Online, it's not going to be much help to you if you can't communicate with your Linux server.

An Ethernet card is a special subset of network card. Luckily, since Ethernet
is the standard today, the vast majority of network cards *are* Ethernet-
compatible. So you can say that all Ethernet cards are network cards, even
if all network cards aren't necessarily Ethernet cards.

Network cards that add strings to your Ethernet

Ethernet cards are specifically designed to work with the TCP/IP protocol.
More specifically for Linux systems, Ethernet cards are more efficient at
breaking your outgoing information into packets. Just as importantly,
Ethernet cards in your Linux box allow for efficient reassembly of incoming
packets into information that your computer can use.

The most common and popular network cards that handle Ethernet connections for Linux — (and can therefore be honestly called Ethernet cards) are
listed as follows:

This list shouldn't be taken as complete in and of itself, but it's what I can reasonably guarantee will work with Linux.

3Com 3C505

3Com 3C503/16

Hewlett-Packard HP27245

Hewlett-Packard HP27247

Hewlett-Packard HP27250

Novell NE1000

Novell NE2000

Western Digital WD8003

Western Digital WD8013

If you choose to shave a few dollars from your networking budget by buying an off-brand Ethernet card from a fly-by-night network card distributor, you're on your own. You may get a bargain, but then again, you should keep in mind a listing that a wise Linux network administrator once had taped to his main network server: "Buy Miracle Network Ethernet Cards! Remember, if it works, it's a Miracle!!!"

Two situations that don't need an Ethernet card

Yes, even after all my dire admonitions to get an Ethernet card, and a brand-name one at that, there are times you can get away with less. Granted, these are very restricted situations reserved for once-in-a-blue-moon for most network administrators. But of course, you never know.

✔ You don't need a network card if you will be connecting to the network over telephone lines. This is a boon to those who like to use portable laptop computers, since a network card takes up valuable room and adds a few more ounces of weight. (True, it's only a couple of ounces, but try carrying around a three-, four-, or five-pound laptop for a full day while jogging between airports . . . you'll be more sympathetic to the idea that a couple of ounces really can count!)

Instead of an Ethernet card, you'll need a fast modem to make a SLIP (Serial Line Interface Protocol) connection. I talk more about SLIP in Chapter 10. As a rule, however, you'll need to have a modem that can run at least 14.4 kilobytes per second.

Considering that a 14.4 modem will cost you less than a McDonald's Happy Meal, don't be foolish and try to beat this baseline requirement. Go ahead, splurge for the price of a large order of french fries and make sure you have a decent modem.

✔ The second situation where you can get by without an Ethernet Card is when you decide to test your local TCP/IP configuration. This is called creating a *loopback,* where in essence you're telling the machine to talk to itself. Rather than proving that your computer needs some company, a loopback is a way that some network administrators use to check the general health of the machine.

This technique is relatively ancient, and today you've got plenty of techniques and tools to check network and machine health. So, while you should be aware of what *loopback* is, you'll probably never encounter it.

You Are Here: What an IP Address Does

An IP (Internet Protocol) Address provides the same functionality as the street address painted on your mailbox in front of your home. And it performs that job with the same pinpoint accuracy that you'll find on a given building map with the logo "You Are Here." (After all, have you ever seen one of those maps that is wrong?)

To your Linux box, whether it's an IBM PC clone or a converted UNIX workstation, the IP address is a unique 32-bit number that identifies your machine to all the other machines on your computer network. All IP addresses are presented in the same format for a human being's comprehension: four sets of numbers, with no more than three numbers in a given set, and each set of numbers separated by a dot. Some examples of valid IP addresses would be:

177.24.12.108

10.240.99.1

169.45.3.103

222.1.1.10

On the other hand, here are some examples of invalid IP addresses. Try assigning these values to a machine and you're headed for Major Error City:

123.4567.10.1977

134.8.99

0.0.0.0

255.16.76.88

Those of you who have sharp eyes will have noticed that the last two sets of numbers look all right at first glance, as they follow the rules for IP addresses (four sets of numbers, no more than three in each set). However, there's one more rule that you need to know: using 255 or zero in an IP address is a *big mistake*. This is because these numbers are reserved for use in the netmask, which we'll learn about shortly.

For now, just don't set up your machines with an IP address of 255.0.0.255 and your life will be much easier.

As you probably suspect by now, the four-number system is more to help poor, number-clumsy humans than to help machines. For a machine, this is too simplistic. Linux, like other operating systems, crunches these numbers up and spits them back out on the network in hexadecimal format.

The four sets of numbers in an IP address serve another purpose for humans: They help organize machines on a network by class of network and also by subnet. Working from the broadest part of the address to the most specific, the first two fields are the general *network component* and the latter two fields make up the more specific *host component*.

The closest comparison I can think of between IP and real world postal addresses is where the broad, network component portion of the address is equal to your state and ZIP code on your letter. The more specific host component would be the equivalent of a street address and apartment number.

Subletting with subnets

For slightly more complex networks, you'll see the phenomenon of *subnets*. A subnet is a logical grouping of machines on a given intranet that share a common number in the third set of the four fields in the IP address.

As an example, the following machines would be on the same subnet.

160.105.80.80

160.156.80.12

176.178.80.92

These machines are all on the 80 subnet.

Usually, these logical groups are created for more than just ordering purposes. If this group of machines is going to be sharing data back and forth more frequently than the rest of the network, then this is a good way to isolate network traffic and allow the rest of the network to operate at a higher rate with fewer Ethernet packet collisions.

Sailing off the edge of the "flat" network

If you don't anticipate a group of software developers doing heavy stress-testing on your network, or if you don't have a group of people who download large files all day, you may want to avoid subnets. In your case, you may want to stick with the simpler network configuration of one subnet for the whole network. This kind of configuration is called a *flat* network — logically — because there are no real divisions between machines.

There are two rules for selecting your networking scheme:

- ✔ Flat networks are easier to administer. They're also cheaper; you don't need as many different network connectors, like switches and routers, to bridge the gap between subnets.

- ✔ A subnet approach is definitely the way to go if you have pockets of heavy users (like developers).

Putting Your IP Address Out in the Best Neighborhood

If you're a budding mathematician, you may figure that although the total number of combinations of the four groups of numbers is very large, there's a high probability that someone will have a duplicate machine IP address. So how do you avoid picking a number that someone on the Internet is already using?

The answer is that for the vast majority of instances, you don't need to worry about it. This is because the majority of Linux you'll be administering, unless you're a Webmaster, won't be found on the Internet. Too many people make the erroneous assumption that since they can *ftp, ping,* and use Netscape with the best, that their machines are on the Internet. Not true.

If your machine isn't a dedicated server/client that is hooked into the Internet (not to be confused with your local network) 24 hours a day, 7 days a week, then it's not on the World Wide Web. Instead, you're on what's called your *intranet,* which is the network that exists inside your own company, university, tool shed, plywood shack, or whatever. This is actually a good thing, for the following reasons:

- ✔ Because you're not out on the public, domain there's less of a security risk.

- ✔ You don't have to worry about your IP address conflicting with someone else's. The majority of systems have only one or two machines that are dedicated to providing Web service, and everyone else connects to the Internet through this one server.

Yes, keeping intranet and Internet straight is tough. My only defense is that I can truthfully state that I didn't make up the terms. Also keep in mind that a machine that's dedicated to providing Web service is usually called, in techno-speak, a *Web server* or *gateway server.*

Since the Web or gateway server *is* on the Web, it's accessible by any member of the public with a modem and a keyboard. This is why hackers describe a machine of this sort as being *in the public domain.*

The Net cops, a.k.a. the InterNIC

A special agency, whose mission is to prevent redundant IP addresses from cropping up, is the Internet Network Information Center (or InterNIC). If you want to connect to the Internet and set up a public-domain server, you'll have to register with them to make sure your address isn't already taken.

If this were April Fool's Day, I could tell you the InterNIC's agents dress in all black clothing, wear dark, mirrored sunglasses, and shadow unsuspecting Linux administrators. Even at night. (Cue the dangerous theme music . . .)

But the fact of the matter is, I don't know *what* they do if you flagrantly refuse to register with them. (Then again, I've never known anyone who *didn't* register with them.) Maybe they have ways to gain your compliance that we don't want to know and shouldn't find out. Or maybe registering is just a handy way to avoid redundancy (how unromantic). So register your address with them, or else . . . well, *something.*

Who was that network-masked machine?

A *network mask* (or *netmask*) is the network component of the IP address set to 255, which is why you can't use value 255 in your IP address — your machine would get confused. The netmask is used to block out the network portion of your machine's IP address so packets that have similar addresses (or similar numbers) won't wind up on the same subnet when they're routed between machines.

You don't have to set the netmask, but it's helpful to know what exactly it does. A netmask could be 255.255.0.0 or 255.255.255.0, depending on the class of the network you're administering.

Keep in mind that you can't change the level of class of your network by muffling the Iron Maiden album playing in the background, draping your box with red velvet carpeting, or lighting scented candles in the network room. A *network class* is defined by the InterNIC according to the size of the network. There are three categories:

✔ Class A networks are fewer in number, and they're reserved for mono-lithic institutions like large corporations (think Fortune 500 and a guy named Bill here) and government.

✔ Class B is normally used for medium and smaller companies.

✔ Class C is pretty much everyone else.

Part of the fun of looking at Internet addresses if you're in the know (and you find pocket protectors incredibly fascinating) is that you can immediately tell what class of network you're connecting to. This is because the different classes are limited in the first field of numbers to certain combinations. See Table 9-1 for the listings:

Table 9-1	Class by Numbers
Number in the First Field	*Type of Class*
1–127	Class A
128–191	Class B
192–223	Class C

Setting Up Your /Etc/Hosts and /Etc/Services Files

If you want to invite guests over to your house or your Linux box (whichever is more suited for entertaining), then you'll need to be a gracious host. And what does a gracious host do if not provide services to his or her guests? In the networking world, this works both ways; if you want to be a welcome guest and actually get work done, you'll need to have your services and hosts files set up on your Linux box.

The hosts and services files reside in the /etc directory of your Linux box. Change directories to /etc and do a "list files" (**ls –l**) to see what's there. You'll see which files you should know about and which ones you might have to tweak with the vi editor.

You have three hosts files to be aware of on a Linux system.

/etc/hosts

vi the most basic of the three, /etc/hosts. This file lists the IP addresses and host names that correspond to a given address for all the machines on your system. On larger networks, you'll probably be using NIS or DNS and you won't see very much here. But on small networks, you're better off making sure that all your machines are represented. For example, let's say that I run a network with six machines, Linuxbox, Unixbox, Mustang, Nova, Colt, and Pinto. Assuming that I'm on my home machine, Linuxbox, my /etc/hosts file would look something like the following sample:

```
# vi /etc/hosts
/etc/hosts
127.0.0.1              localhost        localhost.localdomain
188.111.59.72    Unixbox
188.111.59.5     Mustang
188.111.59.10    Nova
Colt
188.111.59.99    Pinto
```

Note that every /etc/hosts file will begin with 127.0.0.1, which is the default entry for the localhost connection, also called the *loopback*. This is the setting that is tested with the loopback technique described earlier in the chapter, which explains how it can be worked with, even without an Ethernet card.

/etc/hostname

This file is a breeze to edit, but make sure that you don't forget to work with it or you'll go nowhere fast on a network. The hostname file is used to store the name of your local machine. Just make sure that your hostname is in it. For example, on my machine Linuxbox, the file should look as follows:

```
# vi hostname
/etc/hostname
Linuxbox
```

Incidentally, there are two utilities that will give you the hostname of a machine if you've had a sudden onset of amnesia. You can use the **hostname** command to give you a result like this one:

```
# hostname
Linuxbox
```

If your Linux system lacks this command, you can use the **uname** command with the **–n** option, which gives you a similar output:

```
# uname -n
Linuxbox
```

Yes, that's all there is to it. (Didn't I tell you Linux was easy?)

Name that host with /etc/host.conf

The Linux system uses `host.conf` to resolve `hostnames`. It should look similar to this:

```
# vi /etc/host.conf
/etc/hosts.conf
order hosts, nis
multi on
```

In this episode, `host.conf` tells the system to check the `hosts` file, and then to look for a name server if one exists. Unless somebody has commented out one of these lines, you shouldn't have to make changes here.

/etc/services

This is your list of network services. Luckily, you rarely need to touch this file; any software communications package you add will install itself here. Still, it's best to check this file to find out whether any lines are commented out. Unless you specifically want to shut a service off, it's best to leave the lines uncommented. As a rule, a prudent Linux administrator should heed the words of the great Yogi Berra: "If it ain't broke, don't fix it."

The `/etc/services` file should look similar to the following example. We've seen the `/etc/services` file in an earlier chapter, but this is a more detailed example. Now that you're familiar with some of the services available on Linux, such as UUCP and Telnet, if you skim the list you'll see how ports are allocated for the specific service. You'll also be able to tell whether the type of connection uses the UDP protocol, the TCP/IP protocol, or both.

```
#vi /etc/services
/etc/services
# services      This file describes the various services that
              are
#              available from the TCP/IP subsystem.  It
              should be
#              consulted instead of using the numbers in the
              ARPA
#              include files, or, worse, just guessing them.
#
# Version:     @(#)/etc/services
#
#
echo                7/udp
netstat             15/tcp
```

```
qotd             17/tcp          quote
ftp              21/tcp
telnet           23/tcp
smtp             25/tcp          mail
time             37/tcp          timserver
time             37/udp          timserver
name             42/udp          nameserver
whois            43/tcp          nicname              #
        usually to sri-nic
domain           53/tcp
domain           53/udp
gopher           70/tcp                               #
        gopher server
finger           79/tcp
http             80/tcp                               # www
        is used by some
snmp            161/udp
snmp-trap       162/udp
login           513/tcp                               # BSD
        rlogind(8)
who             513/udp          whod                 #
        BSD rwhod(8)
shell           514/tcp          cmd                  #
        BSD rshd(8)
syslog          514/udp                               # BSD
        syslogd(8)
printer         515/tcp          spooler              #
        BSD lpd(8)
route           520/udp          router routed        #
        521/udp too
courier         530/tcp          rpc                  #
        experimental
netwall         533/udp                               # -
        for emergency broadcasts
uucp            540/tcp          uucpd                #
        BSD uucpd(8) UUCP
kshell          544/tcp          cmd                  #
        and remote shell
mount           635/udp                               # NFS
        Mount Service
nfs            2049/udp                               # NFS
        File Service
irc            6667/tcp                               #
        Internet Relay Chat
# End of services.
```

/etc/networks

One more file you should edit when needed is /etc/networks. This file lists
names and IP addresses of your network and any other network you connect
to on a regular basis. You should consider adding an entry here for every

network that you connect to frequently. When adding entries, you'll only need to put in the network's netmask. See this following example.

Note: The only two lines that you must absolutely have are the `localnet` and `loopback` entries, so don't ever delete them.

```
# vi /etc/networks
/etc/networks
#ident  "@(#)networks    1.4
#
# The networks file associates Internet Protocol (IP) network
        numbers
# with network names.  The format of this file is:
#
#       network-name     network-number  nicnames . . .
#
#
# The loopback network is used only for intra-machine
        communication
#
loopback        127
#
# Internet networks
#
arpanet         10              arpa    # Historical
```

Whenever you make changes to these files, be judicious. You'll normally have to be `root` to make these edits.

When you start playing with /etc files of any kind, *always* make a backup copy to fall back on.

Chapter 10

Telnet: Your Window to the World

● ●

In This Chapter

▶ Using telnet to connect to other computers

▶ Using IP addresses with telnet

▶ Controlling machines remotely

▶ Stopping your telnet session

▶ Finding out what else you can do with telnet

● ●

*T*o connect to other computers on the Internet, the handy `telnet` command is at your service. Telnet acts like a telephone network (tel-net, get it?) connection in that you can connect up to other computers with only your user name and your password.

Computers running Linux use telnet to communicate. Computers running UNIX also use telnet. Macintoshes use telnet. Windows 95, 98, and NT computers can use telnet by looking in the Accessories directory. This isn't by accident. TCP/IP based telnet sessions have become the most widely accepted method of opening communication between different computers because telnet is simple, reliable, and easy to use, as you find out in this chapter.

Connecting by Telnet

Telnet is automatically installed on your Linux network as a connection system using the TCP/IP suite of protocols, so you won't have any work to do in that regard. Telnet itself is also fairly well automated. From the moment you execute the `telnet` command your Linux box starts up a daemon (called, sensibly enough, `telnetd`) which will handle the specific byte-to-byte operations of setting up a telnet session with the remote host of your choice.

It's best to keep your terminology straight when you're using telnet or you'll get easily confused. Worse yet, other people who don't know proper telnet terms will confuse you. Some basic points to keep in mind are:

✔ There is no such thing as a telnet server. Remember, a server is a machine that is dedicated to performing one task particularly well, like sharing out files, storing electronic mail, or collecting coffee cup rings. Since any machine can use telnet just as well as another, you can't have a telnet-specific machine.

✔ The machine you start telnet on is simply the place you started your telnet session.

✔ The machine you're trying to connect to is called the *remote host*. It doesn't matter if you're connecting to a machine in Katmandu or one sitting right next to your desk. It's remote from your telnet session machine in that it isn't sitting in the same computer case.

The Best Uses for Telnet

Telnet is at its best when connecting to machines that provide text-based data that isn't sensitive or private. Rarely will you find a company that provides information through an open telnet site.

On the other hand, the following organizations are usually very telnet-friendly:

✔ Libraries

✔ Universities

✔ Public interest groups

✔ Government agencies

Places like these are great for gathering information remotely. But after you find the file you're looking for, how do you get a copy of it on your local machine to print or read at your leisure? The answer: You need FTP — and FTP just happens to be the topic of Chapter 11!

Making the Connection

So let's say that you want to connect to the remote machine Linuxbox, which has the IP address 198.110.75.111. You can make a telnet connection to the machine Linuxbox as follows:

1. From your terminal window, type:

```
telnet Linuxbox.
```

Your machine tells you that it's trying the connection, and then prompts you for your user name, as follows:

```
Trying Linuxbox (198.110.75.11)
Connected to Linuxbox
Escape character is '^]'
Linuxbox login:
```

2. Type your user name and press Enter.

Next you are prompted for your password.

```
Password:
```

3. Type your password.

You can't see on-screen what you're typing — this is a security feature to prevent someone from getting your password by looking over your shoulder. After you press Enter you are either then logged on to Linuxbox or kicked back to the login prompt.

If you type your password and make a mistake, you can't use the Backspace or Delete key to correct your mistake, which means you can't log on. You simply have to start over, as follows:

1. Press Enter.

Linux dutifully tries the incorrect password for a few seconds and then complains that it can't connect to the remote computer. Linux helpfully gives you the login: prompt again so you can try to improve your typing skills by typing the correct information on the second go-around.

2. Reenter your password and press Enter.

Using the Internet protocol address with telnet

Suppose that you didn't know the name of the computer you're trying to talk to (such as Linuxbox in the last example) but you know the IP address. You can use telnet the same way, but type the IP address instead of the computer's name.

Since Linuxbox had an IP address of 198.110.75.111, you would use:

```
telnet 198.110.75.111
```

Sometimes names don't work but IP addresses do. Every now and then, someone incorrectly registers a machine's name so that it's impossible to telnet into it using that name. However, machines are a lot better at numbered addresses than lettered names. After all, the lettered names were created so humans could remember which computer was assigned to which numbered address.

For example, let's say that you try to `telnet` to remote host Linuxbox and instead you get the following:

```
telnet Linuxbox
Trying Linuxbox
ERROR: Cannot locate Linuxbox
```

You might also see your telnet session hang for up to half a minute, as your machine searches for Linuxbox. Eventually, even an operating system as persistent as Linux will give up and hand you the message "Telnet Session timed out."

In cases like this, the machine Linuxbox may actually exist. Test this by using the `ping` command with the IP address. Since both `telnet` and `ping` use the same TCP/IP protocol, if you can use one command, you'll probably be able to use the other.

So when you're trying to `telnet` to a machine without success, try to `telnet` using the IP address instead. You may be pleasantly surprised.

Any port in a storm

There's a small possibility you might run into an access restricted machine when you're busy using telnet, in which case you normally get the error message `Connection Refused`.

Although it's rare, sometimes a machine will be set up to handle telnet sessions on a single, specific telnet port. This was an old way to try and restrict access to a machine for security purposes, and it's so outdated that I've come across only two or three machines that were set up like this in years. However, if you want to talk to a restricted machine, find out what port telnet is using. If the port is 9500, for example, simply telnet into the machine as follows:

```
telnet Linuxbox 9500
```

Having machines do your bidding remotely

The fun part about using telnet is that after you've logged on to a remote computer, it responds just as if it were your own machine in the same room. The machine you're logged on to is in Hong Kong? Make it list its files. It's in London? Have it start up a Web browser. It's sitting in the computer lab two stories above your room? Make it print a copy of its text files.

Telnet gives you what computer geeks like to call a *transparent interface* with the machine you're logged on to. This means you shouldn't notice much difference between being logged on to this remote machine and your own. Okay, there are a few differences.

- ✔ If the remote machine is sitting an ocean away, there might be a time lag between what you type and what the remote machine does.

- ✔ Unless you know the names of the printers that the machine in Hong Kong is connected to, you won't be able to make the machine print anything. (And if you do manage to print something, it will be *really* tough to read all the way over in Hong Kong, no matter what size font you use.)

Back to our old machine Linuxbox. If you're logged on to Linuxbox, you should be able to tell that you're on a remote machine by looking at the prompt. Normally, the prompt should include the machine name as follows:

```
Linuxbox%
```

To do anything on Linuxbox, just type Linux commands as you would on your own machine.

To change to the root directory, type the following:

```
Linuxbox% cd /
```

To list files in the current directory:

```
Linuxbox% ls
```

And, if your memory isn't what it used to be, type the following to find out which user you're logged on as:

```
Linuxbox% id
```

Table 11-1 lists some more telnet commands you might find useful.

Table 11-1	Popular telnet Commands
Command	*Action*
!	Run a shell from telnet
?	Show help
close	Close the current connection
open	Open a new connection

(continued)

Table 11-1 *(continued)*

Command	Action
quit	Exit telnet
z	Suspend telnet

What to do when the computer is ignoring you

What should you do if the remote machine is ignoring your Linux commands? Relax! You haven't created a computer Frankenstein, roaming around the network under its own free will. Instead, you may have connected to a machine that doesn't use Linux.

When you remotely log on to a machine, you automatically begin using its local operating system. You can, however, easily figure whether or not you're using Linux on the remote machine.

This time, suppose that you're starting from a machine called "tinker." Type the following and press Enter:

```
uname -a
```

You'll get a response like this:

```
Linux tinker 2.0.34 Fri July 1 10:05 EDT 1998
```

The uname command makes the computer tell you the type of operating system being used (Linux), the machine name (tinker), the version of Linux (2.0.34), and the system date and time.

Suppose that you decide to telnet into a remote machine. For some reason, your Linux commands don't seem to work. You type **uname** again, and you get the following:

```
Solaris  5.5.1 Fri July 1 10:06 EDT 1998
```

Although your screen looks the same, you're now connecting to a computer that uses the Solaris operating system (which is a form of UNIX from Sun Microsystems), where the commands might be different. Mystery solved.

Don't let the possibility of connecting to different operating systems scare you away from using telnet. Most of the time, the commands in Linux are the same as the different computers you'll be talking to.

Terminating your telnet session

You can end your telnet session the same way you would normally log off your local Linux machine: Type **exit** and you are taken back to your local computer.

If the remote system is not responding, you can exit in the following manner:

1. **Enter the telnet escape command.**

   This is usually Ctrl+] (right bracket).

2. **At the** telnet> **prompt, type** close **or** quit **to end the session.**

Chapter 11

Transferring Files with FTP or UUCP

In This Chapter
▶ Getting files with UUCP
▶ Getting files with FTP
▶ Going wild about wildcards
▶ Setting up your own anonymous FTP site

*Y*ou can use the `telnet` command to get into another computer and look around at all the goodies available. You need different utilities, however, to get hold of what you see.

You have two options to transfer files over your Linux network or between your Linux machine and a completely different network: UUCP or FTP. If you're connecting to another Linux network or a UNIX-based network of any flavor of UNIX, such as Solaris, SunOS, or HPUX, you can use UUCP.

However, UUCP was developed at a time when UNIX machines only talked to other UNIX machines. In today's less snobby computer world, UNIX machines gladly talk to PCs, Macs, and anything else under the sun that's on a network.

Enter FTP, which stands for File Transfer Protocol. FTP is a utility that enables you to copy files either to or from your Linux machine. Because it's one of the most useful tools available, all versions of Linux, UNIX, and PCs come with this utility already supplied.

In this chapter, you'll learn how to use these protocols and the benefits of each.

UUCP: Older Than the Hills but Just as Solid

If you ever need to prove to a Linux user that dinosaurs still walk the earth, introduce him to the UUCP utility. UUCP, which stands for *UNIX to UNIX Copy,* was invented by Michael Lesk of Bell Laboratories in the mid-1970s. UUCP opened the door to cheap, reliable computer networking because its structure was so efficient that it was adopted by ARPAnet.

In Chapter 8, I explain that ARPAnet's work led to the creation of the TCP/IP protocol family. Along the way, the UUCP communication system led to the creation of Usenet newsgroups. And part of ARPAnet's work using UUCP subsequently led to the global phenomenon known as the Internet. (Talk about kicking off revolutions!) Not bad for a 20+-year-old-piece of programming!

UUCP is limited in the sense that it was developed only to allow UNIX machines to talk to other UNIX machines. However, it's still used occasionally in the UNIX and Linux worlds to transfer files. UUCP has been further upgraded over the years to perform vastly greater communication functions, such as handling mail and news. For the purpose of this chapter, I take a quick look at the most common use of UUCP — to transfer large files between machines.

Just a quick reminder: Linux is still a form (or *flavor,* as the techno-wizards like to call it) of UNIX. Therefore, it doesn't matter if you're using UUCP to copy files from Solaris to Linux, Linux to Xenix, HPUX to SCO. It's still a form of UNIX, so don't panic if you see me use the terms *UNIX* and *Linux* together in the same sentence. For simplicity's sake, I assume that in the examples given, both imaginary computers are running Linux.

Using UUCP

Copying files with UUCP is pretty basic. The command structure for UUCP is as follows:

```
uucp <options> <source>(file) <destination>(file)
```

As an example, say that you want to transfer the file `simpleminds.txt` from a Linux machine called Serverbox to another Linux box called All4Me. `Simpleminds.txt` resides on Serverbox's `/var` directory, and you want to put the file in All4Me's `/etc` directory. The command you type at your Linux session window looks something like this:

```
uucp -c Serverbox:/var/simpleminds.txt All4Me:/etc
```

By default, UUCP copies files into the spool directory of your machine, which is normally set to /var/spool. The -c option allows you to bypass this and send the file directly to the location you're aiming for.

Table 12-1 lists the most popular command options you may need when using UUCP to transfer files.

Table 12-1	UUCP Command Options
Command Option	*What It Does*
-c	Bypasses the default setting of copying files to the spool directory. Best used if you're allergic to the mv command.
-C	Tells UUCP to copy files to the spool directory. I've never known anyone to use this because it's already the default place that UUCP copies to.
-d	Creates directories for the copy if you haven't specified any. By default this option is turned on.
-f	This option specifies the opposite of -d: it tells UUCP to not make directories when they don't exist.
-g	Set the grade (a.k.a. the priority) of the job. This option was created when Linux boxes were much slower than they are today, so that a huge copy job would be allocated to a place in line behind or ahead of other jobs. Today, if your job is large enough to slow the system down, just do it after hours when fewer people are using the network.
-j	Print the UUCP job number.
-m	This fun option has UUCP send an e-mail to the user account that started the UUCP job. The e-mail is sent when the job is complete and tells the user that, um, the job is complete!
-n	Like –m, but here you get to specify which user gets the email message. Seriously cool.

Advantages of UUCP over FTP

UUCP's main advantages have disappeared over the years, as FTP became more flexible in communicating with non-UNIX machines and eventually became the new standard in file transfers. However, UUCP is still a more stable method of transferring files between Linux machines if the files fall into the rarely-sighted category of the truly humongous.

Transferring files that are dozens of megabytes in size does take time, even on the speediest of systems. One of UUCP's remaining advantages over FTP is that when you're running these tasks — perhaps out of some strange desire to keep your Linux system in marathon-runner condition — you can monitor its progress. For this, you can use the UUCP utility called uustat.

To check on UUCP jobs running, type the following at your Linux prompt:

```
Linuxbox% uustat -a
```

You can also use the uustat utility to report transfer time rates (a good way to check the health of your network connections), check on a specific user's jobs, or kill an ongoing UUCP file transfer. In each case, just use the appropriate command option.

Table 12-2 lists the uustat command options you can use.

Table 12-2	Uustat **Command Options**
Command Option	*What It Does*
-a	Lists all the queued UUCP jobs on the system.
-c	Use this with the -t option if you want to find out the average time a UUCP job spent in the queue instead of the time it spent actually in operation. (Useful to find out if your copy jobs are stacking up due to overuse of UUCP.)
-d	Again, use this with the -t option to determine the speed at which the UUCP transfers are taking place. -d allows you to specify a set number of minutes during the UUCP transfers to monitor.
-k	Kills UUCP job. To kill a job, you must either own the job or be logged in as root.
-t	Report the system's average transfer rate in bytes per second over the past hour.
-u	Report the status of all jobs for a specific user. For example, if you want to find out job status for Wally the Wonder User, use: uustat -uwally.

Working with FTP

When you use FTP, your machine calls up the remote server you specified and establishes a connection with it. At this point, the remote server will ask you to log on.

Many FTP servers are *secured,* which means you must have a logon name and password that the FTP server recognizes. This is more common if you're trying to access an FTP site containing a company's business-sensitive information or an FTP site at a computer laboratory that doesn't want random users to be taking up computer time on their network.

Most FTP sites, however, are open for all traffic. No matter who you are, what computer you're using, or how bad your credit rating is, you'll be allowed on the server. In many cases, free access is provided through *anonymous FTP.* The user is automatically logged on as anonymous. If a password is necessary, it's often the user's local e-mail address.

Using FTP

Start using FTP by typing the `ftp` command, followed by the name of the remote system you want to connect to. For example, to connect to the FTP server called `idg.dummies.org`, follow these steps to enter your command:

1. **Type** ftp idg.dummies.org **from your Linux session window.**

   This tells your computer to start the FTP process and find the FTP server on the network called `idg.dummies.org`. At this point, you'll see a prompt that looks like the following:

   ```
   Connected to idg.dummies.org.
   idg.dummies.org FTP server ready.
   User Name:
   ```

2. **Type your user name.**

   Next, you'll be asked for your password.

3. **Type your password.**

   Because passwords are meant to be private, you won't see the text on the screen as you type. If you are trying to connect to a secure server and you're not Michaelized to be on the system, you'll be gently turned out at this point.

If you're logging on to an open server, you may get away with pressing the Enter key for the user name and the password.

If you type your password and make a mistake, you can't use the Backspace or Delete key to correct your mistake. Therefore, you won't be able to log on. So if you mess up, it's best to quit FTP and start over. (If you're logging on to an anonymous FTP server, it doesn't care what gobbledygook you enter for the password.)

Another way to log on to a remote FTP server is to type **ftp** and press Enter. When you get the FTP prompt, you type open and the server name, as follows:

```
ftp> open idg.dummies.org
```

When you use FTP, you must type filenames and machine names completely and correctly. If you make a mistake, you usually will get an error message and will have to start over. If you're using FTP with X Window System, you can save some time by cutting and pasting lines of text rather than typing them.

Transferring files

When an FTP server contains files with information you want on your computer, you want to *get* this information. That's exactly the command to use. To get the file, type:

```
get <filename>
```

FTP will tell you that a connection has been established, copy the file into your local directory where you started FTP, and then notify you when it's finished. The ftp> prompt will return, allowing you to either exit the FTP program or continue to copy files.

Need to put a copy of files you already own on the server? Lucky you. FTP has a command for this: the *put* command. The put command works the same way as the get command. If you want to put a file called mysecretrecipe.txt on the server, type:

```
put mysecretrecipe.txt
```

Table 12-3 is a short list of FTP commands that cover most of the situations you might encounter using FTP to transfer files.

Table 12-3	Popular FTP Commands
Command	*Action*
ascii	Selects the ASCII transfer mode, which is usually the default mode for FTP. It's useful for transferring text (which is what ASCII is), but it won't transfer binary files properly.
binary	Selects the binary transfer mode. Always use this to transfer binary files with FTP.
cd	Changes the directory on the FTP server.
close	Terminates the FTP session. You can also use the quit command.
del	Deletes files on the FTP server. Unless you own the files on the server, you're usually not permitted to do this.
dir	Displays the directory on the server.
get	Downloads a file from the server.
hash	Prints # while downloading or uploading to indicate progress.
help	Lists the help files.
lcd	Changes the directory on the client machine.
mget	Downloads multiple files from the server.
mput	Uploads multiple files to the server.
open	Connects you to a named server.
put	Uploads a file to the server.
pwd	Displays the current directory on your machine.
quote	Directly supplies an FTP command.
quit	Terminates the FTP session.

Transferring BIG files: Hashing it out

Part of the benefit (or curse) of Linux is that it doesn't clutter up your screen with a lot of messages. But if you're using FTP to transfer a gigantic file, how can you tell whether the computer is busy working or has gone on strike?

Your best bet is to use the hash command at the ftp> prompt. Using the hash command makes your computer print a string of # characters (called *hash signs* by those in the UNIX and Linux world) while it crunches the numbers.

Suppose that you're logged on to idg.dummies.org and want the text file chainsaws

4dummies.txt. After you enter your user name and password, type the following at the ftp> prompt:

    ftp> hash

Press Enter. Then use the get command like this:

    ftp> get chainsaws4dummies.txt

You'll see a row of hash marks scroll across the screen until the FTP process is finished. Then, you'll be back at the ftp> prompt, ready for your next request.

The Joker's Wild: Wildcards in FTP

Suppose that the text files chainsaws4dummies.txt, bunjeejumping4dummies.txt, and brainsurgery4dummies.txt are all in the Dummystuff directory. Because you've decided that you want all these weird files, why not just use FTP to transfer over the Dummystuff directory?

Unfortunately, FTP doesn't work that way. One of its limitations is that you can't transfer an entire directory at one time. But there's a way around this: mget and mput.

- ✔ To transfer multiple files *to* your machine, you use the mget (multiple get) command.
- ✔ To transfer multiple files *from* your machine to the server, you use the mput (multiple put) command.

No matter what command you use, you need to use *wildcards* instead of typing the complete filenames.

When you want to transfer multiple files, you can use wildcards in your FTP command instead of laboriously typing each filename, one at a time. Creating a filename that uses wildcards is easy:

1. **Find something common in all the names you want.**

2. **Substitute wildcard characters for the parts of the names that aren't the same.**

   The most common wildcard characters are

- ✔ * Stands in for any number of characters

- ✔ ? Stands in for exactly one character

- ✔ [ ] Matches any single character contained within the braces. Example: [Idg] matches an uppercase I, or a lowercase d, or a lowercase g.

- ✔ ' Disables the special meaning of characters enclosed in single quotation marks. For example: *.txt will match *all* files that end in .txt. Using '*'.txt will match only a single file called *.txt.

For example, the three text files I've been talking about in Dummystuff all end in .txt. You can get all these files by typing the following:

```
ftp> mget *.txt
```

Don't worry if you get some other .txt files that you don't want. Linux politely asks whether you'd like to transfer a file each time it's ready, like this:

```
mget chainsaws4dummies.txt?
```

To answer, simply type **Y** for yes or **N** for no. When FTP reaches the end of the .txt files, you'll be returned to the ftp> prompt.

Setting Up Shop: How to Set Up Your Own Anonymous FTP Site

If you'd like to make a bunch of your files available to the public over the Internet, you can create your own anonymous FTP site. The following instructions are a fast, easy way to set up your site without creating a large security risk on your machine.

Creating a user account

You need to create a user account for public access. Start building your FTP site by creating a user account called ftp on your system, as follows:

1. **Log on as root.**

2. **At the prompt, type** adduser.

3. **When adduser asks you for a logon name, type** ftp.

4. **When adduser asks questions about the new user's environment, default shell, and so on, press Enter to accept each question's default answer.**

5. **When adduser finally asks for a password, enter** *.

By entering a wildcard, you're letting someone log on anonymously because they won't have to enter a password.

When `adduser` is finished, you'll be at the command prompt again.

Creating the directory structure

If you're providing public access, you need to organize the information in a directory structure. After following the preceding instructions to create a user account, create the directory structure, as follows:

1. **Change to the home directory with the** `cd /home` **command.**

2. **Create the home directory (**`/home/ftp`**) with the** `mkdir ftp` **command.**

3. **Change to the new ftp directory with the** `cd ftp` **command.**

4. **Create** `/bin`, `/etc`, **and** `/pub` **directories in the** `ftp` **directory with the** `mkdir bin etc pub` **command.**

5. **Change to the new** `/ftp/pub` **directory with the** `cd ftp/pub` **command.**

6. **Create an incoming directory under the newly created pub directory with the** `mkdir incoming` **command.**

7. **Make the incoming directory writable for anyone with the** `chmod ugo+w incoming` **command.**

Establishing permissions

Now that you've built the gate, it's time to put a lock on it. Of course, you don't want users from all over the world exploring every nook and cranny of your network. It's easy to control anonymous users by customizing access for the anonymous FTP account.

After you've used the preceding instructions to create an FTP user account and FTP directories, follow these steps to control anonymous FTP access:

1. **Change to the** `/ftp/etc` **directory with the** `cd /ftp/etc` **command.**

2. **Copy your password and group files with these commands:**

```
cd /ftp/etc
cp /etc/passwd .
cp /etc/group .
```

3. **Open the passwd file with the** vi passwd **command: Use** vi **to delete all the lines in the passwd file except for the line that begins** ftp; **then save the passwd file.**

The file you save should look like this:

4. **Open the group file with the** vi group **command. Use** vi **to delete all the lines in the group file except for the one that begins** ftp; **then save the passwd file.**

For a refresher on what the passwd and group files do, see Chapter 3.

5. **Make the** /ftp, ftp/etc, ftp/bin, **and** ftp/pub **directories unwritable by anyone.**

Use these commands:

```
cd /home/ftp
chmod ugo-w etc
chmod ugo-w bin
chmod ugo-w pub
cd ..
chmod ugo-w ftp
```

Congratulations! If you've followed the three preceding sets of instructions, you've mapped a first-class FTP site. This means that

✔ Anyone can log on as user *ftp*.

✔ All the directories are secure except for /ftp/pub/incoming.

✔ Incoming users can put their own files somewhere if they want to send something to your FTP server.

✔ Files you want to make available to the world go in the /ftp/pub directory.

✔ While other people can get copies of your files, they can't alter your original files on your disk.

Part IV

Administering Office Networks

The 5th Wave   By Rich Tennant

"THAT REMINDS ME—I INSTALLED WINDOWS 95 ON MY 386 LAST WEEK."

In this part . . .

Part IV begins with slipcovers — kidding — actually it covers SLIP and PPP connections, which are among the many ways that Linux machines talk to each other. You get a look at why ISPs (Internet service providers) structure their servers the way they do. And you get a handle on using these vital connections with two programs, `slattach` and `dip`, which work according to whether your connection has dynamic or static addressing (another arcane topic that shall be made clear, seeker).

You also learn about Linux file systems — structures that are absolutely critical to making data available to all the users on your network. You get the skinny on how to create, delete, mount, and unmount file systems.

Chapter 12

Connecting to the Network? Make Your Trip with SLIP

· ·

In This Chapter

▶ What SLIP is all about

▶ Advantages of using the SLIP method to connect computers

▶ Serial ports and how to allocate them

▶ Static versus Dynamic IP Addressing

▶ Setting up a SLIP connection with slattach

▶ Setting up a SLIP connection with dip

· ·

SLIP may sound clumsy, but you'll see in this chapter that there's no better way to connect to your Linux network via a serial line. This chapter discusses the differences between static and dynamic forms of Internet Protocol addressing and how the addressing form affects the kind of connection you'll be using.

Once you're on the network, you'll find that your Linux system more than earns its keep. How? By providing you with the one of the fastest, most stable network connections you can get from any operating system.

Serial Lines: The Network of Champions

SLIP stands for Serial Line Internet Protocol. Despite its odd-sounding name, it has two major advantages.

▶ It's one of the best ways to use a modem or any other serial port device to communicate with your network when you don't have an Ethernet card installed.

▶ Its name is easy to remember.

Incidentally, a serial port has nothing to do with a marina that serves break-fast. It's one of several kinds of ports that all computers come with to exchange different kinds of data. You can think of a port as an agreed upon meeting place to exchange protocols and transmit data.

There are physical ports, such as serial ports for modems, or parallel ports for your printer. More common in the Linux world are the virtual ports, which don't exist in the physical world but are instead programmed rendezvous sections (TCP ports, UDP ports, and so on) of the computer for the electron streams to cross and exchange data.

Although a physical port simply plugs into the back of your computer, you're going to have to allocate a virtual meeting place in your machine to corre-spond to it. That is, once the data packets come into your computer, the computer has to have a rough idea where to send it. Over 90 percent of the time, this is already set for you, but if you need to play with the settings, change directories to /dev and take a look at the files allocated to serial port connections.

Remember the old teletype origins of Linux? Here they are again, as /dev/tty devices. The Linux serial ports you should already have allocated are in Table 12-1.

Table 12-1		Linux Serial Port Files	
Device Number	*Outgoing File*	*Incoming File*	*Function*
1	/dev/ttyS0	/dev/cua0	This is used for your dial-in external modem, if you have one.
2	/dev/ttyS1	/dev/cua1	Direct serial connection to your File Server or Router.
3	/dev/ttyS2	/dev/cua2	For reasons that are lost in the mist of time, this is no longer used. Rumors include UFOs, crop circles, and plots from several *X Files* episodes.
4	/dev/ttyS3	/dev/cua3	This is used for your dial-out line or PPP internal modem.

If you're not able to use your modem with your Linux machine, make sure that you link up your modem device to the right `tty` port. You can do this from the root account by creating a link with the linking command `ln` as follows:

```
ln -s /dev/ttyS0      /dev/modem
```

Or, if you have an internal modem:

```
ln -s /dev/ttyS3      /dev/modem
```

SLIP Connectivity

Although using SLIP is different than using Ethernet connectivity, it's still a far-flung member of the TCP/IP protocol club.

Setting up SLIP is in many ways similar to setting up TCP/IP. You'll need to know about

- ✔ Static versus dynamic IP addressing
- ✔ How the two styles of SLIP programs are set up to interact with the SLIP server

As far as hardware is concerned, you'll need

- ✔ A serial line of some sort to connect with your communication device, unless you have an internal modem.

  Your communication device can be a phone line, an asynchronous line, or a dial-up modem.
- ✔ Access to a dial-in SLIP server.

This kind of service is provided cheaply at most universities and businesses. Keep in mind that SLIP is fairly ancient compared with the newer, hot technologies of ISDN, DSL, and PPP. You may find that your best bet to utilize SLIP service remains in the academic world.

With SLIP, you're only working with two machines to exchange data. SLIP is not something you're going to use to set up a Linux network. That remains an Ethernet and TCP/IP issue, which you can read about in Chapters 8, 9, 10, and 11.

SLIP uses one of two programs to initiate the connection between two machines. Which one you use depends on the kind of connection you're going to be making.

✔ **Slattach:** A relatively old program

✔ **Dip:** A a slightly more automated program

When SLIP establishes a connection with the SLIP server, it sends (like a good, obedient protocol) an IP address that has been allocated for that connection.

✔ **Static addressing:** If the system you connect to uses the same IP address over and over again, then it's called *static addressing*.

✔ **Dynamic addressing:** If the system you connect to uses IP addresses then throws them out like a pack of disposable razor blades, the IP address will be slightly different each time you log on. This is called a *dynamic IP address allocation,* or *dynamic addressing* for short.

Configuring for static IP addressing

Static IP addressing means that your IP addresses need to be entered in the same file locations as your typical Ethernet connection.

✔ The three host files covered in Chapter 9 need to have your machine's name and IP address in them.

✔ Make sure that your IP address is in the startup scripts, /etc/rc.inet1, /etc/rc.inet2, and /etc/resolv.conf.

Pay specific attention to the /etc/rc.inet1 file. You'll need to vi this file to manually edit it to accept the SLIP connection for the slattach program.

If you're using the dip program, your IP address is in the startup scripts automatically. Which is the reason why I strongly suggest that, with a static IP addressing system, you stick with dip. If you're into self-punishment, modify your rc.inet1 file to include the following two lines:

```
IPADDR="Your Machine's IP Address"
REMADDR="The SLIP server's IP Address"
```

Most of the time, you'll find sample lines like this already in your /etc/rc.inet1 file, but commented out. It's there to provide a model for you to follow. As an example here, say that you're connecting from machine Linuxbox, with an IP address 101.28.80.50. The SLIP server you'll be connecting to is called Slippup, with an IP address 238.237.92.85. Your modified rc.inet1 file will look something like the following:

```
IPADDR="101.28.80.50"
REMADDR="238.237.92.85"
```

Never assume that you can interchangeably use a machine's name instead of its IP address in any kind of configuration file. When in doubt, use the address. It's the only kind of address that you can persuade a stubborn Linux box to read.

If you're editing a file like /etc/rc.inet1 where only an IP address will do, you can still make changes that help you remember who's who. Just because computers run this world, doesn't mean that you're not in control! Edit the file the same way as I previously describe, but add comments to the file by inserting a # sign in front of any notes you add to prevent the machine from reading the text as part of the configuration. Your /etc/rc.inet1 file might read as follows, with commentary to help you keep track of who you're talking to on the network.

```
IPADDR="101.28.80.50"        # This is my machine, 'Linuxbox'.
REMADDR="238.237.92.85"      # This is the SLIP server I'm
                             connecting to, also known as
                             'Slipup'.
```

Always make sure that you comment out each line of text you've inserted, even if the text wraps around the end of the screen. Otherwise, you're going to end up with results on your Linux box that will range from interesting to heart-stopping disaster. Each of the two lines in the following comment is commented out with a # sign.

```
# This is the SLIP server I'm connecting to,
# also known as 'Slipup'.
```

Configuring for dynamic IP addressing

If the IP address you connect to changes each and every time, then you won't be putting the server's IP address in any file. Otherwise, you'll only be able to connect up a grand total of once. In this case, you must use a program that automatically inserts the address in the right location each time. Therefore, with a dynamic system SLIP connection, use the dip program.

Attaching to Slattach

When you've got a cable or other kind of line running directly to the SLIP server, you can use slattach. *Slattach* stands for Serial Line Attach and can be configured to run in regular SLIP mode, or CSLIP (Compressed SLIP) mode, for faster connectivity. This is the default mode for SLIP servers today.

To configure your CSLIP connection:

1. **Run the following command as the root account:**

   ```
   # slattach /dev/cua2 &
   ```

2. **If the SLIP server you're attaching to refuses to support the Compressed SLIP mode, retry the** `slattach` **command as follows:**

   ```
   # slattach -p /dev/cua2 &
   ```

   `-p` is the command option you can run with slattach to specify you want the connection set up to handle uncompressed SLIP packets.

3. **Configure your network kernel interface with the following command:**

   ```
   ifconfig sl0 localhosts pointtopoint Procyon
   ```

Ifconfig is a program that every Linux box has installed. It configures and manages kernel network interfaces for you automatically. Ifconfig tells your machine to configure your local host to create point to point connections with ISP Procyon. Of course, point to point connectivity is another way of saying *Use a TCP/IP protocol.*

```
route add Procyon
```

Here, you tell your Linux box to add a network route so you can get to Procyon.

```
route add default gw Procyon
```

Finally, you're telling your machine here to add this route as the default one for your machine to try and connect with this SLIP connection.

When you sign up to use a SLIP server, make a note of the SLIP node and the IP addresses you need.

Dipping into Dip

If you're thinking that the slattach method of connecting is a tad difficult due to all the editing and file checking, you're right. That's why the next step in SLIP evolution, dip, came along. Let's see how much easier the dip connectivity is to achieve.

The dip program automates a lot of slattach's work for you. This is extremely important in a dynamic IP Addressing situation, because with slattach, you'd have to go in and edit files every single time you connect to the SLIP server.

Dip stands for Dialup Internet Program. You can find the binary as /sbin/dip on your system, or it might reside in the /usr/sbin directory. You can run dip with the option that interactively prompts you to enter data. Otherwise, dip will use a special script file, called a chat script, to run.

The lazy person's way to create your chat script

Your chat script will contain all the commands you need to run manually if you wanted to do a lot of extra work. Here's what a typical chat script looks like:

```
# Dialup IP connection support script. (dynamic)
#
# Version:       X.X
#
# Features:      Auto redial when busy
#                Two phone numbers support
#
main:
    #
    # Set serial port and speed.
    #
    reset
    port modem
    speed 57600

    #
    # Should match the assignment from your administrator
    #
    #netmask 255.255.255.0
    netmask 0.0.0.0
    #
    # Send initializing string to modem and print banner
    #
    # get $mtu 576
    send AT&FL1S0=0S7=25S11=45\r
    wait OK 3
    if $errlvl != 0 goto modemerr
    print DIP script for UCR's (X) server 5/96
    print ————————————————————————-
    print
    print Press Ctrl-C to abort

dialsvr:

    send +++\r
    wait OK 3
```

(continued)

(continued)

```
send ATHO\r
wait OK 3
print Trying 787-6400...
send ATDT787-6400\r
if $errlvl != 0 goto error
wait BUSY 25
if $errlvl == 0 goto next
wait CONNECT 25
if $errlvl != 0 goto next
goto login

next:

send +++\r
wait OK 3
send ATHO\r
wait OK 3
print Trying 787-6400 again...
send ATDT787-6400\r
if $errlvl != 0 goto error
wait BUSY 25
if $errlvl == 0 goto dialsvr
wait CONNECT 25
if $errlvl != 0 goto dialsvr
goto login


#
# We are connected.  Login to the system.
#

login:

send \r\r\r
#
# "login:" is my system prompt, change it to yours
#
print Connection established.
wait > 30
if $errlvl != 0 goto error
#
#
print Telneting to CS...
send c cs\r
if $errlvl != 0 goto error
#
wait login 20
if $errlvl != 0 goto error
#
# Tell server our login
#
print Sending user name...
send PLACE_YOUR_LOGIN_NAME_HERE\r
```

```
if $errlvl != 0 goto error
#
# If you must enter shell and type extra commands to enter
        slip mode,
# add your own chat procedure here.
#
wait password 20
if $errlvl != 0 goto error
#
#
print Sending user password...
send PLACE_YOUR_PASSWORD_HERE\r
if $errlvl != 0 goto error
#
# Catch the key word to confirm that IP string will show up
        shortly.
#
print Activating slirp
send slirp\r
if $errlvl != 0 goto error
#
#
wait host 20
if $errlvl != 0 goto error
#
# Get our dynamic IP from strings that sent by slirp
#
get $rmtip remote
#get $locip remote
#get $locip remote 3
#get $local remote 3
wait is 10
if $errlvl != 0 goto error
#
# Get server's IP from strings that sent by slirp
#
get $locip remote
#get $rmtip remote
#get rmtip remote 3
#get $remote remote 3

#
# Set up the SLIP operating parameters.
#
#get $mtu 1024
#get $mtu 576

#
# Set Destination net/address as type 'default' (vice an
        address).
```

(continued)

(continued)

```
  # This is used by the 'route' command to set the kernel
         routing table.
  # Some machines seem to require this be done for SLIP to
         work properly.
  #
  default

#
# Give the connection report !
#

done:

    print Entering slip mode.
    print Dynamic IP assigned by host is $local
    print Remote host connected is $remote
    mode cslip
# mode ppp
    goto exit

error:

    print slip connection failed.
    goto exit

modemerr:

    print Modem initializing failed.
    goto exit
exit:
```

This script is so user friendly, you'll notice that its comments even tell you
what to insert to get it customized for your own use.

Feeling really lazy? Don't worry about typing this script. Use the man command (short for manual) on the program dip.

1. **Redirect the output of the** man **command into a text file on the** /etc
   directory that you can call lazydude. **Do so by using the following
   command:**

   ```
   man dip > lazydude
   ```

2. vi **the file** lazydude.

3. **Find the chat script inside the file** lazydude. **Delete all the lines
   except for the chat script, and then edit the script itself. Save your
   work.**

   Your chat script is all set to run.

A typical dip SLIP session is like this:

1. **Run dip and open your SLIP connection with the following command:**

```
/usr/sbin/dip -v /etc/lazydude
```

   Dip runs in the background.

2. **When prompted, enter your user name.**

3. **When prompted, enter your password.**

   Your automatic connection steps are displayed, like this:

```
slipup>slip
Entering SLIP mode.
Async interface address is unnumbered
Your IP address is 166.123.10.35. MTU is 1500 bytes
Header compression will match your system.
```

4. **At this point, press Cntrl if necessary.**

   The remaining connection steps are displayed, like this:

```
            DIP> get $locip 160.108.276.12
            DIP> get $rmtip 156.77.13.85
            DIP> get $mtu 1500
            DIP> netmask 255.255.0.0
            DIP> default
            DIP> mode CSLIP
```

Once the slip connection is up and going, you can use a telnet session or FTP at will.

In order to hang up the dip connection, do the following:

1. **Use the process search command to locate dip's PID (process identification number).**

2. **Use the** `kill` **command to stop the process.**

Dip is an amazingly tough process to kill, which is testimony to how tenacious a SLIP connection really is.

✔ If dip refuses to die – you can check if it's dead by running another `ps` command – kill it the hard way: Use `kill -9` on its process id number. It should go down.

✔ If you see dip crop up again under a different PID, then something else is kicking it off. Most likely, you're still running a telnet session or FTP session that needs it. Kill the telnet or FTP session and you'll find that dip stays dead.

Chapter 13

Connecting to the Network, Part Two: Using PPP and the DIP Program

● ●

In This Chapter

▶ What PPP is all about

▶ Advantages of using PPP

▶ How to set up a PPP connection with Dip

● ●

*P*PP may sound only marginally less silly than SLIP, but it's every bit as good as SLIP, and then some. This chapter introduces you to the similarities and differences between making a SLIP and a PPP connection. You also see why PPP has taken over SLIP as the new standard in Linux point-to-point connectivity.

You also broaden your networking skills when you discover how to set up your PPP connection and the dip program. Dip is a program that works with PPP to improve its functionality, so if you work with them together, you'll be pleased with the results.

PPP — SLIP for the Next Generation of Linux Users

PPP stands for *Point-to-Point Protocol* and, since its inception, has made its mission to replace the aging SLIP connection protocol. PPP has definitely succeeded in its goal, and it is the new standard when setting up point-to-point connections with Linux. PPP uses many of the same files and scripts that SLIP does, but it's a more flexible and useful protocol to use overall than SLIP.

Advantages of PPP over SLIP

The biggest difference between PPP and SLIP is that PPP is more flexible, with the ability to run on more machines, and it's more efficient (translation: faster) because it's able to work with the newer, higher-speed modems.

PPP is easier to configure than SLIP. It's particularly easy to use if you have a GUI interface and you're making PPP connections with the `diald` program. Once it establishes a connection, the PPP protocol is actually slightly more reliable than SLIP.

The real changes between SLIP and PPP have been made at the next level below the administration standpoint. If you're a real techno-wizard and want to know some more of the details of why SLIP has yielded its place to PPP, it's because:

- ✔ SLIP isn't intelligent enough to know the type of packets that are coming in for it to handle until it unpacks each packet. This creates more "busy-work" for SLIP, making it inherently slower than PPP.

- ✔ SLIP can't handle differently sized packets. In order for it to get a grip on the situation, the SLIP server pads packets or breaks them into less logical breaks to fit what SLIP can handle, which also makes SLIP less efficient.

- ✔ SLIP isn't available in all areas due to its age and the fact that it's no longer a standard. That is, you may find some difficulty getting an ISP with a SLIP server for your connections.

A Picked Portion of PPP Preferences, Please

PPP uses a combination of a triple protocol combo and one daemon to handle the data. PPP is inherently a more complex character than SLIP, because it's more compartmentalized.

- ✔ The PPP packet doesn't need to be all the same size as the one handled by SLIP.

- ✔ The PPP packet can be of more than one type. PPP, the Swiss Army knife of protocols, can handle both serial connections and types of encapsulated packets.

More protocols in PPP than you can shake a stick at

The first of the three protocols that PPP puts into service is *NCP,* or *Network Control Protocol.* NCP acts like a person with a checklist, inspecting each packet that comes into your machine and sees whether the PPP connection can handle it. If your connection speaks any of them, you get the information.

The second of the PPP trio is the HDLC, also known as the High-Level Data Link Control protocol. HDLC is a bit of an oddball when it comes to protocol types. Instead of using control characters to tell when a give packet starts and ends, it uses bit patterns, which helps PPP to be more flexible; instead of relying on set control characters to define when a packet ends, it relies on bit patterns, avoiding the need to "pad" packets with extra zeroes and ones.

The final member of the PPP protocol team is *LCP,* or *Link Control Protocol.* LCP is the actual protocol that establishes the connection, configures it, and tests it. This protocol is relatively intelligent and is the basis for PPP's current dominance over SLIP. LCP is better able to recognize and deal with today's newer, faster modems. This is a good deal for you, but even better, you're never going to have to configure or automatically start any of these processes, because PPP does this for you.

Your local neighborhood daemon, pppd

The pppd daemon is the process that automatically kicks off when a PPP connection is made and verified by the LCP protocol. Your pppd daemon will be the actual workhorse of the processes, shuttling data back and forth over your connection.

pppd, like other daemons, has nothing that you need to start up or configure. It should be automatically installed as part of your installation. If for some reason your Linux network doesn't have it, you can either download it from the Web at the Red Hat Linux site (www.redhat.com), or get it directly off the Red Hat Linux CD-ROM that comes with *Linux For Dummies,* 2nd Edition.

The PPP daemon should be set up as follows in the /usr/sbin directory.

```
-r-sr-xr-x   1 root      root         95225 Jul 11 00:27
             /usr/sbin/pppd
```

Changing directories to /usr/sbin and doing an ls -l is a good way to see if you already have the daemon installed.

If the file permissions for pppd are not set up properly, then you'll have to modify the permissions so you can run the PPP daemon correctly. Here's how:

1. **Use** su **to become the alpha-user on your system; you can use the** root **account to make this a lasting change.**

2. **Once you're root, run the following command:** chmod u+s /usr/sbin/pppd

3. **Edit the remaining files needed to set up PPP. In the** /etc **directory, make sure there's a** root**-owned directory called, appropriately enough, "ppp."**

```
drwxrwxr-x   2 root        root        1024 Oct  9 11:01
             ppp
```

If directory /etc/ppp exists, it will contain a template of your options file called options.tpl. Print it out. Options.tpl notes all of the PPP options available to you. In my experience, they're a little less obtuse than the man pages on pppd, but more importantly, you can use this file as the default method of connecting.

If this directory doesn't exist, create it and then reinstall the PPP daemon and utilities from either the Web, another Linux machine, or the CD-ROM that came with your initial installation. PPP has been around long enough — and is the connection standard — so you shouldn't have much trouble getting a copy.

PPP Dip, a Chip Off the Old SLIP Dip

When you're ready to fire up your PPP session, make sure that you have your dip program ready to go.

Since PPP is more advanced and can handle dynamic addressing in its electronic sleep, it can make full use of dip and its command options. To that end, read over the dip options you may need to use. In particular, the -t and -v options are the most useful, as they can help point you to problems that an otherwise reticent Linux system wouldn't say anything about.

Table 13-1	Command Options You'll Find Useful with Dip
Command Option	*What It Does*
-a	Prompts you for your user name and password.
-i	Has dip act as a dial-in server (see DIALIN MODE below).
-k	Kills the dip process. (I guess if you're tired of typing kill then you should like this alternative.)

Command Option	What It Does
-m mtu	Set the Maximum Transfer Unit (MTU) (default 296).
-t	Runs dip interactively.
-v	Runs dip in "verbose" mode. This makes problem solving easier, as it gives you more clues and even echoes each line of the script as it's executed.

When you're ready to run the dip program, here's a rough idea of what the connection should look like.

```
# /sbin/dip -t
        DIP: Dialup IP Protocol Driver version X.X.X
           (12-12-95).
        DIP> port modem
        DIP> speed 57600
        DIP> reset
        DIP> flush
        DIP> dial 999-9999
        DIP> term
        [ Entering TERMINAL mode.  Use CTRL-] to get back ]

        Welcome to your authenticated dial-in service.
To connect to a host, type the hostname at the prompt fol-
           lowed by RETURN.
```

See where the fourth line from the top of the preceding example says to use 57600? That's the default speed for your modem. Linux doesn't restrict you to this fixed number. If you know that your modem speed is faster, feel free to increase the number to 115200, or whatever your modem can handle.

That's another bonus you get from using Linux. You can sometimes set your own speed limit on the information highway!

Chapter 14

Mounting, Creating, and Maintaining File Systems

• •

In This Chapter

▶ Knowing what file systems are and why you need them

▶ Mounting file systems: Get back into the saddle

▶ Mounting a floppy disk

▶ Creating file systems from scratch

▶ Checking and fixing file systems

• •

*T*o people new to the world of Linux system and network administration, there are few things more mysterious than the concepts of creating and mounting file systems. That's because those who are new to the idea and practice of network computing find it tough to wrap their minds around the notion that entire directories of data can be made to appear and disappear at will. After all, either data exists or it doesn't, right? Well, sort of.

Data exists — or doesn't exist — only on your local machine. To be more specific, data on your local machine that you have *control* over. If you're looking at data on a remote machine and you're not the root account, that gets to be pretty slim.

This chapter will introduce you to the concepts of file systems. More importantly, you'll learn how exactly to create a file system and mount it for one-time or continuous distribution. You'll also see how you can harness the power of mounted file systems for swap space, and the results you get from this wise investment of energy in a few more keystrokes.

What File Systems Are and Why Everyone Wants One

A *file system* is a device that, fairly obviously, is formatted or configured to store your data in the form of files. Files themselves are everything from the data that you create or mail you send to the system files that control and configure the daemons that run Linux. A device that is formatted to hold your files can be an external or internal hard drive, a CD-ROM, or a floppy disk.

File systems come in various types; in fact, it seems that every few months a new file system type is added to the list. Different file systems run by their own unique rules. For example, the MS-DOS file system doesn't allow you to create filenames over eight characters in length and have more than a three-character extension. So, in Linux you might have a file that you can call

```
linux4dummies.txt
linux_4dummies.text
Linux.txt.4.Dummies
```

Under a DOS file system, you'll only be able to save that same file as follows:

```
linux4Ds.txt
L4Dummys.exe
```

From an administrator's point of view, this doesn't really matter very much. You just need to know which file system types that your system can read. By this standard, Linux is a pretty well-read operating system. As a rule of thumb, your Linux network setup should be able to handle the following kinds of file system types:

Table 14-1	Commonly Used File System Types	
File System	*Name of System*	*Notes*
Extended file system	ext	This was the standard Linux file system, until it was supplemented by the newer, Second Extended File System.
HPFS file system	hpfs	Allows you to access the file system that's still used by the OS/2 operating system.
ISO 9660 file system	iso9660	File system used by most CD-ROMs.
MS-DOS file system	msdos	File system used by the older MS-DOS machines.

File System	Name of System	Notes
Network file system	nfs	The subject of Chapter 15, this file-system type allows you easy remote access to mounted systems.
Novell file system	ncps	Allows you to access the file system used by Novell.
2nd Extended file system	ext2	The current standard Linux file system.
System V file system	sysv	Allows you access to files from System V.

Linux, being the infinitely configurable and flexible system that it is, can be enabled to read different kinds of file-system types that aren't on the above list. However, in order to do that, you'll need to start playing around with the base of the Linux system, the *kernel*. Since doing kernel work on a busily running Linux system is similar to doing open-heart surgery to someone at the office, as a rule I don't recommend it.

Saddle Up, Partner: the mount Command

Ironically, the image you need to conjure up with the mount command shouldn't be horses — it should be plants. Remember, all files in a Linux system are in one big tree, rooted at — drum roll, please — the root directory, indicated by a " / " character. The mount command allows you to attach a file system found on a device to the main file tree. Of course, I realize that this command should have been called "branch" or "extension" rather than mount, but then I overslept on the day they made this command and now we're stuck with it.

The mount command allows you to access any supported file system by attaching it to the file tree — even the root directory itself. The "attaching," or mounting, is done at a specific directory of your choice, called a *mount point*. You can create the mount point directory yourself, so long as you have permission to edit a certain directory. (Of course, if you're root, you have no such worries.)

The mount command itself should only be run by root. mount may exist in the user's path so that they may check which disk partitions have already been mounted for them by simply running the mount command without any command options, as follows:

```
Linuxbox# mount
/usr on /dev/dsk/c0t0d0s5 read/write/largefiles on Tue Jun 1
        14:54:12 1999
/local on /dev/dsk/c0t0d0s7 read/largefiles on Tue Jun 1
        14:54:13 1999
/proc on /proc read/write/ on Tue Jun 1 14:54:12 1999
/dev/fd on fd read/write/ on Tue Jun 1 14:54:12 1999
/tmp on swap read/write on Tue Jun 1 14:54:13 1999
```

Mount by itself prints out what the system is already set up to use. For each of the five mounted file systems, Linux tells you the name of the mounted directory and on which mount point or partition it's located. Further detail is provided by the permissioning of the system and the time stamp that tells when it was mounted. Notice that /local is the only mounted directory that does not have the "write" permission, only the "read" permission.

You learned about the read-write-execute permissioning system that Linux uses for individual files in Chapter 3. Linux duplicates that system as closely as possible in the file systems. Of course, you can't "execute" a file system, so that setting isn't available — but in the case of /local, you won't be able to make any changes to files in that file system unless you copy the file and put it somewhere you have write permissions such as /tmp.

Let's say that after running mount, you realize that the directory you really wanted access to is on partition /dev/hda1. The format of the mount command is as follows:

```
mount -t <type> <device> <mount-point>
```

The -t is used to indicate the file system type. Let's say that the file system type you want to access is a bunch of .txt files saved under NFS file system /dev/hda1. You'll need to enter in **nfs** as the type, since the mount command in and of itself isn't smart enough to figure out what type of file system it's dealing with without being told.

Begin by creating the mount point directory as follows:

```
# mkdir mnt
```

Next, issue the appropriate mount command. In this example, you would be using:

```
# mount -t nfs /dev/hda1 /mnt
```

Check to see if your mount command worked by simply running mount again without any command options. If everything worked properly, you should see a display like this:

```
# mount
/usr on /dev/dsk/c0t0d0s5 read/write/largefiles on Tue Jun 1
        14:54:12 1999
/local on /dev/dsk/c0t0d0s7 read/largefiles on Tue Jun 1
        14:54:13 1999
/proc on /proc read/write/ on Tue Jun 1 14:54:12 1999
/dev/fd on fd read/write/ on Tue Jun 1 14:54:12 1999
/tmp on swap read/write on Tue Jun 1 14:54:13 1999
/dev/hda1 on /mnt on <Today's date and Time>
```

Let's say you want to mount a second directory, a System V file system called /dev/hda2, but you specifically want to make it read-only, as you don't want anyone in the user community messing up these files. In order to ensure that the system is mounted as read-only, use the -r option as follows:

```
# mount -t sysv -r /dev/hda2 /mnt
```

Try this and you'll likely get the standard mount error message, Mount Permission Denied: Mount Point Busy. The reason? Well, think of a mount point like a coat hangar in your closet. You can't mount or attach your coat to the closet wall rack without a hanger, or "mount point," which is why you need to create one.

Now, unless you have a really teeny closet, you're probably not stacking two or more coats on each hanger. Why not? Well, unless they're light windbreakers, you're probably going to end up bending or breaking the hanger. The same principle applies in Linux, where mount points are the equivalent of extremely fragile wire coat hangers. Linux simply won't let you mount more than one directory per mount point!

So, to remedy this problem it's best to start by creating a second mount point for the System V file system. Exercising our creative faculties, let's call the second mount point mnt2.

```
# mkdir mnt2
# mount -t sysv -r /dev/hda2 /mnt2
```

Check with the mount command, but this should allow you access to the directory without difficulty. Once it's mounted, you can change directories to /dev/hda2 as you would with any other directory on your Linux box.

The mount command also comes with several other command options you'll find useful as a Linux administrator. Listed here are most of the ones you'll find yourself using.

Table 14-2	mount Command Options
Command Option	**What It Does**
-a	Mount all file systems (of the given types) mentioned in your files system table, located in /etc/fstab.
-h	Print a help menu, listing all the mount command options you could care to use.
-o	Specifies read or write-only options. (See the -r and -w command options.)
-r	Mount the specified file system as read-only. You could also use -o ro for -option, read only, but why expose yourself to carpal tunnel syndrome with unnecessary typing?
-t	Asks the question, "What File System Type?"
-V	Tells you what version of mount you're running.
-v	Verbose mode.
-w	Mounts a given file system as readable and writable. Again, you could type -o ro, but this is the default setting, so save your calories.

You *must* specify the read-only option when mounting media that is by its nature nonwritable. This includes CD-ROMs or write protected disks. So, for a write-protected disk, your command should look similar to this:

```
Mount -t msdos -r /dev/fd0 /mnt
```

Otherwise, you may get the old staple of the mount command's error codes: Permission denied.

Umount? No, Me Tarzan, You Mount!

The umount command is the mirror of mount. Obviously, if you want to free up a mount point that's in use, you'll have to un-mount the file system that's hung up there.

Don't get confused between the terms "unmount" and umount! To my knowledge, there is no command called "unmount," even though that's exactly what you're doing. Instead, for reasons only the Linux gurus know themselves, they foisted the umount command on poor mortal administrators. So don't pull your hair(s) out over trying to find the Eldorado of commands, "unmount," as dozens of Linux administrators have disappeared in their quest to find it.

The format for umount is as follows: umount <mount-point>. This is a bit simpler than the mount command, but then when you remove a coat hanger from the closet, you probably don't need to know too much about the garment that was hanging on it. To unmount either of the examples we used above, you'd use the following commands.

```
# umount /mnt
# umount /mnt2
```

To check to see if your mounted directories have changed, run the mount command again without options. And speaking of options, check out the command options you'll find most helpful with umount (in Table 14-3).

Table 14-3	umount Command Options
Command Option	*What It Does*
-h	Print out the help options for umount .
-n	Unmount without writing a record in the file /etc/mtab.
-r	In case unmounting fails, try to remount the file system as read-only.
-t	Indicate that the actions should only be taken on file systems of the specified type. More than one type may be specified in a comma separated list. (For example: nfs, msdos, sysv.)
-V	Print umount's version and exit.
-v	Operate in verbose mode.

Note that a file system cannot be unmounted when it is "busy" — for example, when there are open files on it, or when some process has its working directory there, or when a swap file on it is in use.

Creating Your Own File Systems

You can create your very own file systems with the mkfs command. Mkfs, like many of the file system commands, isn't smart enough in and of itself to figure out what file system you're talking about unless you specify what you want. Therefore, you'll want to create file systems with the following command syntax:

```
mkfs -t <type> <device> <blocks>
```

The type of file system you create depends on your need, of course. If you're going to use the standard Linux file system, then use `ext2` for the type. The `device` option will be the device you select to actually hold the data, whether it is a hard disk partition or a floppy disk. *Blocks* refers to the size of the file system you're planning to make. One block in Linux is 1024 bytes, so 1440 blocks is the equivalent of a standard 1.44 MB floppy disk.

To avoid errors when making a file system (of any type) on a floppy disk, make sure that you're not specifying a file system size over 1440 blocks. This frustrates the computer since it can't cram the setting onto the relatively small disk and it could have the Linux equivalent of a nervous breakdown. This can be very nasty, so try to avoid unnecessarily antagonizing your Linux system.

Unlike `mount` or `umount`, by and large you won't be using many command options with `mkfs`. However, to be complete, here's a list of command options which you can try using with `mkfs` at your leisure.

Table 14-4	mkfs Command Options
Command Option	*What It Does*
`-c`	Specifies that `mkfs` check the device for bad blocks before building the file system. Rarely used, but if you're working on an old, semi-decrepit disk drive it can be useful.
`-t`	The type of file system to be built, such as ext2, or msdos.
`-v`	Run `mkfs` with verbose output.

As an example, say you want to create a standard Linux file system on `/dev/hda2`. If you'd like to make the file system size around 3MB, you would use the `mkfs` command as follows:

```
mkfs -t ext2 /dev/hda2 3000
```

Remember, when you create a new file system on a previously used device, you're going to wipe out all existing data files to lay down your new file system! So be safe and check the preexisting file system before you end up blowing away anyone's personal mail files or doctoral thesis.

File System Maintenance without Getting Data All over Your Hands

File-system maintenance is the easiest task we're discussing in this section, because file systems on Linux come with their own Mr. Fixit: Fsck.

Fsck, though it looks vaguely insulting, is actually one of the most potent, intelligent utilities Linux has to offer. Merely by running fsck as root, you can do the equivalent in Windows of a combined Disk Scan, Disk Check, and Defragmentation in one fell swoop. To use, follow the command format fsck -t <type> <device>

As examples, you could use fsck to maintain the two examples we've been using with the following command syntax:

```
# fsck -t nfs /dev/hda1
# fsck -t sysv /dev/hda2
```

Notice that unlike the umount operation, we're specifying the device name, but not the mount point. To continue with the wardrobe analogy we've been using, when you're checking your coat for patching, you're not going to worry about the hanger (mount point) during that task.

Some of the command options you'll find useful with fsck are:

Table 14-5	Fsck Command Options
Command Option	**What It Does**
-A	Directs fsck to go through all the mounted file systems listed in the file system table (/etc/fstab) in one run. This option is a real time-saver compared with running multiple commands for checking a single file system each time.
-a	Automatically repair any file system error found without prompting the user with questions. This is a real time-saver, but only if you're prepared for the worst case scenario, which is where you'd lose all your data.
-R	When checking all file systems with the -A flag, skip the root file system (in case it's already mounted read-write).
-r	Interactively repair the file system (ask for confirmations before repairing and possibly deleting data).

(continued)

Table 14-5 *(continued)*

Command Option	What It Does
-t	Specifies the type of file system to be checked. When the -A flag is specified, only file systems that match that file system type are checked.
-V	Run in verbose mode.

On some rare occasions, you may find that the -v (verbose) option doesn't work or it spit out gibberish instead of returning meaningful exit codes. This is a known bug with some of the older or more esoteric versions of Linux, and there's not much you can do to work around it unless you decide to upgrade your Linux version. This shouldn't be difficult — just buy a recent edition of *Linux For Dummies,* which always comes with a CD-ROM of Red Hat Linux.

Part V

Network File and Machine Sharing

Look, all I said was, "FTC for Mr. Gates," and this nerdy guy with big glasses comes out and tells me he's not afraid of me, I can investigate him all I want, and he'll see me in court with his attorneys.

In this part . . .

In Part V, moving boldly into a higher level of complexity, you learn to use two premier network and file-distribution mechanisms — NFS (the Network File System) and NIS (Name Information System). NFS offers a quick, convenient way to make file systems available while providing system security. NIS boosts your efforts to make network organization and configuration both more consistent and reliable. When you get to know them, these systems can become your steadfast Linux allies.

Finally, this section gives you the key to setting up the most common shared devices on your whole Linux network. What are these devices? Printers! These seemingly simple machines can (and will) take up a good deal of your time as an administrator if you aren't familiar with how to work with them — because what's the first thing users do when they have an important document? Yep — print it out. You learn to pick up your queues (so to speak), manage print jobs according to their importance, spot glitches, size up the equipment, and maintain your printers with more than just paper trays and replacement ink cartridges.

Chapter 15

The File-Distribution Master, NFS

● ●

In This Chapter

▶ Telling NFS apart from NIS

▶ Tracing the origins of NFS, the Network File System

▶ Examining the NFS Daemon and Export components

▶ Befriending the File System Table

▶ Using and Configuring NFS on your Linux network

▶ Using the `Showmount` command

▶ Telling the Automounter what to do

● ●

*T*his chapter introduces you to the most powerful file-sharing program in Linux computing — NFS, the Network File System. It's a straightforward name for a system that has a straightforward purpose; to share out files over the entire Linux network.

NFS and its cousin NIS have similar purposes in life, in that they help you distribute data by means of the horde of protocols you learned about in Chapters 8, 9 and 10. At the same time, no matter how many similarities they share, they are different programs and must be treated differently.

Overall, people have more misconceptions about NFS and NIS than about any other aspect of the Linux file-sharing system. So to start off, I want to demolish a few of the myths that crop up again and again about NFS and NIS, then show you what they're all about.

✔ First, NIS and NFS are *not* the same program. They're not even related, so if someone tries to tell you that NIS is an "updated version" of NFS, you have my permission to smack them with a copy of this book.

✔ NIS and NFS do not have to be running on the same network at the same time. You can have a network that runs NFS without NIS just fine, and vice versa. In fact, smaller systems will probably run just fine without the extra overhead of NIS.

✔ NFS cannot be invoked, configured, fed, bathed, petted, or taken for walks by anyone except the `root` account. Don't let users tell you that they're running NFS on their own systems if it's connected to your Linux network. It ain't gonna happen.

✔ Finally, NFS is pronounced *enn-eff-ess* and not *noofus*. (Then again, *noofus* might make a great term for someone who mispronounces — or misunderstands — Linux terminology.)

Why NFS Could Make You Diss Mount

Using NFS, you can change directories to an NFS-mounted file system as if it were a locally mounted file system. You can read or write files, and even execute scripts and programs, exactly as if you had the files right on the machine your keyboard is attached to.

Why saddle yourself with NFS when you can use mount?

You may be thinking, "That's all very well and good, but since we learned the `mount` command in an earlier chapter, isn't this all redundant?"

True, using NFS when you have the `mount` command may *sound* redundant, repetitive, and even like using the same thing. But NFS has some crucial advantages that the well-worn, tried-and-true `mount` command does not. Among other things, NFS has the edge over the older `mount` command in that:

✔ NFS allows you to store user-critical data in a centralized, easy-to-administer area. Data accessed by a significant portion of your users — say, expense forms, office memos, or Mom's Secret Recipes for Key Lime Chili — can be kept on a central host. Clients can mount this directory automatically at boot time.

✔ For example, you can keep user account information on the NFS server and have all Linux client accounts mount their individual `/user/home` directories from that server. If you run NFS in conjunction with NIS, your users can then log in to any host on the system — and still work on the same files.

✔ Data that requires large amounts of disk space can be kept on a single host. For example, let's say you have all the files for your `widget` project department on hosts `Timbuktu` and `Kalamazoo`. Instead, you can consolidate — keep all these files on your NFS server and make sure the `widget` group can access it.

With NFS, you can keep administrative files, scripts, and programs on a single host. No need to use rcp to install the same file on 20 different machines; doing the task once is enough. Also, since you're not copying files multiple times, you're saving lots of hard drive space and getting the maximum bang for the buck out of your hardware.

NFS, unlike the mount command, is *user-transparent*. Now, that doesn't mean that you can't see the files you're mounting. (You wouldn't believe how many people ask me that when I talk about "transparent processes" on the Linux network.)

Transparency means that regular users can't see what's actually going on, so they can concentrate on their tasks at hand without worrying about what you're doing. (I'm sometimes reminded of the scene in *The Wizard of Oz* where Dorothy and company finally approach the Wizard's lair and see the powerful sorcerer is merely a man in a curtained booth. User transparency is a more subtle way of saying, "Ignore the man behind the curtain!") Since the user doesn't actually have to mount anything — it's done automatically by NFS — there's no perception of having to go to a central server. Files are where the user expects them to be, and whether they're local or remote doesn't matter at all.

From the administrator's point of view, NFS is also more useful than the mount because you control the *exporting* of file systems. This allows you to decide what machines and users on your Linux network get direct access to the disks that contain data or programs that are safe to share.

NFS — an all-you-can-eat network buffet table

Remember the analogy we've been using for the client-server system and the network protocols, where the clients are diners and the servers are the waiters at the fine eating establishment of Chéz Bubba? We can continue working with that comparison here with the Network File System and how it really operates to your advantage.

Imagine that there are so many diners (clients) who want to get to their favorite dishes (stuffed data, broiled data, data fondue, and data au gratin) that the waiters simply can't get to everyone fast enough. Bringing out dishes one at a time, to each client, is creating a huge backlog of orders and the whole system rapidly grinds to a halt somewhere between the corner booths and the salad bar.

Solution? The creative, Linux-like management of Chéz Bubba — create a veritable data smorgasbord by using a buffet table instead of waiters. It's a much more efficient way to provide instant access for hordes of hungry users. And unlike a real restaurant, nobody complains if they get data that's been sitting under a heat lamp or on a steam table for a few hours.

Know These Parts of NFS Before You Run It

NFS is pretty simple to understand, once you get the idea that it's a way to automate the mount command for users on client boot-up. What most people neglect to learn — but not you, of course! — is that there are three pieces of the NFS puzzle that have to be on the table before you start making decisions about what to mount to where, and to whom.

To run without crashing, freezing, or otherwise misbehaving, NFS must have two daemons running; you'll also have to create a special directory in the /etc directory on your NFS server.

The NFS "server" and "client" terms

NFS terminology can be stickier than a cinnamon roll iced with white glue. *NFS server*, for example, means any machine that has been assigned to share out its files. On the other hand, *NFS client* means a machine specifically configured to mount file systems off a NFS server — in other words, it doesn't export data. It merely receives it when a user wants to work on a file.

This doesn't mean that a user can't keep any files locally on their own machine. NFS doesn't block any of the traditional avenues of file access, especially alternate ways to store and access files. Rather, it adds an extra dimension to how your users can update and get to their work.

Both daemons can be started directly from the command line or from the initialization of the Internet daemon, `inetd`. However, your best bet is to place them into the system's startup scripts to be started automatically. Therefore, it's important to read through the options you might want to use and set for each daemon, because you won't be able to change either daemon's options on the fly, while they're running.

If you change your mind as to what switches you want on or off, you'll have to make the changes, shut the NFS server down, and bring it back on line. Doing this during work hours on your network will create only slightly less havoc than the San Francisco Earthquake, Godzilla attacking Tokyo, or the release of the next *Star Wars* movie.

Try to avoid this if at all possible. Besides being unsightly, havoc has the nasty side effect of turning your hair gray.

Mountd — the daemon doorman

Mountd is the first of the three main NFS pieces, and it fits nicely into the restaurant analogy we've been using. Even though a fine eating establishment like Chéz Bubba's operates with a buffet table, it's not a buffet table that lets just anyone join in and chow down. Both an incoming client and the particular section of the buffet table have to be *permissioned* so that the client can step up to sample the data. You'll be learning how to permission client and server areas shortly. But for now, you should think of mountd, the "nfs mount daemon" as the doorman (or if you wish, the bouncer) for your Linux NFS server.

Don't confuse the mountd daemon with the mount command that you learned about in Chapter 14. They sound similar but are (in fact) two different kinds of Linux entities, which do completely different things. The Linux mount command lets you see and mount a particular file system; mountd is not a Linux command but a daemon that *checks* the mounting of those file systems specifically use NFS for networking.

When mountd receives a request for data from an NFS client, it checks the request against the list of exported file systems. If the client is permitted to mount the requested file system, then mountd creates a file *handle* for the directory. The handle is an entry added by mountd to a file called /etc/rmtab.

The rmtab (for *remove table*) command is one of the few files that the Linux system creates and deletes one-hundred-percent automatically. When the mountd daemon receives a request to unmount the system (as from a umount command), mountd removes the client's entry from the /etc/rmtab file.

You should keep in mind that a client may still be able to use the file handle in the /etc/rmtab even after a request for un-mounting the file system is processed. For example, a client may mount the same remote file system on a second, differently-named mount point.

One serious problem can result from a related situation: Suppose a client reboots without notifying mountd. For example, a user in a hurry might simply flick the *off* switch on the local Linux box without logging off or properly shutting down the machine. Result: A stale entry remains in rmtab, possibly preventing that user from mounting that file system (or any file system that resides on an NFS system) despite his or her piteous cries.

This is yet another argument for training your user community to "respect the law" by proper logins and logouts, no matter how pressing the need to jump up and go when the urge strikes. It will save you hours of wasted administration time on easily avoided problems such as this. Incidentally, to fix this, simply go to the /etc directory as the root user and blow away the /etc/rmtab file with the rm command.

Keep in mind that mountd can be started when inetd is invoked, rather than at system boot time. This can be accomplished by adding the following two lines to the Internet Daemon configuration file, /etc/inetd.conf:

```
mount/1-2 dgram rpc/udp wait root /usr/sbin/rpc.mountd
        rpc.mountd
mount/1-2 stream rpc/tcp wait root /usr/sbin/rpc.mountd
        rpc.mountd
```

Overall, running mountd automatically on boot-up is preferable. One reason for this is that when you run mountd from inetd, the mountd will terminate after a certain period of inactivity. Few things will annoy your user community more than if whole file systems just "disappear into the ether" when someone steps out to get a cold Coke from the vending machine down the hall.

Table 15-1 offers a list of command options you should consider implementing (keeping in mind the needs of your Linux user community). Remember, you can change these settings for mountd, but the new settings don't take effect until you reboot the NFS server.

Table 15-1	Mountd Options	
Command Option	*Function*	*Default*
-f	This options specifies which file that mountd should read when searching for the list of clients that this server is prepared to serve and apply to each mount request.	By default, the list is read rom the /etc/ exports file.
-d	Log each transaction verbosely for debugging purposes. This can be useful when you're trying to figure out the cause of a mountd-related problem.	By default, log output is sent to /etc*/syslogd unless the daemon runs in the foreground.

Command Option	Function	Default
-F	When this is requested, the mountd runs in the *foreground*. This allows the log messages to be sent directly to the screen instead of to a log file. Only use this when you're attempting to debug something; This runs in the background.	
-h	Provides you with a short help summary.	
-P	Makes mountd listen on a specified port.	By default, mountd will listen on the mount/udp port specified in the /etc/services file. If undefined, Linux selects an arbitrary port number below 1024.
-p	Operate in *promiscuous mode* so any host on the network will be served.	

The maître d' of daemons — nfsd

The second of the NFS trio, nfsd (for NFS Service Daemon), is like the maître d' you encounter after the doorman (mountd) admits you to the plush confines of Chéz Bubba. The nfsd program handles clients' file-system requests.

As with mountd, nfsd starts by default at system-boot time. However, you can also invoke it from inetd by adding two lines to /etc/inetd.conf:

```
nfs/2 dgram rpc/udp wait root /usr/sbin/rpc.nfsd rpc.nfsd
nfs/2 stream rpc/tcp wait root /usr/sbin/rpc.nfsd rpc.nfsd
```

Just as with mountd, you have to keep in mind that when you run nfsd from inetd, your inetd will terminate after a certain period of inactivity. And to complete the parallels with mountd, you should familiarize yourself with the options that come with nfsd. Because changes made to nfsd again require you to go through the tiresome, possibly career-limiting move of shutting down and restarting the machine you've selected as your NFS server. Table 15-2 lists the most-often-used options that come with nfsd.

Table 15-2	nfsd Options
Command Option	**What It Does**
-f	This option specifies which file that nfsd should read when searching for the list of clients that this server is prepared to serve and apply to each mount request.
	Default Setting
	By default, the list is read from the /etc/exports file.
-d	*D* for debugging, by creating a verbose log.
	Default Setting
	By default, you're provided with less information, allowing nfsd to operate more efficiently.
-F	Used with -d, this puts nfsd in the foreground for easy log display.
	Default Setting
	Normally this runs in the background, out of sight.
-h	Provides a short help summary.
-l	This *log-transfer* option watches all files retrieved from or written to the NFS server. For each stored or retrieved file, a line is written to the system log with the client's IP address and filename.
	Default Setting
	The system log is not written to, allowing nfsd to operate more efficiently.
-P	Makes nfsd listen on a specified port number instead of some random port.
	Default Setting
	By default, it listens on the mount/udp port specified in the /etc/services file. If this is undefined, Linux selects an arbitrary port number below 1024.
-p	Operating in promiscuous mode. (Come on now, stop that snickering! You wanna go to the principal's office?) Putting the server in promiscuous mode means it will serve any given host on the network.
	Default Setting
	Restricted list of hosts.

Command Option	What It Does
-v	Tells you the current version number of the mountd program you're using.
	Default Setting
	Nfsd assumes you know this already, so it won't tell you!

Giving nfsd and mountd a boot

Although you've learned how to start nfsd and mountd from the inetd.conf file, you're still better off having them run from one of your Linux system's startup scripts. By specifying them in the startup scripts, you keep them from being managed by inetd; they start up at boot time, and register themselves with the system portmapper program.

The simplest way to add the NFS daemons to the startup routine is to edit the rc.inet2 script in your /etc directory. Add the following lines to the script:

```
if [ -x /usr/sbin/rpc.mountd ]; then
/usr/sbin/rpc.mountd; echo -n " mountd"
fi
if [ -x /usr/sbin/rpc.nfsd ]; then
/usr/sbin/rpc.nfsd; echo -n " nfsd"
fi
```

In order for this to take effect, you'll have to reboot the machine. Once the machine comes back up, do the following:

1. **Use the ps command to check for the nsf daemon:**
```
Linuxbox% ps -aef | grep nfsd
```
2. **Use the ps command again to check for the mountd.**
```
Linuxbox% ps -aef |grep mountd
```

Both the nfsd and mountd should be running under either the system account or as root.

NFS imports and exports, without tariffs

The third and final piece that you must have in place to run NFS successfully on you Linux network is the /etc/exports file.

Contrary to popular belief, this directory does not automatically come into being when you implement NFS! If you're the new administrator taking over an established Linux network, never assume that this directory is there — check for it, and go through each entry in the file to see what should be exporting to where. Otherwise, you may find yourself with a heap of user complaints on your desk by the following morning, which is something that will really begin to cramp your work style.

The /etc/exports file lists the file systems you've selected as worthy (or unworthy, as the case may be) to be exported to the NFS client machines on your network. The exports file is read by the NFS mount daemon (mountd) and the NFS file server daemon (nfsd).

As a matter of course, you should always check the contents of this file when you administer a new system. Begin by changing directories to /etc and **vi** the exports file. A sample exports file might look something like the following:

```
# sample /etc/exports file
/            linuxbox(rw) pinto(rw, no_root_squash)
/wonderbread   @wonderusers(ro)
/medical/cases   med_files* (rw)
/public/ftp   (ro, all_squash)
   /super/secret   (noaccess)
```

Each line in /etc/exports lists the following information on each line as follows:

```
Mounted Directory    Machines allowed to mount the file system
/              linuxbox(rw) pinto(rw, no_root_squash)
```

Here, the root directory is the mounted one, while machines linuxbox and pinto are allowed to mount the root directory.

Depending on the specific permissions you might wish to grant each machine, each machine name can be followed with a list of mount parameters specified inside a set of parenthesis.

Machine names can be listed in several different formats in the /etc/exports file. How you list a machine can save you a lot of typing, particularly if you have a large Linux network with several hosts that have similar names. For example, you can use wildcards to indicate a large number of machines which are spelled similarly, as opposed to typing each machine name out by hand. See Table 15-3 for this information.

Table 15-3	Options for Listing Machines in /etc/exports
File Option	*What It Does*
single host	The most common method of machine listing. You specify a host either by the machine's name, or the machine's IP address.
netgroup	When using NIS, a netgroups parameters may be used with the @ wildcard, as in @group. The 'host' part of all netgroup members is extracted and added to the access list.
IP network	You can export directories to *all* hosts on an IP (sub-) network. This is done by specifying an IP address and netmask pair as address/netmask.
wildcards	Client machine names in /etc/export can contain the wildcard character *.

For example, say you want to give the same export permissions for the Linux machines med_files, med_files_ah, med_files_achoo, and med_files_gesundheit. The entry med_files* matches all the med_files hosts listed in the domain, which is nothing to sneeze at.

In addition, you also have a wide variety of parameters you can use to tailor the accessibility of each file system in the exports directory. Some of these parameters range from the understandable to the seriously bizarre. Table 15-4 lists the aspects of each:

Table 15-4	Options for Files Listed in /etc/exports
File Option	*What It Does*
Noaccess	This makes everything below the exported directory inaccessible for this particular NFS client. This can be useful when you want to export a directory hierarchy to a client, but exclude certain subdirectories.
	Default Setting
	Every subdirectory below an exported directory is accessible.
link_absolute	Leave all symbolic links as they are.
	Default Setting
	This is actually the default parameter; you don't have to list it. We list it here so you'll know about it.

(continued)

Table 15-4 *(continued)*	
File Option	**What It Does**
ro	Allows only read-only requests on this NFS-mounted file system.
	Default Setting
	By default, NFS allows you to write permissions to these directories as well. You can choose to make this an explicit permission with the rw option, listed below.
rw	Allows read and write requests on this NFS-mounted file system.
	Default Setting
	This is the default, but I recommend that you make this explicit, so that you can tell what is writable by just glancing at the /etc/exports file.

Squash isn't just a root vegetable anymore . . .

Another option that you should be aware of in the /etc/exports directory handles such an important function that it deserves its own subheading. That option is squash. Whether or not you like squash is totally irrelevant, since like any healthy, good-for-you vegetable item you were forced to eat as a kid, you're going to have to get used to it.

If you've inherited a traditional Linux network, you'll have a group of Linux machines with one root account. That root account will have only one password held by the system administrator (that's you), or a group of trusted folks like fellow system administrators, bank guards, and politicians running for president. However, even on a traditional Linux network, some people may have *local root* access. That is, if they log in as root, they can effectively act as the root account (omnipotence and all that) on their machine only.

Normally such delusions of grandeur needn't concern you much; those would-be emperors can't damage anything that resides elsewhere than on their local machines. *Unless* you run NFS.

Imagine, if you will, a world where anyone who runs as root on a client machine is also treated as root when accessing files on the NFS server. (If you didn't gasp in terror, your imagination may be asleep. Grab that morning cup of java and review my definition of "havoc" earlier in the chapter.)

To avoid this horrible fate, Linux automatically maps uid 0 (the root identi-fication number) to a different user-identification number (uid) — namely, the so-called anonymous or nobody user ID. This mode of operation is called *root squashing*. It's the default setting, but you can turn it off with the follow-ing parameter: no_root_squash (If you want a closer look at the elusive uid 0 and nobody, see Chapter 5.)

There are a few situations where you might consider using this setting — for example, a *really* small Linux network with few machines and users who don't normally access — or even know about — the root account. (This isn't an unreasonable assumption. After all, until you really started taking an interest in Linux beyond simple text editing, how much did *you* know about that all-important system account, root?)

By default, the network file system daemon (nfsd) tries to obtain the anony-mous uid and gid (group identification number) by looking in the passwd file at the system startup time for user nobody. Incidentally (if you're curi-ous), if you haven't created or inherited a nobody account, the system assigns you a uid and gid of –2 automatically. So you don't have to sweat it if anybody hasn't had somebody create nobody, since not everybody has to worry about it. (Say what? Just trust me on this one.)

Here's the list of squash options you have available — in handy, easy-to-read Table 15-5.

Table 15-5	Squash Options to Use in the /etc/exports File
File Option	**What It Does**
root_squash	The default setting. Maps requests from user id number 'zero' to the anonymous uid.
no_root_squash	Turn off root squashing.
squash_uids, squash_gids	These options specify a list of user IDs or group IDs that are subject to anonymous mapping. A valid list of IDs might look as follows:
	squash_uids=0, 1, 2, 10-15
	squash_gids=0, 100, 200-500
all_squash	This maps user requests to the 'anonymous' uid by speci-fying the all_squash option. All_squash maps all uids **and** gids to the anonymous user.

Note: This is useful when you have to export NFS-mounted public FTP directories or news-spool directories. The default option, is no_all_squash.

Putting it all together: Reading the /etc/exports file

This is a lot of information to digest at one time. But then, not many files in Linux are so infinitely configurable as the exports file. This level of detail is needed because exports can be amazingly important if you want to distribute data easily on your network. So let's look at some examples from a sample exports file and translate them for practice. We'll reuse the example from earlier in the chapter:

```
# sample /etc/exports file
/           linuxbox(rw) pinto(rw, no_root_squash)
/wonderbread   @wonderusers(ro)
/medical/cases   med_files* (rw)
/public/ftp   (ro, all_squash)
   /super/secret   (noaccess)
```

The first line exports the entire file system on your Linux NFS server without even breathing hard. How can you tell? Because the first symbol is / (which, as duly chronicled in Chapter 3, means the root directory that everything else resides under). This is one *major* mount. According to the file, this root mount has been made to only two machines — linuxbox and pinto. linuxbox has been given full permissions to read and write to the root directory. Its sidekick pinto has the same permissions, and has all uid-squashing turned off.

The third line of code shows an entry by netgroups. Entry @wonderusers allows exports to all machines in the wonderusers net group. Note also that although these hosts are allowed to read the exported /wonderbread directory, they aren't allowed to write their own changes to it. (Freedom of speech is all well and good, but there's a limit.)

On the third line is an entry for the * wildcard, which is set up here to cover all hostnames starting with med_files. Each of these hosts will be allowed permission to read or write to the /medical/cases directory.

The fourth line exports the entire contents of the public FTP directory (here, /pub/ftp) to the public, executing all the user requests from the nobody account in the /etc/passwd file. One smart move made here is to make sure that this directory is read-only. A writable public FTP file is just asking for trouble; a mischievous user could mess up files that *everyone* needs.

The last line in the sample file explicitly denies all NFS client access to the directory/super/secret. I've actually come across this very setting on one Linux system, which made me wonder: If this directory is so secret, then why call attention to it? (I include this line as a good example of restricting access to NFS mounting, though maybe not such a good example of common sense.)

Centralize, centralize, and centralize, preferably in the center of things

Where NFS is concerned, Linux follows the same rule as real estate: The three most important things to keep in mind are *location, location, and location*.

Ideally you should strive to centralize your mounted files on *one* server (it makes the question of *location* so much simpler). NFS system functionality is happiest and most robust on just one machine.

If you're starting to build your Linux system from scratch, select one machine from which you expect to do the bulk of your administrative work — and make that one your NFS server. If possible, your selected machine should have the following qualities:

✔ It should be the biggest, baddest, fastest machine on your network. As a bare minimum for a network of, say, a dozen machines, your NFS server should have double or triple the computing power of the clients.

You can most accurately estimate computing power on your machine by getting data on your machines from your files (or the prior administrator's files) on the chips in your machines, the chip's clock speed, and the amont of RAM installed on each box. If you're unfaniliar with whether Model A is faster than Model B, check your vendor's documentation or their Web site. Whether you run a Sun box or an IBM PC, you'll be able to find rough benchmarks on the relative speed of a machine.

✔ You should be able to get to the physical machine easily if nessesary. Even better, *you* should be able to get to the machine easily, but it should be incredibly difficult for *anyone else* to get to the machine. Consider renting a walk-in vault next to Fort Knox.

✔ The NFS server must have more than one network card to handle the network traffic from multiple subnets. (If your network has a *flat* name structure in which every file is a rugged individualist whose name has nothing to do with other names, you can probably get away with fewer network cards.)

✔ Load up on RAM: Too much is barely enough.

✔ The NFS server should have enough hard drive space to store all the files you plan to put on it. That means all the files you have now *and* all the files you're ever going to have (well, okay, within reason).

✔ If you have to choose between buying a single, huge internal hard drive and several smaller external ones, go for the big one. You'll have fewer problems with network connections and points of failure, so administration is easier.

On a related note, all this centralization does entail more vulnerability to failure should the system go down. Therefore, make sure to set up a routine to *back up* files on tapes or alternate disks. The amount of time and money you spend on such a system should depend on:

✔ How valuable the stored data is.

✔ How much money you're allocated to spend on equipment.

✔ How much you love your job.

Of course, the real world can often be a kludge-on-the-cheap; budget constraints or other practical obstacles may keep you from centralizing to your heart's content. Fortunately, it isn't absolutely *essential* to cram all your network data onto one box. If you simply must use multiple NFS servers, save your sanity by categorizing them according to the information they store. For example, you could make sure that one NFS server just exports the Human Resources files while another exports the user community's directories.

The -r option for the network file-system daemon allows you to export remotely mounted file-systems — but be careful. This maneuver amounts to *re*-exporting NFS mounts that are then "looped back" because the mount point has been reused. ("Incoming . . . !) One unhealthy and ugly result can be a deadlock between the NFS client and the NFS server. Visualize the entire system locking up. And that's just the start of more administration nightmares. Brrrr.

At Last, Some Action: Setting Up and Testing Your NFS Mounts

Mounting an NFS file system is very similar to what you already learned in Chapter 14. As with other kinds of file systems, you invoke mount by using the following syntax:

```
# mount -t nfs <nfs volume> local dir options
```

For example, say you want to mount your users' home directories from a machine named hearthstone on the /home mount point. You might use a command like this one to do the job:

```
# mount -t nfs hearthstone:/home /home
```

You *could* invoke the mount command from the command line, but for NFS, you want to avoid invoking mount. Having the exported NFS file system automatically mounted for you when the client boots up is *so* much more civilized. You can perform this bit of hocus-pocus by editing the /etc/fstab entry for the NFS exported file system. You can specify options in the fstab file the same way you do from the command line. In either case, you can use multiple command options so long as you use commas to separate them from each other.

Options that you specify on the command line of a mount command will always override those created in the /etc/fstab file!

Taking an fstab in the dark

The file /etc/fstab is the location of the *file system table*. Your Linux machine is automatically configured to look in this location for the list of file systems that have been mounted on the client machine.

In a way, this file is the flipside of the /etc/exports one. Where exports tells the server what to place on the network for others to view, fstab tells the client what it must try to retrieve automatically from the Ethernet jungle. Great feature. Even greater potential for mishaps and misconfiguration — which means that only you, as root, can edit this file most of the time (ah, make that *the vast majority* of the time).

The fstab file contains four fields. Of the four, the first three must be configured or the file system won't be mounted. The fourth accepts defaults, but you're still advised to set it. The lineup of the fields is listed in Table 15-6:

Table 15-6	Fields in the /etc/fstab File
Field	*What It Is*
Volume	Volume is the NFS mounted directory that you've set on the NFS server itself, by using **vi** on the file /etc/export.
mount point	The field mount point is the directory created on the client as the "coat hanger" on which you hang the directory.
type	The type field tells the Linux system what kind of file system it's trying to mount. (The many different possibilities are listed back in Chapter 14, under Table 14-1.)
options	Any options you wish to specify with regards to the reading of the mounted file system are specified here. (The available options are listed in Table 15-7. Read on.)

As with the /etc/exports file, the command options in the fourth field vary from the common to the truly esoteric. Our friend fstab has another vital similarity to the exports file: Any changes made to fstab won't take effect until the client machine is rebooted — which means it's prudent policy to understand what's available and set it right away so you can prevent excessive client downtime. Fortunately, Table 15-7 provides this information.

Table 15-7	Options to Use in the /etc/fstab File
File Option	*What It Does*
timeo=<*number*>	Times out a request. The timeo (*time-out*) option sets the interval that an NFS client will wait for a request to complete. The default value for this is 0.7 seconds.
hard	Explicitly marks this file system as a *hard-mounted* one (which is the default setting). *Hard mounting* means the system is hard-nosed about accomplishing a mount. In the event of a problem with mounting off the NFS server, the system will continue trying to mount it.
soft	*Soft-mounts* the file system. Unlike hard mounting, soft mounting means the system tries only once to mount, chickens out if it doesn't get the job done, and won't even tell you whether it was successful. For this reason, I don't like using soft mounts.
intr	Allows signals to interrupt an NFS call. This option gives you a way to stop the NFS mount attempt if the server doesn't respond.

Hard-mount at your own risk . . .

I recommend that you always use hard-mounting with an intr option whenever possible. The idea is to prevent possible sticky situations when there's an NFS server problem. Without intr, the Linux client will try to mount the volume until the universe comes to an end, even during an NFS problem or power outage. If you've determined that waiting for cosmic implosion might take too long, you'll probably end up having to do a rather gory reboot if you don't have that handy intr option in place.

Each option shown in Table 15-6 directs the client to act a certain way *if it has trouble contacting the NFS server*. To begin with, when the client machine boots up and attempts to mount the NFS files listed in its /etc/fstab file, it uses the timeo option to determine when the operation is to finish.

If the client machine doesn't get a confirmation within the set time limit, it makes a second attempt to reach the NFS server. By default, if the second attempt fails, the client machine prints a message on-screen to describe the difficulty, usually with a message like this one:

```
NFS host Linuxbox unreachable: retrying.
```

A hard-mounted file system can keep "retrying" forever unless you've set the `intr` option. Without the `intr` entry, you won't be able to locate the mounting processes and put them out of their obsessive misery. Then your only option is to hit the power switch. Messy.

Whether you hard- or soft-mount a given file system depends on what kind of information you want the system to contain. Data that isn't accessed frequently (or isn't very important) won't suffer if you've soft-mounted. NFS-mounted news partitions or FTP archives, for example, normally don't hold earth-shattering info; you may as well soft-mount them so they don't suddenly hang your session if remote machine is temporarily down. (Administrators think like that. It's a good habit to develop.)

If your network connection to the server is slow (for whatever reason), you should take the following measure: Increase the initial time-out parameter using the `timeo` option. This will avoid problems caused by retries when the NFS server is available, even if the network connection seems to clump toward completion on lead feet.

Sample fstabs

In general, when you see a table or sample entry, file, or command line, you're learning the model way to do things. However, when you're being shown how easy it is to make a mistake in certain areas, we'll let you know. This is one of those times. Some sample entries in a machine's `/etc/fstab` might include the following. However, while all the entries look fine, most of them are example of the *wrong* way to do things. Explanations on which are good (and which are not) follow.

# volume	mount point	type	options
linuxbox:/med_ cases	/achoo	nfs	hard, intr
home:/usr/ wally	/local/wally	nfs	hard
thread:/usr/ spool	/local/spool	nfs	timeo=14
pillow:/cases	/stuffing	nfs	soft, intr

The first entry is properly set up; the second is a recipe for disaster. Why? Take a look at /med_cases, for example: It's set up to be mounted on the local directory achoo, and although the mount is hard, it's *also* interruptible if it fails to contact the NFS server linuxbox. So far, so good. But if the client can't contact the NFS server home when it tries to mount the exported directory /usr/wally on /local/wally, it's gonna get obsessive about trying to mount. And you won't have a way to stop it short of rebooting the machine.

Therefore, heed well: Either change the option to soft so the client tries only once to mount, or add the intr option so you can mercifully kill off the process if need be.

Line three is correctly set. Notice that it's the only mounted file system that does *not* accept the default time-out setting. Since the setting is higher, it's probable that the thread NFS server is on a slow connection. Now for a curve ball: The final line is incorrectly set, but it won't cause problems. The inter option is set so the machine won't get stuck, but why bother? The mount point is *soft*; it won't be trying repeatedly in any case.

As with the mount command from the command line, you can't mount directories without creating a directory for a mount point. When you create an entry for your /etc/fstab file, it doesn't mean that you just *created* the mount point — it means you just told the machine to *look* for one. For example, take a look at this fstab entry:

```
pillow:/cases          /stuffing          nfs          soft
```

You're telling the machine to look for the mount-point directory stuffing. But until you actually go in there and use the mkdir command to create the stuffing directory, it's not going to exist. Which means the only thing you'll be stuffing up is your Linux machine.

The mount daemon keeps track of the directories that have been mounted, and knows which hosts mounted them. This information can be displayed using the showmount program.

Showmount: the Jerry Maguire of Linux commands

The showmount command displays mount information specifically for an NFS server. It does this by querying the mountd daemon on a remote host. Then showmount lists the set of clients mounting from that host. Considering how useful showmount is, Linux users everywhere can consider themselves lucky that it's already included in the NFS package that comes with all Linux releases.

The most useful command options you'll come across for `showmount` include those shown in Table 15-8.

Table 15-8	Showmount Options
Command Option	*What It Does*
`-a`	The *list all* parameter. Lists both the client hostname and mounted directory in *host*: *dir* format.
`-d`	Lists only the directories mounted by at least one client.
`-e`	*E* is for `exports`. Shows the NFS server's export list.
`-h`	Provides a short help list. Like most Linux help lists, it's not very helpful, but there's just no help for that.
`-v`	Tells you the current version number of the program you're using.
`-no-headers`	Suppresses the descriptive headings from the `show-mount` output. (Hey, if you *like* reading cryptic stuff, this is for you.)

The automounter

If you're running a Linux network where you're going to have excessive NFS traffic, you might consider using the `automount` facility — a program that runs on the later versions of Linux. If you don't have it on your system, you can do a search for it on the Web and download it.

The `automount` program runs a daemon (called, creatively, the `automountd`). It automatically mounts any NFS volume as needed, and then unmounts it after it hasn't been used for some time. This cuts down on your NFS traffic and eases the load on your servers.

Your best bet is to use the `automount` facility when one or more of the following conditions exist (or are soon to exist) on your network:

✔ Your network contains more than four or five NFS servers, each of which are accessed mutiple times a day.

✔ One or more of your NFS servers have to mount half a dozen different directories to allow users to access vital information.

✔ You have over 100 users, and the majority of them need active access to files stored daily on the NFS servers.

✔ You have a very slow network connection.

✔ You have one or more very slow NFS servers.

Unfortunately (and you've heard this before), no program is perfect; I have two caveats about using `automount`.

✔ **Documentation is scarce and pretty unreliable.** Because of this, I strongly advise you to use `automount` only if it's already been installed with your version of Linux. If not, then when you upgrade to any form of Linux that's less than five years old you should get it automatically.

✔ **At times, the `automount` program can be a real pain to work with.** If, for example, you want to unmount a directory that the program believes should stay mounted, you'll play Linux tug-o-war with the process unless you kill it. (Ropes and dueling pistols, anyone?)

Whichever way you choose to implement the network file sharing, you'll be able to get data from all over the network.

Chapter 16

The Network Distribution Master, NIS

. . . .

In This Chapter

▶ The origins of NIS, the Network Information System

▶ Calling from the YP area code

▶ Maps and domains

▶ How to use and configure NIS on your system

. . . .

*T*his chapter introduces you to NIS, the *Network Information System*. It's a rapidly changing area within Linux and therefore worthy of learning about, even if you don't have it yet on your system. NIS helps you distribute data by giving organization to your Linux network. There are a few things you should keep in mind as you're learning about NIS and how to play with it.

✔ NIS and NFS do not have to be running on the same network at the same time. NIS runs just fine without NFS around. However, NIS carries more overhead than NFS, which is why you'll tend to find NIS implemented on larger Linux networks.

✔ NIS cannot be invoked, configured, pruned, watered, fertilized or re-potted by anyone except the root account. Don't let users tell you that they're running NIS on their own system if it's connected to your Linux network. It's not possible.

✔ Finally, NIS doesn't rhyme with hiss. It's pronounced Enn-Eye-Ess. You can spot a Linux pretender a mile away if they start talking about NIS while sounding like a puff adder.

The Raison D'etre (Reason for Being) of the Network Information Service

NIS stands for Network Information Service. NIS's purpose in life is to provide information that has to be known by all machines on the Linux network. More specifically, NIS centralizes administration of this information and keeps it consistent between all machines on the network.

The key concept to help you differentiate NFS (the Network File System, talked about in detail in Chapter 15) and NIS is that NFS helps you distribute data to different users on the Linux network. NIS is more of an administrator's toy. It affects users when they log in and when they connect to the network, but it really doesn't touch any of their more immediate concerns beyond that.

NIS won't alter their work, touch their files, or help them print, so it's pretty much an invisible system so far as they're concerned. Of course, as far as you're concerned, it's a pretty big deal, since without a properly functioning NIS system you'll either be inefficient at your job or you'll be administering a chaotic jumble of machines and passwords.

NIS keeps vital data such as user account information synchronized between the client machines on your system. Another kind of organizer which specializes in host name resolution is DNS (the domain name service). DNS can often be confused with NIS, because they use many of the same concepts — such as domains, servers, hosts, and clients. However, they're completely different, which is why DNS gets its own chapter.

One thing to keep in mind is that if you manage a small(ish) Linux network with little or no Internet connectivity, setting up DNS is a lot of trouble for many administrators without much gain in return. Although DNS predates NIS, this is the reason that many small to medium size Linux networks were having problems with their administration. "Too big for personal knowledge; too small for DNS" became a lament expressed by more than one administrator in these Dark Ages of Linux.

The Shadowy Origins of NIS

Sensing a niche market about to be born (and concurrent profits to be generated), Sun Microsystems stepped into the picture. Sun Microsystems is one of the big UNIX corporations. Among other things, it's the producer of Sun's UNIX operating system, known as SunOS and/or Solaris, depending on which marketing material you prefer to read.

Sun Microsystems filled the product niche by developing NIS. NIS was a hit from the start, as it provided a kind of generic database that NIS servers used to distribute information contained in critical files to all hosts on the network. This effectively makes the network operate as a single system containing the same user accounts on any and all hosts.

Information that NIS is usually set to distribute include:

- ✔ User login names
- ✔ User account passwords
- ✔ User home directories
- ✔ Group information (pulled from the /etc/group file)
- ✔ Hostname information (pulled from the /etc/hosts and distributed to all machines on the network)

For example, you might change your login name and password on your Linux network. Using NIS, the change is recorded in the NIS password database. NIS synchronizes the information — in effect it's distributed to each host on the system. You'll be able to log in to any and all machines that have the NIS client programs running.

Incidentally, you'll hear old Linux gurus talk in hushed tones about the "dark origins" of NIS. Truth be told, NIS does indeed have some twisted legal history wound about it. Way back when a 9600 baud modem was thought of as pretty cool, NIS came into being as a system called the "Sun Yellow Pages," or *YP* for short.

But although popular, NIS was not to have an easy time of it in the world. Unknown to most of the world (and, apparently, Sun's legal department) the name Yellow Pages was and is a registered trademark in the United Kingdom. The company British Telecom had complete legal rights to what many people in the U.S. consider a synonym for the "Ma Bell" book. And British Telecom wasn't about to cede over rights of the term to an upstart software company who, for all they knew, wrote software for American Revolution.

Tempers flared about as much as they do in these kinds of disagreements. The end result was that the Yellow Pages became known as NIS, though you'll see that many of the remaining NIS commands and processes still retain the YP naming conventions.

Incidentally, if anyone reading this knows why British Telecom objected to Sun Microsystems using the term Yellow Pages but *didn't* complain about huge American telephone companies using it, do me a favor and let *me* know. . . .

YP Reborn as NIS — How It All Works Together

NIS is widely available today. Linux being the freethinking operating system that it is, you can even find free versions of it. In fact, one of the freeware versions of NIS was developed from a public domain implementation donated by Sun Microsystems.

NIS is simple in concept but a little trickier in execution. In order to best understand it, you'll see how all the pieces work together before we actually start configuring files to our heart's delight. First things first though — on any NIS network, there must be at least one machine acting as a *master* NIS server.

Of course, you can have multiple NIS servers, each serving different NIS "domains." Alternatively, you can have a hierarchical system of NIS servers. In this kind of system there is still only one master NIS server. As for the other servers, they are the so-called *slave* servers, which act both as backups and as relay stations which receive updated NIS information, such as new group IDs, changes to user passwords, and additions to the /etc/hosts file.

NIS Domains — The kings of this particular type of hill

An NIS network "domain" is the name that the Linux wizards have given to the collection of all hosts that share a part of their NIS system configuration data. The term *domain* causes some confusion for people, because both NIS and DNS use the same terms. Worse, NIS domains have absolutely nothing in common with DNS domains.

If you're unfortunate enough to run DNS as well as NIS, the best way to keep the two straight in your mind is to remember that NIS domains are purely administrative in purpose. NIS domains are mostly user transparent — the most that users will note is that they are able to log in from any machine on the network with the same password and account.

Because NIS is administrative in nature, the NIS domain name is really only important to a network's administrator or system administration team. Any name or alpha-numeric combination will work, as long as it is unique to your local network.

I suggest that you select domain names that will help you to remember the function of the grouping of your machines. For example, let's say that you administer three Linux networks (poor you!) at a university for the physics, marine biology, and music departments. You might divide up the three domain names by department as well, calling them `einstein`, `cousteau`, and `pavarotti`.

What's in a name, part two

While it's common for administrators to use the DNS domain name for NIS domain name, I strongly advise you not to do this. It causes a lot of confusion, especially when you're trying to work with other administrators. If I call both my local NIS domainname `Watt` and my DNS domain name `Watt`, then when I schedule administration tasks, nobody I talk to is going to know which `Watt` when, and why.

Also, don't be silly and go the exact opposite direction by using a really weird naming scheme, like `000101010100` or `Findor_DragonKill_Domain`. Not only are these hard to remember, they're really, really annoying to try and type.

On the other hand, if I select NIS names to complement DNS names, then I have the best of all worlds. Creating DNS pairs like `Batman and Robin`, `Bonnie and Clyde` and `Null and Void` are both easy to remember and distinguish when administrations tasks must be performed on one domain and not the other.

To display your current NIS domain name, use the `domainname` command. `Domainname` is one of the more useful commands as it also can tell you information about DNS domains. The format for the domainname command is:

```
domainname [-F filename] [—file filename] [name]
```

When invoked without any command options, it prints the current NIS domain name.

On some Linux systems that run both NIS and DNS, you might want to double-check the validity of the result by running "domainname –y." `domainname` with the `-y` option specifies that domainname check for an `NIS` domainname only, and not a DNS one.

To set the domain name, you should run the `domainname` command during your selected server's boot time. You can also change the domain name with the `domainname` command from the command line as follows:

Make sure to su to root first:

```
Linuxbox% su root
Password: ******
#
```

Select a name for the domain. Let's say that the DNS domain is batman and you want to choose a related NIS domain name, such as robin.

```
# /bin/domainname robin
```

Check the result by using the domainname command with the -y option. You should get a result as follows:

```
# /bin/domainname -y
robin
```

domainname also gives you even more information about the hosts (client machines) under a specific domain. Some of the other command options that you're going to find useful as a Linux administrator with domainname are as follows:

Table 16-1	domainname Command Options
Command Option	**What It Does**
-a	If a host has an alias in addition to its official name, display it.
-F	Read the host name from the specified file.
-f	Display the FQDN (Fully Qualified Domain Name). A FQDN consists of a short host name and the DNS domain name. Unless you are using bind or NIS for host lookups you can change the FQDN and the DNS domain name (which is part of the FQDN) in the /etc/hosts file.
-I	Display the host's IP address.
-s	Display the short host name. This is the host name cut at the first dot. (For example, batman.com will come back as "batman.")
-v	Be verbose and tell what's going on in excruciating detail.
-y	Make sure to display only the NIS domain name as opposed to the DNS one.

Don't be tempted into using the -d option with domainname. This command option will display the name of the DNS domain, not the NIS domain. This can cause you lots of wasted hours of confusion. Instead you should use the command dnsdomainname instead. You'll be shown all the different uses for this command in Chapter 17.

NIS domains determine which NIS server a user will connect to. A client host finds out which server to connect to with a daemon using the UDP protocol. NIS clients use a special daemon called ypbind (there's that Yellow Page connection again!) to detect an NIS server in the selected NIS domain. Before being able to perform any NIS functions, each host must be able to find and bind to a server found by ypbind's initial query.

ypbind looks for NIS servers by broadcasting a query to the local network. Remember back in the chapter on UDP and TCP, where we likened the unfocused broadcast UDP to standing up in a crowded cafeteria and shouting, "Is anyone here an NIS server?" Of course, instead of getting strange looks, on a computer network all the machines ignore the request, unless they're NIS slave or master servers.

The first NIS server to respond is assumed (using impeccable machine logic) to be the fastest server. From then on, the client is *bound* to that server, which will be used in all subsequent NIS activities. Of course, if the server becomes unavailable, ypbind will begin to broadcast for other servers, hoping to hook up with a live one.

The NIS maps that guide users around

NIS servers keep information in *maps* containing key-value pairs. Maps are stored on a central host running the NIS server, from whom clients may retrieve the information. Although any database administrator worth his or her salt will object, you can consider these maps (also called *ypmaps*) as a kind of primitive database of all the information that must be kept in sync across the network.

Ypmaps can be generated from certain system files such as /etc/hosts or /etc/passwd. Also, there are certain files and maps you may find in some NIS packages and not in others. These may contain special information such as a bootparams map for applications like a BOOTP server. However, you'll more commonly find your maps in the /var/yp directory.

Maps can be created only on the master server. From there, they are distributed to all slave servers (if you have any) and onward to the clients when the clients request data. Slave servers store only copies of the NIS ypmaps and receive these copies from the master NIS server.

Slave servers are kept in sync with master servers when they are notified of any change to the NIS maps. The updating is done via the yppush program, which directs the slave servers to automatically retrieve the updated information needed in order to synchronize their ypmaps. NIS clients don't need to do this since they will always bind to their local NIS server to read the information stored in the ypmaps.

NIS updates aren't "Fire and Forget"

Keep in mind that while clients don't have to be updated when you change the ypmaps, that's because they rely on the master or slave NIS servers to give them their information. And a major misconception that some Linux administrators have is that slave servers are automatically updated when the master server registers a change. This is not the case. You'll be learning how to make sure everything is in sync later in this chapter, when we cover the yppush command.

Starting to Configure Your System to Handle NIS

First off, you'll need two daemons running on your system: the portmap and the ypbind. ypbind functions as you just learned. portmap wasn't covered because technically, it's not part of the NIS system. The RPC (Remote Procedure Call) portmapper is a server that converts RPC program numbers into TCP/IP protocol port numbers. Since NIS uses these *calls*, you'll need to make sure that the portmapper is running in order to use the NIS functionality.

Number, please . . .

If you're interested, here's how portmap works when a Remote Procedure Call (a C programming term) is made. When a client makes an RPC call, it contacts portmap on the server machine to determine the port number where RPC packets should be sent.

The RPC tells portmap what port number it is listening to, and what RPC program numbers it is prepared to serve. The portmapper then fulfills its namesake by hooking the two ports up. I suppose you can think of the portmapper as the electronic equivalent of the old-time telephone operators who used to connect people by physically plugging in telephone switchboard connections.

Do a process search (ps) to see if these two processes are running on your machine. If they are, you'll get an output like the following:

```
root  1092     1  0  Apr 28  ?     0:00 /usr/sbin/portmap
root  1053  1052  0  Apr 28  ?     0:00 /usr/sbin/ypbind
root  1029     1  0  Apr 28  ?     0:00 /usr/sbin/cron
root  1752  1707  5  14:12:02 pts/00:00 ps -aef
```

If it's already running, you don't need to do anything except skip to the next section of the NIS chapter. If you still need to start portmap, you've got a little more work cut out for you.

Most Linux distributions already have the code in the /sbin/init.d/ or /etc/rc.d/ files to start up this daemon. If this is the case, go to the inetd.conf file and you should be able to locate the portmapper entry. If it's not running then you most likely have to uncomment it (remove the # sign in front of it). All you have to do now is to reboot your Linux machine.

Next, change directory (cd) to the /var directory and do an ls to see if you have a yp directory. If not, create the directory /var/yp or ypbind will go on strike and refuse to work for you.

Once this is completed, you can start up the ypbind daemon from the command line as follows:

```
#/usr/sbin/ypbind &
```

Note that you'll probably have to be root to do this.

Do two more things to make sure all is working as it should. First, perform another ps to ensure that portmapper and ypbind haven't decided to lie down on the job. Next, use the command rpcinfo -p localhost to check if ypbind was able to register with the portmapper. The output should look something like:

```
program versproto        port
9999    tcp    844  portmapper
9999    udp    124  portmapper
9999    udp    234  ypbind
9999    tcp    811  ypbind
```

Depending on the ypbind version you are using, the output may vary slightly. You can perform a final check by running rpcinfo -u localhost ypbind. This result should be something like:

```
program 999999 version 2 ready and waiting
program 999999 version 2 ready and waiting
program 999999 version 1 ready and waiting
```

Once ypbind is ready to go, make sure your NIS domain name is set — Linux systems have been known to throw tantrums if they have to connect to an empty domain name. Use your trusty domainname -y command for this, as follows:

```
# /bin/domainname -y
freshly_created_domainname
```

If it all works, perform a final test by rebooting the machine. Watch the boot messages to see if ypbind is automatically started. If not, you'll have to change your startup files so that ypbind will be started at boot time and your system will act as a proper citizen of the NIS domain.

Setting Up an NIS Client

Although you'll be working on client machines instead of your server for these specific tasks, make sure that you become root. You'll need the unearthly powers of root at your disposal or you won't be able to get into all the sensitive files that need editing.

Speaking of sensitive files, you'll first need to delve into one of the most sensitive of all, the /etc/passwd file. Add the following line to the passwd file and make sure to save the change.

```
+::::::
```

The + signifies that access is granted, while the colons signify that the field is left to the default, which is that all users are allowed access. This may sound like a bit of a security hole, but then NIS is by default supposed to make information more, not less available.

You can customize access by adding additional lines including the + and - characters. For example, let's say that you want to grant access to everyone, but deny access to an especially mischievious bunch of users with the user account names groucho, harpo, chico, and zeppo. Your /etc/password file should then contain the following lines:

```
+::::::
-groucho
-harpo
-chico
-zeppo
```

If you decide that you don't want to grant access to everyone, then don't insert the +:::::: sign. However, keep in mind that if you follow that course, you'll have to grant every single user or user groups access individually. (Note also that when you grant people access, you'll need to also add the colons.)

```
+bob::::::
+joe::::::
+carol::::::
+janet::::::
```

. . . and so on, and so on, and so on . . .

One file, two ways to look at it

I recommend that you avoid cluttering up your /etc/passwd file with NIS
and user password lines intermingled. Consider changing your password file
if it looks as follows:

```
-groucho
-harpo
-chico
-zeppo
root:EIUiuh654DSA:0:0:Root User:/:/bin/csh
averagejoe:128939JY:100:101:A.
        Joe:/usr/home/averagejoe:/bin/csh
kiko:654KLQWER:105:108: Kara 'Kiko'
        Karlson:/usr/home/kiko:/bin/csh
loki:ZXCE302822:100:132:Loki, God of
        Mischief:/usr/home/loki:/bin/csh
nobody:OOWAJHQL2:105:122:Dummy
        Account:/usr/home/nobody:/bin/sh
wally:TROI8761111:105:161: Wally the Wonder
        User:/usr/home/wally:/bin/sh
```

Or, heaven forbid, like this:

```
-zeppo
root:EIUiuh654DSA:0:0:Root User:/:/bin/csh
averagejoe:128939JY:100:101:A.
        Joe:/usr/home/averagejoe:/bin/csh
-groucho
kiko:654KLQWER:105:108: Kara 'Kiko'
        Karlson:/usr/home/kiko:/bin/csh
loki:ZXCE302822:100:132:Loki, God of
        Mischief:/usr/home/loki:/bin/csh
-harpo
-chico
nobody:OOWAJHQL2:105:122:Dummy
        Account:/usr/home/nobody:/bin/sh
wally:TROI8761111:105:161: Wally the Wonder
        User:/usr/home/wally:/bin/sh
```

Your best bet for sanity's sake — and if you ever need to edit things in a
hurry — is to leave a separate section for your NIS entries and leave a couple
lines of space between the NIS and the regular password lines.

Consider placing a comment in the no man's land between the two so you know the score.

```
root:EIUiuh654DSA:0:0:Root User:/:/bin/csh
averagejoe:128939JY:100:101:A.
         Joe:/usr/home/averagejoe:/bin/csh
kiko:654KLQWER:105:108: Kara 'Kiko'
         Karlson:/usr/home/kiko:/bin/csh
loki:ZXCE302822:100:132:Loki, God of
         Mischief:/usr/home/loki:/bin/csh
nobody:OOWAJHQL2:105:122:Dummy
         Account:/usr/home/nobody:/bin/sh
wally:TROI8761111:105:161: Wally the Wonder
         User:/usr/home/wally:/bin/sh
# The following lines are for NIS Permissioning Only.
+:::::::
-groucho
-harpo
-chico
-zeppo
```

You can also control access by user groups, using the @ sign. For example, let's say that you have two permissioning issues to deal with. First, the user group gummo is following the lead of the four users you're having problems with (groucho, harpo, chico and zeppo) so you want to restrict their access. Meanwhile, although users groucho et al are a lot of trouble, the rest of the users in their group, which is called marx are a fine bunch of upstanding users. You can edit the restrictions as follows:

```
-@gummo
-groucho
-harpo
-chico
-zeppo
+@marx:::::::
```

Additionally, you can also force changes on certain users of an NIS system. Let's say that you want the user group gummo to use the Korn shell, while you want user groucho to use the Bourne shell on your system. If your Linux network uses either of these shells as default, you don't need to set this. But for the example, let's say you run C-shell but for your own bent and twisted reasons you want to force this user and group to use other shells. Simply add the shell designation to the passwd file entry, as you would to a user's .cshrc file. The result should look something like this:

```
-@gummo/bin/ksh
-groucho/bin/sh
-harpo
-chico
-zeppo
+@marx:::::::
```

Of course, the rest of your users will still be using the C-shell by default. Incidentally, if you do end up making these changes, it's best to notify the users so they don't become concerned that their shell prompts look strangely different when they next come in to work.

The Nsswitch.conf file

The /etc/nsswitch.conf file has a sort of Simon Says quality to it. Nsswitch.conf determines the order of the lookups that are done when the NIS client requests NIS specific information. For example, if your nsswitch.conf file contains the line:

```
hosts: files nis dns
```

Then your lookup functions will first look in the /etc/hosts file local to the machine. Next, it will perform an NIS lookup and finally through the DNS (domain name service) files such as /etc/resolv.conf. If no information is found at any of the three places an error is returned.

If you lack an /etc/nsswitch.conf file, you won't be able to run NIS properly. You can download a file off the Web, or use the following one — at least for reference:

```
# /etc/nsswitch.conf
#
# An example Name Service Switch config file. This file
         should be
# sorted with the most-used services at the beginning.
#
# The entry '[NOTFOUND=return]' means that the search for
         an
# entry should stop if the search in the previous entry
         turned
# up nothing. Note that if the search failed due to some
         other reason
# (like no NIS server responding) then the search continues
         with the
# next entry.
#
# Legal entries are:
#
#       nisplus              Use NIS+ (NIS version 3)
#       nis                  Use NIS (NIS version 2),
         also called YP
#       dns                  Use DNS (Domain Name
         Service)
#       files                Use the local files
#       db                   Use the /var/db databases
```

```
#        [NOTFOUND=return]          Stop searching if not found
         so far
#
passwd:       compat
group:        compat
# For libc5, you must use shadow: files nis
shadow:       compat
passwd_compat: nis
group_compat: nis
shadow_compat: nis
hosts:        files nis dns
services:     nis [NOTFOUND=return] files
networks:     nis [NOTFOUND=return] files
protocols:    nis [NOTFOUND=return] files
rpc:          nis [NOTFOUND=return] files
ethers:       nis [NOTFOUND=return] files
netmasks:     nis [NOTFOUND=return] files
netgroup:     nis
bootparams:   nis [NOTFOUND=return] files
publickey:    nis [NOTFOUND=return] files
automount:    files
aliases:      nis [NOTFOUND=return] files
```

Setting Up an NIS Master Server

Setting up an NIS server is actually slightly easier. To begin with, do a process search and make sure the portmapper is running. (If it isn't, follow the same instructions above to kick it off.) Once you've determined that portmapper is on the job, edit the file /var/yp/Makefile to add, change, or remove the ypmaps that you'll be using on your system.

Next, you'll want to start the server process, ypserv. You can execute this from the command line as root:

```
#rpcinfo -u localhost ypserv
```

As a result, you should get a standard output similar to:

```
# program 100004 version 1 ready and waiting
```

There are two command options for the yp server process that you'll find useful at one time or another. They are:

Table 16-2	ypserv Command Options
Command Option	*What It Does*
-d	This is the most useful command option to run if you're able to get the NIS processes to function, but are still having problems. The -d option causes the server to run in debugging mode. In debug mode, the server does not background itself and prints extra status messages directly to the screen for each request that it monitors.
-p	This option specifies the port that ypserv will bind itself to. This streamlines network traffic and makes it possible to have a router filter packets to these specific ports so that access to the NIS server from hosts on the Internet can be restricted.

Next, you'll generate the NIS ypmaps, the database of the NIS world. All yp maps are built from scratch, either from the information you've entered, or from the ASCII data base files in /etc. In order to build these maps, you'll need the ypinit command. ypinit has only two options, but they're important ones:

Table 16-3	ypinit Command Options
Command Option	*What It Does*
-m	Set up your machine as the master server!
-s *<master server>*	Set up a slave server with the maps from the master server. Keep in mind that you'll have to also put in the name of the master server, so it knows where to get the master's maps.

So, on the master server, run the following command from the root account.

```
#/usr/lib/yp/ypinit -m
```

You're now running the NIS system, with a master server. Remember, if you want to create slave servers, you *must* perform these steps first. A slave server without a master server to get the map files is about as useful as an open CD-ROM drive used as a cup holder.

Setting Up an NIS Slave Server

The NIS yp map database used by the slave server is set up by copying an existing one from a running server. When setting up a slave server, you must make sure that the command ypwhich works with the -m command option.

ypwhich returns the name of the NIS server that supplies the NIS services to an NIS client or slave server. When ypwhich is invoked with no arguments, it names the NIS server (slave or master) local machine has bound to. If a hostname is specified, that host is queried to find out which NIS master it is using. The command options you should be most aware of for the ypwhich command are:

Table 16-4	ypwhich Command Options
Command Option	**What It Does**
-d *<domain name>*	Specify a domain other than the default domain you're in.
-m *<master name>*	Find the master NIS server for a map. No hostname can be specified with the -m option. If the master name is omitted, ypwhich will produce a list of available maps.

If ypwhich works properly, then your slave server is set up to use NIS in the correct way and you can run the ypinit command from root to set it up:

```
#/usr/lib/yp/ypinit -s <master server name>
```

Go back to your master server and add the new slave server name to the file /var/yp/ypservers. Run the make command in the /var/yp directory to update the yp map as follows:

```
# make
```

And I bet you thought this would be difficult! That's all you'll need to do to create an NIS slave server.

Adding a New NIS Slave Server

You can add a new NIS slave server at any time.

To prevent unnecessary duplication, you shouldn't add new slave servers just whenever you feel like it. Add a new one whenever you are adding a new subnet or when you notice significant lag time between altering a map on the master server and the implementation of the change on the existing slave servers.

To begin with, make sure that the new slave server has permissions to contact the NIS master. Then, go through the checking procedures you learned about when setting up an NIS client — portmapper, et cetera.

When all that checks out, run the same command as you did for creating the original slave server:

```
% /usr/lib/yp/ypinit -s <name of master server>
```

Finally, on the master server, add the new slave server name to the file /var/yp/ypservers and run the make command as before in /var/yp to update the map.

Updating Yp Maps with yppush

As your Linux network grows, you'll find that you'll be altering the /etc/passwd and /etc/hosts files more and more often. Since you're running NIS, you'll have to make sure that these alterations get passed on to the various clients and slave servers so that all the data is synchronized.

The most useful command to keep things in sync is yppush, which yppush copies updated NIS yp maps from the master server to all slave servers in a given NIS domain. yppush reads the NIS map ypservers in the domain to determine the names of the slave servers. Use yppush as follows when you're the root account:

```
# /usr/sbin/yppush
```

Yppush has many command options you can specify, but for most administration purposes, you'll need to reference only two:

Table 16-5	yppush Command Options
Command Option	*What It Does*
-d <domain name>	Specifies a particular domain to 'push' the maps out to. The NIS domain of the local system is used by default. You can find out what other domains you have available by using the domainname command referenced earlier in this chapter.
-t <time in seconds>	The timeout controls how long yppush will wait for a response from a slave server before sending a map transfer request to the next slave server in the list. By default, yppush will wait 90 seconds. For big maps, this is not long enough. (Incidentally, this is a good way to tell when you need to add more master or slave NIS servers!)

If you need to update a map, you can also run `make` in the `/var/yp` directory on the NIS master. This will update a map if the source file is newer, and push the files to the slave servers. However, the `/var/yp/Makefile` does not invoke `yppush` by default. To use this method, `vi` the Makefile and comment out the following line:

```
NOPUSH="True"
```

Whichever method you use, don't use `ypinit` to update your maps. I don't know where or when the rumor started that this was suitable to update yp maps. But don't believe it unless you enjoy creating administration problems for yourself.

The ypcat's Meow

The `ypcat` command is not, as some Linux administrators will tell you on April 1, a rare breed of feline that eats ASCII text cat food. In fact, `ypcat` is a very useful command in the NIS world, both for verifying that your NIS installation is working properly, and for querying your network for hostnames. Hence its name, which is short for `yp catalog`.

`ypcat` is where you let your "fingers do the walking" through your own electronic phone book. For example, if you want to reassure yourself that the proper files are being exported by NIS, use a command like the following: (And for once, you don't have to be root!)

```
% ypcat passwd
```

Running this will give you the entire contents of your NIS-exported `/etc/passwd` file. You can also use this NIS built-in command to locate hosts on your network, which is very useful when you're a new administrator or if you take care of a gazillion Linux machines.

Gazillion is a technical term meaning "a whole bunch." It's interchangeable with the terms *whole-lotta, mucho grande,* and *jumbo pack*.

The most common use of `ypcat` is to locate hosts. These hosts can be looked up either by host name or by the machine's IP address. For example, let's say you wanted to find out if you have a machine that's rumored to be hidden on your network, called `nessie`. Running the following `ypcat` command will give you `nessie` (if it exists) and `nessie`'s IP address:

Get pushy with yppush

One very good use of the cron daemon (see Chapter 4 for review) might be to edit root's crontab settings on the master server as follows:

```
00    1    *    *    sun
    /usr/sbin/yppush
```

In case you were too busy to go back and review Chapter 4, this commands the master server to push out its ypmaps every Sunday night at midnight. This will help ensure that your NIS yp maps are kept synchronized, even if a slave server was down at the time the update was done on the master server.

```
Linuxbox% ypcat hosts | grep nessie
Linuxbox% nessie 133.102.67.18
```

Here, the ypcat command is directed to search through the hosts files kept by the local NIS server. Alternatively, you can use ypcat to search via the IP address, which is also very useful. Let's say you get an urgent message saying that host 133.102.67.18 is overloading the network with TCP traffic. Since you don't memorize these machines by numbers, you run the following to get the host name:

```
Linuxbox% ypcat hosts | grep 133.102.67.18
Linuxbox% nessie 133.102.67.18
```

Remember, if you're running on a machine that is bound to a slave server that hasn't had the latest ypmaps pushed out to it yet, you'll get different results. That's why as an administrator, you can use the ypcat utility to test whether information has been properly synched up.

Chapter 17

Master of the Linux Domain: DNS

*1*n this chapter, you learn about another network organizer extraordinaire, *DNS* — or *Domain Name Server*. DNS is what many Linux administrators call a *black box* kind of program. Unfortunately, that doesn't mean it's well-nigh indestructible, like the black box on an airliner. Instead, it means DNS is a mysterious, hard-to-understand utility.

This bemusement is understandable; DNS *is* pretty strange in spots. Although we can't go into complete detail on all the functions and quirks of DNS — whole tomes are devoted to DNS in the Linux world — this chapter can help you master the basics.

DNS adds organization to your network by helping you resolve those four-bit IP addresses into recognizable, plain-English hostnames. This makes it a completely different program from NIS (dissected in detail in Chapter 16). Part of the confusion surrounding DNS is that it uses many components and terms that are uncannily similar to those in NIS. The facts are:

✔ DNS and NIS both use the terms domain. DNS domains are not inter-changeable with NIS domains. For this reason, I suggest that you keep the domains supplied with different names to distinguish the two.

✔ DNS cannot be invoked, configured, tuned up, or have its oil changed by anyone except the root account. If a user tells you that they're running DNS on their own system, they're sadly mistaken.

✔ Finally, although DNS can be a dense subject, it's *not* pronounced "dense" — it's pronounced "dee-enn-*ess*." (Granted, anyone who tells you differently may *be* dense . . . .)

Black Box of the Linux Networking Universe: DNS

DNS stands for the Domain Name System, and is a regular feature of the Linux landscape on large Linux networks. But, you may wonder, if NIS and NFS are more common on small-to-medium-size systems, why is DNS so popular on the economy-pack-size networks?

The answer provides the key to the origins of DNS. First off, all Linux systems put the host machines' names and addresses in /etc/hosts. When you add, remove, or change a hostname, you (or whoever you assign as the hapless administrator) has to update the /etc/hosts files on every machine on your network. Try this on more than a dozen machines and you'll appreciate why early Linux administrators cried out for a better way.

A better way came from Sun Microsystems: a system that made switching machine names around as easy as reading a phone book. This system, originally known as the Yellow Pages, ran afoul of British legal action and was renamed NIS. As duly recounted in Chapter 16, NIS stores information such as hostnames and passwords in a series of simple databases, called ypmaps. This information is kept on a central *master server* and assorted *slave servers* (from which the clients may retrieve it as needed).

On still bigger networks — we're talking the early Internet here — address information was stored in a centrally administered file called HOSTS.TXT. The NIC (or Network Information Center) maintained the file, which had to be downloaded and installed by all participating sites.

As the network grew, this cumbersome scheme began to fall apart. The load on the servers that distributed the information grew out of control. Contributing to the problem was the fact that *all* names had to be registered with the NIC; part of the NIC's mission in life was to ensure that early machine names weren't duplicated (which could cause some serious network malfunctions). DNS, invented by Paul Mockapetris in the mid-1980s, attempted to solve these problems.

DNS host resolution — being kind to humans

DNS provides two major services on a given Linux network. The first, lesser-known function is to convert machine names to IP addresses and vice versa. This DNS process is also called hostname resolution by those Linux folk in the know. You can think of hostname resolution as an association the kindly machine makes for us poor humans, connecting a machine name (like `ftp.megastuff.net`) with an equivalent numeric code that Linux boxes prefer to use (such as `123.45.67.89`).

DNS domains: the most recognizable feature of the Internet

The second big function that DNS provides is the organization of hostnames in a hierarchy of domains. The simplest kind of domain is a collection of Linux hosts that are related, because taken as a whole the machines form a typical Linux network. This is the kind of relationship that also defines an NIS network.

The free-thinking program DNS isnt so restricted with its definition of a domain, which is why we as an Internet-savvy world are more familiar with the most visible portion of DNS, the domain name grouping. With DNS, hosts can be grouped together because they all belong to a certain organization like a university, company, or state/federal government. The domain could be created because the hosts are in the same geographical area.

The largest groupings of these domains are called *top-level domains*, which you've seen if you've ever ventured within eyeshot of the World Wide Web. Some top-level domain names you see most frequently include those listed in Table 17-1.

Table 17-1	Top-Level Domains
Domain Name	*What It Signifies*
com	You're looking at a domain belonging to a commercial organization or company. Don't just sit there, buy something!
edu	Educational institutions like universities, colleges, vocational schools, and kindergartens. (I hear they do their Java scripting after naptime.)
gov	U.S. government institutions at either the federal or state level. The gov name is used exclusively in the United States.
mil	U.S. military institutions. The mil designation is also used exclusively in the United States.

(continued)

Table 17-1 *(continued)*

Domain Name	What It Signifies
net	Gateways, administrative hosts, and ISPs (Internet Service Providers) on a given network.
org	Noncommercial organizations. Unlike the com domains, you'll probably find less merchandise on sale here — but you *are* likely to find people with similar interests who are drawn to what the org is dedicated to.

Farther abroad, each country generally uses a top-level domain of its own, named after its two-letter country code. England, for instance, uses the uk domain, fr is used by France, and ca by Canada. Below the top-level domain, each country's NIC organizes smaller domains in a manner similar to the United States in only one respect: They try to avoid duplication within that domain. Therefore, while you'll never see

```
example.site.uk
example.site.uk
```

You might see two legitimately named sites, each with the same name, but under a different country's domain.

```
example.site.uk
example.site.us
```

DNS allows you to act like your own country and let you subdivide your top-level domain into several subdomains. For example, consider the problem faced in Chapter 16 with NIS domains, in which you, the courageous administrator, have to administer the Physics, Marine Biology, and Music Departments. Your school is proudly named Wossamatta University, so you've called your domain wossamatta.edu. You then create three subdomains or zones and name them in accordance to their function: physics, marinebio, and music.

Name lookups with DNS

Splitting up networks into domain and zones may seem chaotic to the novice Linux administrator. Well, on some levels it is! DNS manages to keep order, however; like NIS, it acts as a simple distributed database. DNS supplements its work by connecting to *name servers* (which, like the NIS slave servers are dedicated to supplying information on a given domain or set of domains).

Each zone (or *subdomain*) has at least one name server that holds information on hosts in that zone. You can access this information via the `nslookup` command. `nslookup` is used to query domain name servers on the Internet. `nslookup` has two modes: interactive and noninteractive. Interactive mode allows the user to query name servers for information about various hosts and domains or to print a list of hosts in a domain.

Noninteractive mode is used to print just the name and requested information for a host or domain. Using the `wossamatta.edu` example, your command and output may look like this:

```
# nslookup
Default Server:  localhost
Address:  127.0.0.1
```

Table 17-2 lists some of the most important command options you can use with `nslookup`.

Table 17-2	nslookup Command Options
Command Option	*What It Does*
`all`	Prints the current values of the frequently-used options to set. Information about the current default server and host is also printed.
`domain`	Changes the default domain name to a specified name. The domain search list contains the parents of the default domain if it has at least two components in its name.
`port`	Changes the default TCP/UDP name server port to a specific port value — the system default is 53.
`retry`	Sets the number of times that `nslookup` will try to reach a name server. When a reply to a request is not received within a certain amount of time, the timeout period is doubled and the request is re-sent. The default is four seconds.
`timeout`	Change the initial timeout interval for waiting for a reply to number seconds. Each retry doubles the timeout period.

`nslookup`'s real strength is as a diagnostic tool for your DNS domain. If the lookup request was not successful, an error message is printed. In each case, the error gives you a valuable clue as to what may be wrong with your domain.

✔ **Timed out** — The server did not respond to a request after a certain amount of time and a certain number of retries.

✔ **No response from server** — No name server is running on the server machine.

✔ **No records** — The server does not have resource records of the current query type for the host, although the hostname is valid. The query type is specified with the `set querytype` command.

✔ **Non-existent domain** — The host or domain name does not exist.

✔ **Connection refused** — or **Network is unreachable** — The connection to the name server could not be made at the current time. This error most commonly occurs with ls and finger requests.

✔ **Server failure** — The name server found an internal inconsistency in its database and could not return a valid answer.

✔ **Format error** — The name server found that the request packet was not in the proper format. It may indicate an error in `nslookup`.

The `nslookup` command works because the DNS name servers hold all information on hosts within a domain. To provide accurate data within the subdomains, the master and name servers must be fairly well synchronized. As with NIS, the primary server (which loads its zone information from data files) must update the secondary servers by transferring subdomain information to them at regular intervals.

The main reason to have several name servers is to eliminate a single point of system failure. Another reason is to distribute workload on extremely busy networks. DNS, like NIS, has a certain amount of fault tolerance; if you lose one DNS server, the hosts will connect to the next one up the chain of DNS servers.

A time to live, a time to die . . .

When you combine the updates, `nslookups`, and client requests, it looks like a lot of network traffic is being generated for just looking up hostnames and IP addresses. However, compared to the amount of data that was being transferred in the HOSTS.TXT days, the number of packets going to and fro is pretty small.

To improve server response time, DNS name servers store the information they've obtained in a local cache. The next time someone wants to look up the address of a host in the local domain, the name server simply goes to the local domain's name server directly.

The name server doesn't keep this information in its cache forever. (Imagine the disk-space headaches you'd have after a few days!) Instead, the DNS server discards it after a set period. This expiration interval is called *time to live*, or *TTL*. Each DNS database is assigned such a TTL, which can be set manually.

The Daemon with No Name (d)

In the Linux world, the Internet-domain name-server daemon resides in the `/usr/sbin` directory; it's a program called `named`. If you don't supply command options to `named`, it will read its default configuration file, which is kept in the `/etc/named.conf` file. When the `named` daemon has been fully initialized, it starts responding to initial incoming information, and then begins listening for user queries.

Any command option you specify when you activate `named` from the command line will override what `named` has been configured for in the `/etc/named.conf` file.

Unlike most daemons (which are mostly handled automatically at system startup), you have more control over how you want to run the name daemon. Like the `nslookup` utility, the output produced by `named`, which you can view in the `/var/adm/messages` file (or `/var/log/messages`), is very useful for debugging and tracking down potential network problems. Your most useful command options are listed in Table 17-3.

Table 17-3	Named Command Options
Command Option	**What It Does**
`-b` *<filename>*	Use an alternate configuration file instead of the standard `/etc/named.conf`. This argument is overridden by any configuration file which is specified at the end of the command line.
`-c` *<filename>*	Ditto.
`-d`	Sets the debugging level. The debug level is a number determining the level of messages printed.
`-p` *<number>*	Use a specified remote port number to send queries.
`-r`	Turns recursion off in the server. Responses to queries come only from local DNS zones. The default is to use recursion, but this can be useful to zero in on an error that you think is in the local domain zone.

Starting the name daemon can be a little tricky. If you're using a dial-up connection, you have to dial up and connect, or the name daemon doesn't have much to do. One way to kick off the `named` is to type **ndc start**, without any command options, and press Enter. If that doesn't work on your system, try **/usr/sbin/ndc start**. If you **vi** either the `/var/adm/messages` file or the `var/log/messages` file, you should see something like this:

```
Dec 21 15:30:17 linuxbox named[834]: starting.named 8.1.1 Sat
        Dec 14
Dec 21 15:30:17 linuxbox named[834]: cache zone "" (IN)
        loaded (serial 0)
Dec 21 15:30:17 linuxbox named[834]: master zone
        "0.0.127.arpa"
(IN) loaded (serial 1)
Dec 21 15:30:17 linuxbox named[834]: listening
        [127.0.0.1].53 (lo)
Dec 21 15:30:17 linuxbox named[834]: Forwarding source
        address is [0.0.0.0].1040
Dec 21 15:30:17 linuxbox named[6092]: Ready to answer
        queries.
```

If there are any messages about errors, do a process search and grep for named, use a kill command on the process ID number, and then go back to check the /etc/named.conf file for stray characters or other problems. The procedure for doing this would look similar to the following:

```
Linuxbox% ps -aef | grep named
<OUTPUT FROM MY MACHINE>
Linuxbox% kill <PID>
Linuxbox% cd /etc
Linuxbox% vi named.conf
```

When you have named running, start the nslookup utility to examine your handiwork. If you get a result like the following, you're in business!

```
Linuxbox% nslookup
Default Server: localhost
Address: 127.0.0.1
```

Try querying a machine that's either close to your network or another machine on your network. For example, let's try a DNS query to the machine dense.test.edu. If all is working properly, you should get back a result like the following:

```
> dense.test.edu
Server: localhost
Address: 127.0.0.1
Name: dense.test.edu
Address: 160.101.24.2
```

The DNS caching operation in action

nslookup performed the querying task by using the name daemon to look for the machine dense.test.edu. The name daemon, in turn, pulled the information in from the /etc/resolv.conf file on one of the name-server machines.

New resolve in the /etc/resolv.conf file

The *resolver* is a set of routines in the C library that provides access to the Internet Domain Name System. You don't have to do anything to install or invoke it. However, the /etc/resolv.conf file is a valuable resource. The resolver's configuration file contains the list of domains to be read by the resolver routines when a process like nslookup invokes the routines for the first time. The file is designed to be legible to most human beings (which you can't really say about a lot of other Linux files).

Depending on how many domains you listed in your /etc/resolv.conf file, it might take a few seconds for an answer to be returned. (For really big networks, it might take up to *half a minute* during peak times!)

If you make the same request a second time, you'll get an answer much more quickly. However, if you look at the result, you'll see that it's just slightly different:

```
> dense.test.edu
Server:   localhost
Address:  127.0.0.1
Non-authoritative answer:
Name:     dense.test.edu
Address:  160.101.24.50
```

The Non-authoritative answer: response on the second request is, in effect, a red flag; it tells you that the name daemon is pulling the information out of the DNS information cache — but that cached information might be out of date.

Apparently data was a lot like French bread in the old days — without the preservatives. Hence, a trade secret: Real Linux gurus never use the phrase "out of date" to describe data. The proper, yeasty description is to call the data *stale*.

This red-flag response is a very useful function of the DNS utilities: You're notified that there's a possibility your data is not quote accurate; you also get an immediate indication that your cache is functioning. Compared to a lot of Linux utilities, this treatment is equivalent to getting the company car with the power windows, power brakes, power door locks, and 12-CD-changer sound system: Very plush.

A Simple DNS Domain and How to Duplicate It

When starting out on something like setting up an NIS or DNS domain, do some basic network tests. Make sure you can ping, telnet, and successfully make all kinds of connections to the net. One specific test you should perform is telneting to IP address 127.0.0.1 and get your own machine. Make sure you have the following files, and that they are not only readable/writable by you as `root`, but also free of extra or corrupt characters:

- ✔ `/etc/nsswitch.conf` (`/etc/host.conf` will also do)
- ✔ `/etc/resolv.conf`
- ✔ `/etc/hosts`

Let's see how a name server operates, using the name from our earlier example: dense.test.edu. From this example, you can duplicate the creation of the defined DNS domain `arpnet`, and then define a couple of machines under it.

Keep in mind that DNS, unlike most of Linux, is *not* case-sensitive! For example, DNS sees no difference between `dense.test.edu` and `Dense.TEST.EdU`.

Look for a paragraph of text in `named.conf` that's similar to this one:

```
zone "0.0.127.arpa" {
        type master;
        file "density/127.0.0";
};
```

This stanza is important because it tells you how the domain will be defined. Here, the zone is set as `0.0.127.arpa`. It also indicates that the configuration file set up for the appropriate master server is in a file called `density/127.0.0`. If you look into this file, it will read remarkably like the following:

```
@               IN      SOA     ns.dense.test.edu.
        hostmaster.dense.test.edu. (
                               1        ; Serial
                               8H       ; Refresh
                               2H       ; Retry
                               1W       ; Expire
                               1D)      ; Minimum TTL
                      NS      ns.dense.test.edu.
        1             PTR     localhost.
```

This stanza tells DNS that the name server of the domain 0.0.127.arpa is ns.dense.test.edu. ns is a customary designation for name servers. By contrast, Web servers are usually named www.something.

The line containing SOA indicates that you're looking at the selected zone name. There should be one of those in each file. Here, it shows that the zone originates from ns.dense.test.edu.

Start your named and use nslookup to examine the domain:

```
Linuxbox% nslookup
Default Server:  localhost
Address:  127.0.0.1
> 127.0.0.1
Server:  localhost
Address:  127.0.0.1
Name:    localhost
Address:  127.0.0.1
; Zone file for dense.test.edu
;
; The full zone file
;
@       IN      SOA     ns.dense.test.edu.
            hostmaster.dense.test.edu. (
                            199802211          ; serial, todays
            date + todays serial #
                            8H                 ; refresh,
            seconds
                            2H                 ; retry, seconds
                            1W                 ; expire, seconds;
                            1D )               ; minimum,
            seconds
                    TXT     "Dense.test.edu, your DNS
            consultants"
                    NS      ns                 ; Inet Address of
            name server
                    NS      ns.mail.meeto
                    MX      10 mail            ; Primary Mail
            Exchanger
                    MX      20 mail.meeto. ; Secondary Mail
            Exchanger
   localhost        A           127.0.0.1
   gw               A           192.168.196.1
                    HINFO   "BayNetworks"
                    TXT     "The router"
   ns               A           192.168.196.2
                    MX      10 mail
                    MX      20 mail.meeto.
                    HINFO   "P6" "Linux 4.5.2"
   www      CNAME   ns
   mail             A           192.168.196.4
                    MX      10 mail
                    MX      20 mail.metoo.
```

```
                    HINFO    "P6" "Linux 4.5.2"
    ftp             A        192.168.196.5
                    MX       10 mail
                    MX       20 mail.metoo.
                    HINFO    "P6" "Linux 4.5.2"
```

Remember that while you're in the `named.conf` file, *don't* put periods after the domain names. Doing so will cause the network some serious confusion, just as if you tried to pay your bills buy writing dollar amounts on checks but moved the decimal point at random intervals.

Shifting into Reverse DNS

With DNS, programs can convert the names in `dense.test.edu` to addresses that they can connect to. Now, you have to make sure that reverse DNS also works. That is, you have to make sure that the functionality of your DNS server allows programs to convert IP addresses into machine names.

This capability is actually used by lots of servers of different kinds (FTP, IRC, WWW, and others). For full access to all services on the Internet, a reverse zone is required. So let's include the following in the `named.conf` file:

```
zone "196.168.192.arpa" {
        notify no;
        type master;
        file "pz/192.168.196";
};
```

Restart the `named` daemon again. You should get something similar to the following from your `nslookup` command:

```
> 192.168.196.4
  Server:  localhost
  Address:  127.0.0.1
  Name:    mail.dense.test.edu
  Address:  192.168.196.4
  [localhost]
  $ORIGIN 196.168.192.arpa.
                      1D IN NS
          ns.dense.test.edu.
  1                   1D IN PTR
          gw.dense.test.edu.
  2                   1D IN PTR
          ns.dense.test.edu.
  3                   1D IN PTR
```

```
donald.dense.test.edu.
  4                          1D IN PTR
              mail.dense.test.edu.
  5                          1D IN PTR           ftp.dense.test.edu.
8H              ; refresh
                                  2H                    ; retry
1W              ; expiry
1D )            ; minimum
```

Setting Up a Secondary (Slave) DNS Name Server

If the primary/master server has address 127.0.0.1, then **vi** the named.conf file to include a stanza similar to the following:

```
zone "dense.test.edu" {
          type slave;
          file "sz/dense.test.edu";
          masters { 127.0.0.1; };
     };
```

Believe it or not, that's all there is to do for this particularly cryptic portion of DNS. Take off your wizard's hat and take a break.

Should You Let an ISP Run DNS for You?

Another way to ask that question: Is there an easier way to use DNS? Short answer: Yes! But you'd better put your wizard hat on.

Here's a thumbnail sketch of an area of Linux that's complicated enough to bring nightmares to all but the hardiest Linux system administrators. If you truly want to delve into this area and become a master of the occult side of Linux, then I advise you get a book that's dedicated to the subject, like O'Reilly's *DNS and BIND*, 3rd Edition, by Paul Albitz and Cricket Liu.

However, DNS should be the one area you "outsource to" (biz-speak for *fob off on*) your ISP (Internet Service Provider). Not only is it easier, it just makes more sense. As a rule of thumb, you should only consider running DNS yourself if the following three conditions exist:

✔ You run a large network of Linux machines over a very slow network link, and you have many peak traffic times during the day.

✔ You truly want to control the DNS system within your domain.

✔ You don't have a connection to the Internet!

While I'm sure some networks fall into this category today, I have yet to see one that's large enough to qualify for DNS service and *didn't* have a connection to the Internet. Perhaps that kind of arrangement was more common a few years ago, when ISPs weren't as sophisticated and the Internet wasn't as ubiquitous. These days you're better off handing this headache over to someone you're going to pay for World Wide Web access anyway — and if you can, that's one heck of a freebie.

OK, How Do I Get My Own DNS Domain on the World Wide Web?

A final question is always asked of me when I finish advocating outsourcing DNS functions to an ISP: *How can I get my own Web domain?* (This is always asked with a little gleam in the eye, as if the magic act of putting up www.yournamehere.com will somehow make people send you money.)

Again, a Web domain of your very own is a benefit you get from an ISP. Contact yours and have them either work with you or direct you to the InterNIC (a.k.a. the NIC, or the Net cops we kidded about in Chapter 3). For a fee, you'll be able to register a domain name with InterNIC.

The system is much like one from the Department of Motor Vehicles. The fee is for them to do the checking in your country's domain to see whether your proposed name has been taken or reserved.

If the name you want is taken, you're out of luck and you'll have to come up with something else that's more original. In other words, if www.fred.com is taken, you might be able to come back and get www.phred.com instead. Alternatively, you could try registering your domain name with a different country, as with www.fred.nz (New Zealand), or any other country domain where Fred is a slightly less popular moniker.

NFS, NIS, and DNS — nice plunge into pure networking, wasn't it? If you're ready to get your hands dirty again with real-world attachments to the network (the best way to get data off is to use Lava soap), then wade into the next chapter, where we talk about hooking up print servers and other such tools of network mayhem.

Chapter 18

The Linux Print Shop

*I*f I had to rate the importance of which chapters you should learn in this book, this chapter would land in the top three.

Shock! Horror! As a budding Linux administrator, you're probably wondering what happened to all the cutting-edge network stuff you were learning about in the last few chapters. Well, next to the basic administration of the Linux system (to make sure that your expensive computer equipment is worth more than a series of plastic aquarium cases), printing is the key.

Trust me on this one. Of all the problems you'll be called in to handle on a Linux network, around half will be printing-related. There is some good news buried in that statistic, however. Let's say that of one hundred problems on your Linux network, fifty involve printing. Of that fifty, about four out of five of the problems will be non-Linux-related. The printer will have suffered a paper jam, a cord will have been pulled from the wall, or someone will have put the toner cartridge in upside-down. All these problems require absolutely zero Linux knowledge, but keep in mind that you're still getting paid the same wage. So there are some compensations to the job.

Linux Universe, PostScript World

Linux can handle nine out of ten kinds of printers on the market today, partly because the technology has become more standardized in recent years, but also because Linux is a printer-friendly operating system. Essentially, if you can plug the printer into a serial or parallel port, it should be able to communicate with Linux.

Mission: Unprintable

From time to time, you may get a mission (should you choose to accept it) that requires you to get a printer working with Linux that absolutely refuses to cooperate. If you do get one of these choices, immediately opt for sick leave or exile. Linux is very good about working with most printers, but there are several that will cause you untold grief and heartache.

Some of the older NEC printers cause an agonizing problem when they steadfastly refuse to print out at any resolution sharper than 300 dpi. In case you didn't know, *dpi* stands for *dots per inch,* a standard benchmark for how fine the printing is. 300 dpi is better than having a third-grader drop crayons on a piece of paper on the floor, but not by much. You're shooting for 600 dpi and better.

By far the biggest headaches can be from the nonstandard generic printers that many vendors throw in with a network purchase. These are sometimes called "Windows" printers or "Winprinters," because the vendor will usually provide a Windows-only printer driver and happily sell only to Windows users. The worst part is that some or all of the printer's setup procedures and basic mechanisms aren't documented (at least in a language that vaguely reads like English).

About the only way to get one of these Winprinters going is to search the Web for similarly afflicted souls. With luck, one of these folks is also a programmer on the side, and has written a driver for your uncooperative printer. If you find someone with this skill set, beg, borrow, or steal a copy of the driver from him or her. Then be aware that this person has very likely saved your life, or at least reduced your stress level. Consider sending a large box of chocolate-chip cookies. At least.

By default, your best choice is to buy a printer with native PostScript support. Unless you're running a really esoteric version of the Linux kernel, you'll be able to produce legible output in PostScript. The only downside to a PostScript-friendly world is that PostScript was developed for laser printers, and it may well remain in that realm. For networks that support inkjet or (poor you) dot-matrix printers, PostScript support is less than abundant and may be a costly option on your vendor contract (in the neighborhood of $100 to $150 per printer).

PostScript became the *de facto* Linux standard because it's open (as with Linux, anyone could write stuff in it), and very "device-independent" — which means that PostScript output will look roughly the same if you print from a vector screen, a fax machine, or almost any printer mechanism.

Identifying the old dot-matrix monster

If you have dot-matrix printers on your network, you'll be better off if you can phase them out. These old dinosaurs break down more often and cause more Linux network problems than newer printers — especially whenever you do a Linux upgrade. The drivers that run them went out of style with Nehru jackets and muumuus.

You have a dot-matrix printer if it exhibits any one of the following traits:

- ✔ The printer makes an extremely annoying chatter-chatter sound instead of a laser's steady hum or whine. That's because it's slugging away at the paper to make letters (the *impact printer* principle).

- ✔ The printer comes with a dial on the side to move paper back and forth through the printer's print area.

- ✔ Your printer's paper has holes on the sides; after printing, you have to peel the perforated edges off both sides of the page.

Note that there are some exceptions to the rule: Many invoice and payroll systems still have dot-matrix printers that are admirably suited to their task. As a general rule, if the matrix printer uses special paper (such as carbon) to make several layers of copies at once, then you're better off leaving it alone.

Ghostscripting for ghostwriters and more

An alternative to springing for PostScript printer is to use a printer that works with the PostScript interpreter program Ghostscript. Because Ghostscript is freely available, yet never really found a home with a vendor, many of the available copies that come with Linux are somewhat out of date.

Due to the lack of a true vendor (hence a lack of a clear "latest version"), your best bet is to get your Web surfboard out of storage and get looking for a copy on the Web off a Linux hacker's Web site. Keep in mind that although Ghostscript will come with installation instructions and a myriad of tips, it is free. And you may very well get what you pay for. So if you can't convince your superiors (or yourself, if you're on a budget) to get a PostScript printer, the watchword should always be *caveat emptor* (buyer beware).

How the Linux Printing System Works

The driving force behind the entire print process is the Line Printer Daemon, also known as lpd. This complex program bears more similarity to such semiintelligent program systems as NIS and NFS than it does to the one-shot, one-function daemons like `cron` or `telnet`.

As `root`, you have the power to send files directly to the printing device, using the `cat` command. `cat` is short for *concatenate* (ah, whoever invented that one had a sense of humor) and simply reads your entire file out to the screen, another file, or a device on your system. Here, the `cat` command is harnessed to send a file — in this example, the file `hairball.txt` — to the default print device, `/dev/lp`.

```
#su
Password: ******
# cat hairball.txt > /dev/lp
```

Only users with `root` privileges should be allowed to access the files that directly operate the printer, so don't start using the `chown` command indiscriminately. If you simply award those rights to all your users and call it a day's work, you've got a potential security problem. Fortunately, commands such as `lpr`, `lprm`, and `lpq` were created to get around the problem. Your users will be using a command called `lpr` to print their files.

In a nutshell, when the system boots, `lpd` is run. Lpd scans the `/etc/printcap` file to find out which printers it will be managing spools for. Then, when a user makes a print request, the `lpr` command takes care of all the initial work needed to print the file. Lpr then hands control over to the line printing daemon (`lpd`). The line printing daemon then tells the printer how to print the file.

Printing Configuration Made Easy

Unless you have a fetish for hard, possibly frustrating work, you should accept that the length of human life is finite and use the easy method of Linux printing. In any of the Linux versions sold through vendors (Red Hat, Caldera, and Slackware come to mind), you'll also get a GUI-style print-configuration tool. For example, here's what you'd do when working with the Red Hat Linux `printtool` program:

1. **Become `root`.**

2. **Enter the following `xhost` command to make sure you'll be able to open the `printtool` window on your system:**

```
xhost +
```

3. **Set your environmental display variable as follows:**

```
setenv DISPLAY :0.0
```

4. **Start up Red Hat's utility, `printtool`, which gives you the rest of the program in GUI format.**

5. **Click Add, and click OK to select a local printer.**

6. **Enter the printer's device name, which is usually** `/dev/lp1` **or** `/dev/lp0`.

   You should also fill in the input filter by selecting a printer type, resolution, and paper size, which you should know by looking at the labels on your printer and the stacks of printer paper you're using.

7. **Restart the Line Printer Daemon.**

Of course, each print tool is slightly different, but as a species they're so easy to use that it's not worth taking up much space in a ...*For Dummies* book. (Even I get bored just telling you to point and click!) Of course, you'll still probably want to read along to see what your machine is doing behind the scenes for you. Or perhaps you can look at how much work you've saved by *not* using the manual configuration (coming up next, you lucky person), and have a nice laugh while you kick back in your lawn chair and enjoy your margarita.

Printing Configuration Made Not-So-Easy

The first step in setting up your Linux print system is to add a print queue that `lpd` can read. To do this, you must add an entry in `/etc/printcap`, and make a new `spool` directory under `/var/spool/lpd`.

Entries in `/etc/printcap` can looks pretty cryptic. Here's an example that defines a spool called `lp`, `dj`, or `deskjet`, prints to device `/dev/lp1`, and spools print jobs in the `/var/spool/lpd/dj` directory.

```
# LOCAL djet500
lp|dj|deskjet:\
        :sd=/var/spool/lpd/dj:\
        :mx#0:\
        :lp=/dev/lp0:\
        :sh:
```

The `man` page for `printcap` will give you a lengthy list of the different types of add-ons you can use to customize the `printcap` file for whichever printers you're using.

Next, enter in the names of the hosts that you want to have access to your network printers in the `/etc/hosts.lpd` file. Once this is done, you can either kick `lpd` off from the command line or just restart your system. The vast majority of Linux machines will either already have lpd running, or it will be automatically started once the /etc/printcap and /etc/hosts.lpd files have been edited.

For the truly paranoid, you can check which permissions are set on the important files. They should be set up with the following permissions:

```
-r-sr-sr-x    1 root     lp       /usr/bin/lpr*
-r-sr-sr-x    1 root     lp       /usr/bin/lprm*
-rwxr-r—      1 root     root     /usr/sbin/lpd*
-r-xr-sr-x    1 root     lp       /usr/sbin/lpc*
drwxrwxr-x    4 root     lp       /var/spool/lpd/
drwxr-xr-x    2 root     lp       /var/spool/lpd/lp/
```

If things aren't set up to your liking, become root, and then chmod the ones that aren't up to snuff with the rest. (For a review of chmod, see Chapter 3.)

Executing Print Jobs

When lpr is executed, it first copies the specified file to a directory called the spool directory where the file remains until the line printer daemon gets around to printing it. Once lpd is told there's a file to print, it creates a copy of itself (which techie types are more apt to call *spawning*). This newborn lpd will print the file while the original copy waits for more requests.

The danger of free spawning

Spawning, that most organic process, is actually among the more common errors that crop up with the Line Printer daemon. Sometimes the newly spawned lpds won't gracefully die after fulfilling their Purpose In Life, which is to get a file printed.

These spare lpds hang around in the Linux ether like delinquent teenagers, soaking up resources without doing much of anything. If you notice slow-downs or freezes in your print jobs, always run a process search for lpds; you may find a few have taken up residence on your computer. Banish these processes with a kill -9 command.

The syntax of lpr itself is pretty simple:

```
Linuxbox% $ lpr [ options ] [ filename ]
```

If a filename isn't specified, lpr expects input to come from standard input, such as the keyboard. The lpr command accepts several command-line arguments that allow any user, not just an administrator, to control how it works. Some of the more useful command options include those in Table 18-1.

Table 18-1	lpr Command Options
Command Option	*What It Does*
#<*number*>	Specifies the number of copies lpd should print.
-h	Suppresses printing of the header, or *burst page*, thereby saving a sheet of paper. Great for the budding Linux environmentalists out there!
-P<P*printer*>	Specifies which printer to use. Note that there is no space between the -P and the name of the printer! So, to print to printer closeshave, you'd use: lpr -Pcloseshave
-s	This creates a symbolic link instead of copying the file to lpd's print-spool directory, which can be useful when you're printing large files.

Let's say that you want to print file hairball.txt from something other than cat. (Do gerbils get hairballs? Never mind.) This following example will add the file to the spool directory for the printer named closeshave. The line printer daemon would then print out two copies of the file:

```
Linuxbox# lpr -#2 -Pcloseshave hairball.txt
```

Controlling, Checking, and Managing the Print Queue

When you have multiple print requests, Linux stores each request in a sort of delivery room, where each line printer daemon patiently waits its turn to get the job done and expire. This storage process is called *spooling,* probably after the early technique of spooling rolls of printer paper on large metal or plastic spindles. The electronic "spool" itself is actually called a *print queue* ("queue" is the Queen's English for "stand in line" or "a line to stand in"). Your print jobs are queued up as they wait patiently to be sprayed, pressed, or burnt into the waiting page of paper. (Talk about a stiff upper lip. . . .)

At times, you'll want to view the print queue — for example, if you need to delete waiting jobs to free up processing power, or move a critical document ahead of the plethora blocking the way. In either case, being able to see and manipulate the print queue comes in very handy.

If you want to view the contents of the print queue, use the lpq command to examine the spooling area and report the status of specified print jobs. When you issue lpq from the command line, the default setting returns the current contents of the default printer's queue. Here's what a sample return from lpq may look like.

```
Linuxbox% lpq
lp is ready and printing
Rank      Owner           Job        Files
          Total Size
12   wally               active     wonderuser.txt
          45768 bytes
```

Two case-sensitive lpq command options should be part of your print-monitoring repertoire; Table 18-2 describes them.

Table 18-2	lpq Command Options
Command Option	**What It Does**
-P	Specifies a particular printer's print queue. Otherwise the default line printer's queue is the one checked.
-l	Prints out information about each of the files comprising the job entry. By default, only as much information as will fit on one line is displayed.

Let's say that your users tell you that printer gutenberg is not printing out files. You use lpq on the printer gutenberg and get the following:

```
Linuxbox% lpq -P gutenberg
lp is ready and printing
Rank      Owner           Job        Files
          Total Size
12   wally               active     wonderuser.txt
          45768 bytes
13   laura               waiting    thesis.txt
          45768 bytes
14   mac                 waiting    anotherthesis.txt
          45768 bytes
15   joyce               waiting    important.txt
          45768 bytes
16   pat                 waiting    deadline.txt
          45768 bytes
17   steve               waiting    longwait.txt
          45768 bytes
18   mark                waiting    longerwait.txt
          45768 bytes
```

Since all the jobs are waiting for user wally's to finish, then wally's job is the one holding up the print queue. Further checks show that the printer has enough paper and toner, that wally's file is not large — and what's more, `wally`'s job isn't printing, either. So most likely the `lpd` process taking care of `wally`'s job is ailing badly. Your best bet is to delete `wally`'s print job, let the rest of the queue finish, and then have `wally` reprint his job.

To cancel `wally`'s printing, use the command `lprm` to remove the job from a printer's spool queue. For security purposes, the print-spooling directory is normally shielded from user interference. However, you don't have to be `root` to run `lprm`. So long as the user owns the print job, `lprm` is normally the only method by which a user can delete that job.

Let's say that user `wally` decides to `kill` his print job. He can do that simply by running this command:

```
Wally_on_Linuxbox: lprm -
```

Normally, our friend Wally would have to use the `-P` option, specifying a printer, or include a job number so that `lprm` knows which job to delete. However, Wally has decided to use a more blanket-style `lprm` command; he has only one job running in any case. The `-` command option cancels *all* print jobs owned by the user who issued the command.

You have a potential overkill problem brewing here. If you run `lprm  -` as superuser, you *can* empty the entire spool queue without meaning to. Of course, that might sometimes work in your favor, but keep in mind that this command acts more like a shotgun than like an aimed rifle.

How to print to a printer over the network

One of `lpd`'s handiest features is that it supports printing over the network to printers that are physically connected to a different machine. One of your best choices is to use the `rlpr` utility to send a print job directly to a queue on a remote machine. When you use `rlpr`, you won't have to go through the hassle of configuring `lpd` to handle it.

- ✔ Unlike `lpr`, `rlpr` does not require that the remote printers be explicitly known to the machine you wish to print from. This approach is considerably more flexible than the plain-vanilla version of the print daemon `lpr`.

- ✔ `rlpr` can filter just as well as the standard `lpr` so that clients executing a program on a remote machine can print to your local machine with little difficulty.

Printing from a remote Linux host (or any host that runs a UNIX OS)

Allowing a remote machine to print to your networked printer is extremely easy if the host is running Linux or any other variant of UNIX. Simply vi the /etc/hosts.equiv or /etc/hosts file and be sure to add the host's name and IP address.

If your machine has both the /etc/hosts and /etc/hosts.equiv file, then to be on the safe side, edit both of them.

Printing from a remote Windows host

To print from a Windows client to a Linux server, you'll need to go through the Samba software package, which also supports Windows-to-Linux file sharing.

Your best bet is to look for and install a printer-specific driver on your Windows machines. Relying on Windows drivers usually results in better output, particularly if you are using PostScript printers. Samba includes excellent, detailed documentation on the best way to configure Samba to adapt to specific Windows printers.

Printing from an Apple client

Here your best bet is to local a copy of a utility called Netatalk. Although Netatalk doesn't have a steady vendor at this time, even the older versions of this program should work for you. Netatalk allows you to print from Apple clients over Apple's Ethertalk utility.

When you pick up Netatalk from the Web, check out its HOWTO page for details on its setup. However, be warned: In my experience, you'll save yourself a lot of headaches if you migrate away from Apple to a more Linux-friendly operating system.

Setting Up Different Printers on Your Network

If you're connecting a Linux network to a different flavor of UNIX (such as Solaris or HP-UX), you shouldn't have a problem. These printers all use Ethernet connections, and they'll be able to take requests directly from the line printer daemon. Of course, check your printer's documentation for more specifics if you *do* run into trouble; printer-versus-network trouble is usually more easily corrected from the printer end of things.

Printing to a remote Windows printer

For Windows 95, 98, and Windows NT, again your best answer is to use Samba. With Samba, lpd can queue print jobs through Samba's smbclient program. Samba includes a script to do this called smbprint.

Of course, you should refer directly to the Samba documentation for the best way to set this up, but here's how a sample /etc/printcap file would look when configured to run an smb-enabled printer.

The /etc/printcap entry goes like this:

```
lp|remote-smbprinter:\
    :lp=/dev/null:sh:\
    :sd=/var/spool/lpd/lp:\
    :if=/usr/local/sbin/smbprint:
```

Printing to a remote Apple printer

When you print to an Apple printer, the solution is the same as connecting with an Apple host: Use Netatalk to communicate with the Ethertalk system. Once again, I have to add a disclaimer about Netatalk: I can't vouch for how well it's been kept up-to-date. If you can find it, configure your system with the HOWTO files that come with it.

How to Select Your Print Software

Linux is flexible enough to run any kind of word-processing software that UNIX uses. However, only three word processors can run directly off the Linux box with 100-percent compatibility *and* are prevalent enough to find on nearly all Linux systems. There are Adobe's Acrobat Reader, Applix's Applixware, and Corel's WordPerfect.

Applying Applix

Applix's word processor usually comes bundled as part of Applixware's Applix suite of products, which is a sort of Linux version of Microsoft Office.

The suite comes with a word processor, spreadsheet program, and network mail program, for starters.

This should be your primary choice if people on your network favor Framemaker. Applix's word processor seems able to mimic most of what Frame does. My only caveat is that Applixware comes with a license-key setup that you have to update from the vendor at certain intervals, which can be a minor pain.

Flipping for Adobe Acrobat

Adobe's Acrobat Reader software is available for all versions of Linux. To use, download it from their Web site at www.adobe.com. Again, as with all free items, I advise *caveat emptor,* but I have rarely heard of anyone being really displeased with Acrobat.

Perfect WordPerfect

Corel distributes a basic version of WordPerfect 8 free for Linux. Information on how to get this is on Corel's Web site at www.corel.com. Since the freeware version lacks certain features, Corel makes it convenient for you to purchase the full-blown version and support. Of the three kinds of Linux word processors, WordPerfect is the most adaptable, allowing you to port your WordPerfect files from a Linux box to a PC. If you want the full benefits of the package, you're going to have to spring for the full version. If your needs go beyond basic letters and memos, go ahead and purchase the entire suite.

If you're contemplating any kind of Microsoft-Word-to-Linux transfers, here's a word to the wise: Save your documents as Text Only if you want a reasonable chance at reading your Word file on a Linux environment.

Part VI
Electronic Mail, News, and Web Browsing

The 5th Wave   By Rich Tennant

"This part of the test tells us whether you're personally suited to the job of network administrator."

In this part . . .

*1*f you're familiar with how the Internet works, you'll meet some old friends in Part VI — in their UNIX form, they've been part of the Net almost forever — but here you get to see them from a whole new angle. You learn about the most common utilities in use on the typical Linux network: e-mail, newsgroups, and Web browsers. (It's déjà vu all over again!)

Electronic mail (or, as most cubicle-dwellers know it, e-mail) has become the standard mode of communication in the corporate world — making an office memo as dated as a windup wristwatch. In this part, you see how Linux considerately (and automatically) sets up default daemons to service your mail. You learn how to check on those mail daemons and resurrect them if they die unexpectedly.

You also learn the startling truth that *old can be faster* when you meet the three main mail programs that come with Linux. These are the old Berkeley `mail` program and the newer `pine` and `elm` programs. (No, I don't know why two of them are named after trees, unless it's to remind you how much paper you're saving by using e-mail.) Although these humble helpers are normally overlooked as part of the administration process, you should know each of these programs well enough to answer your users' questions and recommend one suited to their needs.

Although few know about it (yet), Netscape is enhancing the Linux side of the Force by bundling its Web-browsing program with all recent Linux installations. This combination may be the best free software to come along in years — especially considering how easily it installs. You also get a crash course in how to search the Web for additional resources (complete with hints on how to get to the sites we recommend in Part VIII of this book).

Finally, you have a look at network newsgroups — which are like a cross between the electronic bulletin boards of the PC Stone Age and the America Online chat groups common in more recent times. You explore setting up subscriptions to a select set of newsgroups that can provide access to *even more Linux information* — which should help you keep your network vital, productive, and (oh yeah) running reliably.

Chapter 19

Mail Transports and Programs

*G*o ahead, throw out your stamp collection. In this chapter, you find out how easy it is to set up and use electronic mail *(e-mail)* in the Linux environment. You also learn what to look for in case of an electronic mail outage and how to get things moving again.

You take an in-depth look at the three most common e-mail programs you can use with Linux: `mail`, `elm`, and `pine`. Although you can't restrict users from using one program over the other, you should be conversant with each of the three programs. In this manner, you can recommend to new users which programs to use, and you can answer any of the how-do-I questions that invariably accompany a new user's first encounters with any e-mail program.

The Main Piece of the E-Mail Puzzle

The current standard mail transport agent in the Linux work is the pragmatically named `sendmail` program. About ninety to ninety-five percent of all Linux networks today have some version of `sendmail` set up on their systems. You don't have to worry about installation or setup; both are done for you during the main Linux installation procedure.

The default `sendmail` program set up with the initial Linux install will be placed in the startup scripts area, `/etc/rc.d/init.d/sendmail.init`. On boot-up, this script starts up the `sendmail` daemon as follows:

```
echo -n "Starting sendmail: "
daemon sendmail -bd -q1h
echo
touch /var/local/subsys/sendmail
```

Using the `touch` command (chronicled in Chapter 3), `sendmail`'s startup script creates a directory — in effect allocating itself some space to run undisturbed by other processes. In addition, `sendmail` commandeers a portion of the `/var` directory, creating directories with the path `/var/spool/mail/<username>`. Since `sendmail` runs with `root` privileges, it automatically creates a new directory each time a new user receives an e-mail message for the very first time. The mail is then held (or *spooled*) in the directory until the `sendmail` daemon can send it to the user.

This hold time is specified by the `-q1h` command option set in the default `sendmail` setup. q1h tells the `sendmail` daemon to make a sweep though the `/var/spool/mqueue` directories once every hour to send any mail messages that may have built up over the interim. This is especially useful should a server down the line go down, preventing mail from being sent until later in the day.

The `-bd` command option is equally important; it specifies that the `sendmail` program should run as a daemon and that the daemon should run in the background. I've never heard of anyone running the `sendmail` program as anything but a daemon, so you shouldn't have to worry about running it as anything else.

And speaking of changing or altering `sendmail` in any way, shape, or form:

Don't.

Of all the programs on your Linux network that it's best not to fool with, `sendmail` is a major kahuna. A lot of thought and care went into setting up `sendmail` as a default installation with Linux. If you change it, you run the risk of destroying your system's e-mail capacity. Not worth it.

If you truly want to get into the innards of `sendmail`, then you'll need to slog through a number of very thick, very dense books. Retooling the amazingly complex `sendmail` process is outside this book's range. (Was that a sigh of relief? Can't blame you.)

Spotting and resolving sendmail daemon problems

If multiple users start complaining that the e-mail isn't working, the most likely problem is that a server on a subnet has gone down. Your next most likely suspect is a router or other kind of network connection. However, every now and again the sendmail daemon is at fault. Once you exhaust your most likely problems, take a good look at your sendmail daemons.

Verify that the sendmail daemon is running by connecting directly into the TCP port number 25, which is the default port set aside on Linux systems for mail transport. **su** to root and use the telnet command to do this:

```
# telnet localhost 25
Trying 127.0.0.1...
Connected to localhost:
Escape character is ^H
<OUTPUT APPEARS HERE>
```

If sendmail isn't running, the telnet connection hangs, gives no answer, and eventually times out. If this is the case, your best bet is to reboot (which should start the sendmail daemon) or go to the /etc/rc.d/init.d directory, locate the script that runs sendmail, and run it manually.

Of course, if sendmail is running, your next move should be to change directories to the /var directory. Check to make sure you have enough space on this directory by using the **df** command (presented in Chapter 3). If you get a result like the following, then you're out of space!

```
# cd /var
# df -k .
<OUTPUT APPEARS HERE>
```

To free up space, start going through the various directories and deleting files you don't need. (Hint: What are they doing besides taking up space?) Be sure to look in the /var/spool/mail directories. The sendmail daemon might have left the system earlier without leaving a forwarding address, allowing the unsent mail to pile up to truly disturbing proportions.

Rounding Up the Usual Suspects: Your Three E-Mail Candidates

Your basic Linux mail utilities are pine, elm, and mail. They've been included with Linux installations for quite some time. The binaries are automatically installed in the /bin directory, or /usr/local/bin. From there, the user just decides which to use. No extra work on the part of the administrator is necessary.

When a user wants to send or receive mail with appropriate utilities such as mail, elm, or pine, Linux starts the sendmail program, which takes care of the electronic connections. When you sign up for service with an ISP, they will provide you with the name of the mail server they use.

An ISP's dedicated mail servers act like a main post office in a city. It's the job of the mail server to take the e-mail address that you've put on your piece of e-mail, decode it, and send it to the right destination.

By the way, techno-wizards don't refer to old-fashioned letters as *regular mail*. Instead, because it gets to its destination so slowly compared to e-mail, it's referred to as *snail mail*.

Selecting the Best E-Mail System for Your Users

E-mail programs must always trade off between efficiency and user-friendliness. Of course, many users prefer programs that are more user-friendly, even if they're a few seconds slower in sending or fetching e-mail. To prevent users from constantly bombarding you with how-to questions and to reduce overall user frustration, it's best to take a minute and decide which e-mail program you're going to make the *de facto* standard on your Linux network.

The forest for the trees: mail, elm, and pine

In this section, we'll take a look at the three most popular e-mail programs, from least user-friendly (`mail`) to most user-friendly (`pine`). If you don't like what you see at first, skip ahead to one of the later programs.

The older, faster, and less helpful e-mail programs such as `mail` and `elm` were designed when computers were a lot slower in finishing tasks. Newer programs such as `pine` work just as well as the older programs, and although they have more bells and whistles, they're also a lot easier to figure out on your own.

Using mail

`mail` is the oldest, most primitive form of e-mail program. `mail` is automatically installed off the Linux CD-ROM. It's a very old binary that's been included in Linux installations for years. You can usually find it in `/bin` or `/usr/local/bin`, but you can execute it from anywhere. It has the advantage of speed, making it ideal for running on very old computers. It also doesn't require a GUI system such as X Window System. Another version of the mail program you may run across on a Linux platform is mailx, which behaves similarly.

Here's how you would send e-mail to hypothetical user Kara Jones, using the mail program. At the command line, enter the command **mail**, followed by Kara's e-mail address:

```
mail Karajones@anytown.com
```

Press Enter. mail responds with the Subject prompt. Type the subject of your e-mail and press Enter a second time. For example:

```
Subject: Ain't Linux cool?
```

Now type your e-mail message just as you would a regular letter. Here's what I typed:

```
Hi Kara,

I've been learning how to administer Linux on my system. I
thought it might be difficult at first, but I have a Linux
Administration For Dummies book and it's all becoming clear to
me now.
```

After you finish your letter, press Enter, type . (that's a period) on a line by itself, and then press Enter a second time. This is the way you tell mail that you've finished writing your e-mail message and you want to send it. mail puts the letters EOT (end of text) on-screen and sends your message on its way:

```
.
EOT
```

To retrieve mail using the mail program, simply enter **mail** on the command line without any arguments. mail will list information about itself, the location of your stored e-mail, and the e-mail messages you've received. mail also gives you the & prompt so you can enter more mail commands to read, save, or delete your messages.

```
mail
Mail version 5.5 : Type ? for help.
"/var/spool/mail"; 1 message 1 new
>N Karajones@anytown.com Wed Jan 10 1999 "Linux is Cool!"
&
```

To quit the mail program, type **x**. For the complete list of commands that mail uses, you can type **?** while in mail or check out Table 20-1.

Table 20-1	mail Command Options
Command Option	**What It Does**
+	Moves to the next e-mail message
-	Moves back to the previous e-mail message
?	Shows a list of mail commands
R	Replies to the sender
d	Deletes an e-mail message
h	Shows the list of e-mails
n	Goes to the next e-mail message and lists it
q	Quits and saves e-mails
r	Replies to the sender and all the e-mail's original recipients
t	Lists the current message
x	Quits without saving e-mail messages

Using elm

The elm program is the next step up in user-friendliness. The elm mail reader was developed when computers could handle more robust programs than mail. A lot of users still prefer elm over other mail programs.

The elm program is slower than mail but still faster than pine. It was the first mail program to incorporate the alias feature. It's also intuitive if you like using the vi editor.

To send or receive e-mail using elm, simply type **elm** at the command prompt. elm displays a list of commands for you to use at this point. I provide a list of those commands for your reading enjoyment in Table 20-2.

Table 20-2	elm Command Options
Command Option	*What It Does*
d	Deletes mail
u	Undeletes mail
m	Mails a message
r	Replies to a message
f	Forwards mail
q	Quits elm

elm has an additional feature your users should become more acquainted with, called *aliasing*. Suppose you have a friend you like to e-mail regularly. The only problem is that his e-mail address is on the huge side:

Delhaviland_Shushkilides@thebiggest_thebest_
websiteintheworld.com

Rather than typing this mess each time you send him an e-mail message, you can create an *alias* for him in elm, as follows:

1. **Type** elm **to start up the elm mail program.**

2. **When** elm's **main screen comes up, type** a **and the** aliases **menu appears.**

3. **Type** n **to create a new alias.**

4. **Follow** elm's **instructions. The** elm **program leads you through the process of creating a new alias by asking for the person's first and last names, e-mail address, and what you want the alias to be.**

   Keep your aliases simple but long enough so that you remember who you're sending mail to. For this example, I might use Delhav, Delshush, or Dshu.

5. **Type** r **to exit the alias menu and return to** elm's **main screen. When you're ready to end the** elm **program, type** q.

Boughing Politely to pine

Now on to pine, the friendliest mail program. The pine program was developed by the University of Washington to replace elm. Although not as fast as mail and elm, pine retains all their qualities and adds two new advantages:

- ✔ pine is very user-friendly.

- ✔ pine has no problem working with *attachments*, which are files you send to someone along with the e-mail message you've composed.

To start pine, simply type **pine** at the command line. Because pine effectively lists all its commands on the screen, I don't need to list much here. One command you should be aware of, however, is the **o** command. When in pine, if you can't find the command you're looking for, type **o** (for *other commands*); pine will display the lesser-used commands for you to go through.

Attaching a file to an e-mail message is like paper-clipping something to a letter before you send it. Your users only need to identify the file you want to attach; pine takes care of the rest:

1. **Type** pine **to start the** pine **mail program.**

2. **Compose your e-mail message. Don't forget to type the e-mail address and** Subject **line.**

3. **Move the cursor to the third line from the top of the screen, labeled** Attchmnt.

4. **Press Ctrl+J.**

   Another menu appears, and pine asks you for the file that you want to attach.

5. **Enter the name of the file you want to attach.**

   pine prompts you for a comment. You don't need to add one, but it's handy when you want to tell the recipient something like the following:

   ```
   This is URGENT!
   For your eyes only.
   Whatever you do, don't read what I just sent you.
   ```

6. **Press Enter, and your e-mail message (plus the attachment) is on its way.**

7. **When you've finished sending and receiving e-mail, simply type** q **to end the** pine **program.**

Now that you're familiar with the various Linux mail programs, you're ready to take a break from all the heavy-duty network stuff. Ready to go surfing? You can put away the board wax. You'll be learning how to surf the Web with the best Linux freebie in the book.

Chapter 20

Setting Up Your Free Web Surfboard

· ·

In This Chapter

▶ Understanding what the World Wide Web really is

▶ Using Netscape Communicator, the ultimate freebie for Linux

▶ Deciphering URLs

▶ Finding stuff on the Web

· ·

*U*nless you've been stuck on a desert island for the last decade, you've probably heard of the World Wide Web, or the Web for short. It has nothing to do with giant spiders, so you don't have to save the coupon for the six-pack of insecticide.

The *Internet* is simply the total number of computers hooked up to a network that spans countries and even continents. Back when the Net was new, most of the information available was just in text form because computers weren't fast enough or powerful enough to handle anything else like graphics and movies.

As computers became speedier, someone got the idea of putting together pages of data that included pictures as well as text. To the techies in the computer labs, this was the greatest thing since tint-control color monitors! A new computer language called HTML grew up around putting these pages together.

By the way, learning how to use HTML is not only useful for creating your own Web pages, it's also a lot of fun. If you want to find out more, check out *HTML 4 For Dummies,* 2nd Edition, by Ed Tittel (also published by IDG Books Worldwide, Inc.).

As people could do more and more over the Internet, something was bound to happen. It was time for the Internet to go commercial. And that's the World Wide Web — it's the Internet all grown up, complete with pictures (courtesy of HTML), motion (courtesy of Java), and lots of things to see, do, and buy (thanks to corporate America).

In this chapter, you find out how to set up your free Web browser, Netscape. You also find out about URLs (pronounced "earls" or "you-are-ehls") and why they are so important for navigating the World Wide Web. And I'll give you a few pointers on how to find whatever you want on the Web.

Setting Up Your Free Web Browser

A *Web browser* is a program that gives you a GUI (graphical user interface) to navigate from one Web address to the next. A GUI is also useful because it displays pictures as well as text on your screen. One of the best Web browsers is from Netscape.

Linux users benefit from a cool decision made at Netscape: to make their Web browser freeware. Freeware is just what it says: It's software that you can download and use for no charge. As a result, you can expect to see a lot more Netscape involvement with Linux. The current version of the browser, Netscape Communicator 4.0, is included with the latest Red Hat Linux CD-ROMs.

If you're lucky enough to have this CD-ROM, it should be installed at the same time you put Linux on your computer. You can skip ahead to the section on what URLs are all about. Otherwise, you have to download your free copy of Netscape from the Web itself. Be warned: Download times can be lengthy, especially if you're on a slow (33.6K) PPP connection.

To reduce your download time, try to do this installation during off hours, such as very late at night or very early in the morning.

Installing Your Copy of Netscape Communicator

If you purchased the book *Linux For Dummies,* 2nd Edition (written by Jon "maddog" Hall and published by IDG Books Worldwide, Inc.), it comes with Red Hat Linux 5.2. Bundled into your Linux package is Netscape Communicator 4.0.7. When you completed your Linux installation, you automatically installed Netscape. So you should be able to start up Netscape by typing **Linuxbox% netscape** at the command prompt.

Of course, if you didn't get that book, you didn't get the CD-ROM; therefore, you'll have to get Netscape off the Web by yourself. You'll need to do the following:

1. **Log on to Linux as root.**

2. **Start your ISP (Internet Service Provider) connection.**

   When you sign up for an ISP, it normally provides setup software. After you install the software, you normally only have to click a button to connect to the Internet.

3. **Navigate to Netscape's home page.**

   The address of the Netscape home page is `http://www.netscape.com/download/client_download.html`.

   Alternatively, you can go to `ftp://ftp.netscape.com`.

4. **You can download Netscape for Linux by clicking the appropriate links on the page.**

   As of this writing, the kind folks at Netscape have made this even easier by leading you through a four-step process to select the right software version.

   The file will download as a `.tar` file. This means it will be compressed to make it smaller and easier to download. You'll need to uncompress the file with the `tar` command to use it.

5. **Create a temporary directory called `tardir` for storing the tar file.**

   Suppose that the `tar` file, called something like `netscape.tar`, was placed in your `/home/user` directory. To create a temporary directory, type **mkdir tardir**.

6. **Move the `tar` file into `tardir` by typing** mv netscape.tar tardir.

7. **Change directories to `tardir` by typing** cd tardir.

8. **Uncompress the `tar` file (you use the `tar` command to do so) by typing** tar xvzf netscape.tar.

   The uncompressed file has become a number of larger, ready-to-use installation files.

9. **Start the installation by executing the Netscape installation script by typing** /ns-install.

   The script asks you some simple questions and then extracts the required files that you just de-tarred. By default, the browser installs itself in the `/opt/netscape` directory, which it also created.

From now on, you'll be able to start Netscape Communicator from the command line of your terminal window by typing **/opt/netscape/netscape**.

Do you have any more questions? Netscape has its own Help guide. You can view this on the command line by typing **Linuxbox% netscape –help**.

To start visiting other parts of the Web aside from Netscape's own home page, you can click the areas of the screen that Netscape indicates on its home page. Alternatively, you can type URLs in the blank bar located about two inches below the top of the screen, labeled either *Netsite* or *Location*.

A link to less typing

If you're feeling ambitious, you can configure Netscape so that it starts with a little less typing. You do this by creating a symbolic link, which is a file name that points like a road sign to another file.

You create a symbolic link using the `ln` or `link` command, with the `-s` command option to make the link symbolic:

```
Linuxbox% ln -s
    /opt/netscape/netscape
```

```
/usr/local/bin/netscape
```

Linux by default looks for programs in the `/usr/local/bin` directory. By putting in the "road sign" for Netscape in this directory, you're making Linux execute a program that exists in a completely different directory. You can now start Netscape from the command line by typing **Linuxbox% netscape**.

Sure, you save only a little typing. But believe me, you'll appreciate it in the long run.

So, what is this mysterious thing called a URL?

URL stands for Uniform Resource Locator. A URL is a Web address that enables you to find a specific piece of information on the Web. Typical examples of URLs are:

```
http://www.uedakota.edu/chemistry/exams/cheat.txt
http://www.idgfanclub.org
http://ticktock.bigbenclocks.uk
http://www.topsecret_govtagency.gov
```

A URL consists of three main parts:

- ✔ The hypertext transport protocol, which is `http://`
- ✔ The server name, such as `www.uedakota`
- ✔ An *extension* that names a file on the server, such as `/chemistry/exams/cheat.txt`

HTTP servers are used for displaying text documents and Web pages, because a HyperText Transport Protocol server is a cheap, reliable way to put pages on the Web.

As you may have read in Chapter 17, server names are a way that humans can easily navigate the Web without using difficult-to-remember server addresses, such as 111.96.55.51. For the server at the University of East Dakota, for example, you'd have a much easier time remembering `http://www.uedakota.edu` than four sets of random numbers.

The extension on a Web address also clues you in to the type of file stored on the server. For example, the `.txt` ending on the Web address for `http://www.uedakota.edu/chemistry/exams/cheat.txt` tells you that it's a text file. Judging from the rest of the extension, it looks like someone decided to sneak a look at the professor's chemistry exam.

A glance at a URL can sometimes give you a hint about how long it will take to load a Web page from the server. As a general rule, an address with any of the following endings takes longer to load:

- ✔ uk tells you that the server is located in the United Kingdom. If you're in the United States, anything you see on your screen has to be transmitted by satellite or transatlantic cable.

- ✔ edu is a university or other academic site. Traditionally, these sites are busy around the clock with students doing class work, homework, or lab experiments.

- ✔ gov tells you that this site belongs to a United States government agency, such as the DMV or the U.S. Postal Service. Need I say more?

How can I find stuff on the Web?

The Web gives you access to everything that humanity has seen fit to put on a computer. To find something, your best bet is to use a Web search engine. It isn't a motor that sits out on the network, chugging away on low-octane gas and spitting out data. Rather, a *search engine* is a software program that searches the Web for you by looking for Web sites that contain certain words or phrases you're looking for.

Netscape's default home page has links to a few of these search engines, such as Excite, Lycos, and Infoseek. Click one of these links and you'll be taken to the search engine's home page.

A *link* is a connection from one Web site to another that has already been set up for you. Most links are placed on Web pages as pictures: If you see a blue button that says `Press to go to Lycos`, then it's probably a link. Click on the button, and you'll automatically be transported to that Web page.

From there, you'll be directed to type some words for the search engine to look for. For example, suppose you're using Netscape late at night and are thinking about your next vacation. You think a trip to a national park would be just the ticket. You click on the Excite link, and are taken to the Excite home page. From there, you type **national +parks**.

You can find out about that + (plus sign) as well as other advanced search options from Excite's help section.

You click the Search button (all the search engines have one, usually right next to where you type in your request) and get back a list of Web links to click for more information.

More than likely, your request is going to give back so much information that you could spend hours looking at all the sites dedicated to national parks. But when you're searching for information, too much is almost always better than too little.

Chapter 21

Setting Up Network News

· ·

In This Chapter

▶ What is network news?

▶ How news works

▶ How NNTP works

▶ NNTP installation

· ·

*S*etting up your Linux network to handle newsgroups may not be on par with getting e-mail and your printer working, but it's still important. You'll learn in this chapter that the vast majority of user communities still want access to all that the Internet has to offer, and that includes the ability to keep informed with newsgroups. You'll see what exactly this news phenomenon is all about, where it came from, and how to set the whole system up.

Not the Five O'Clock News

Incidentally, if you're not familiar with network news (also known as Usenet), don't think of it as the low-budget version of CNN. News is not a formalized broadcast to bring in news from around the world. News is more like a gigantic discussion board that relates to specific topics of interest to the users in the group. You learn more about what you can subscribe to in Chapter 22.

How does this whole news thing work?

Believe it or not, the whole process starts when a user writes a message on his or her topic of interest and posts it to the Net. This message is usually either called a *post* or an *article*. (Oddly enough, you'll hear people asking, "Did you post that article?" But you'll never hear anyone ask, "Did you article that post?")

Articles can be posted to one or more newsgroups. Existing newsgroups are organized in a kind of hierarchy, with each group's name indicating its place. At the top level, news hierarchy is determined at the first part of the name, such as:

alt.	A sort of catch-all hierarchy name
comp.	Devoted to computers of some type
rec.	Recreational activities

Within each major division, you'll see subdivisions splitting topics into smaller areas, sometimes *extremely* small areas. For example, you might see divisions in the comp section as follows:

```
comp.os.linux
```

```
comp.os.linux.questions
```

```
comp.os.linux.really_hard_questions
```

```
comp.os.linux.really_hard_nfs_questions
```

Articles generated or received by the local news system are forwarded to the other news servers that carry that site. To distinguish articles and recognize duplicates, articles carry a message identification section that combines the posting site's name and a serial number into a special field. The news system logs this identification field into a history file. Any incoming articles are checked against this field and thrown away if they are duplicates.

The normal news storage area is kept in the /var/spool/news directory, under which each newsgroup is stored in a separate directory. To prevent the disk from filling up, articles are routinely discarded after a period of time. This process is called *expiring,* which makes me wonder if those who designed news got their ideas while shopping for milk.

News changes with the times: UUCP to TCP/IP

Network news came about in the late 1970s, back when UUCP (UNIX to UNIX Copying) was still all the rage. Using a network built on UUCP and shell scripts, news distribution really represented no more than easy file copying across the system. When the demand for this new service grew, the UUCP system was eventually replaced with a proper program to handle the information that was flowing across the network.

This new program went through multiple phases, called (with a marvelously efficient naming scheme) News A and then News B. In the late 1980s, programmers Geoff Collyer and Henry Spencer put news through one more iteration, called C, or C-News. A C-News version is currently included in most Linux releases.

C-News is the most efficient implementation of news on the older UUCP-dependent Linux networks. For today, the more prevalent scheme is TCP/IP, which you read about in Chapter 8. In order to take advantage of TCP/IP's qualities (such as virtual circuit reliability), a new protocol was developed.

The new protocol, *NNTP*, or Network News Transfer Protocol, was developed in 1986. NNTP is based on TCP/IP network connections, but on today's faster machines, it can approximate the older C-Net's speed. Since the new protocol is the current standard for Linux systems today, you'll need to learn how to set up the NNTP system, so keep reading.

NNTP — Your News Net

NNTP is more than just a particular software package — it's an Internet Standard. NNTP is based on a TCP/IP stream-oriented connection between a news client and a news server on a host that keeps net news in its disk storage.

The new kind of connection allows the client and server to transfer news articles while cutting turnaround delay to an absolute minimum. This in turn reduces the number of duplicate articles.

With the faster data transfer rates available today, news postings can reach the net community in under an hour. Compare that with an average time of over a week under the old system, and it's easy to see why NNTP has rapidly moved to the forefront of Linux news systems.

NNTP does have a nasty security leak in that it allows hackers to insert articles into the news stream with false sender information. This is known as *news faking*. You don't have to take any precautions on your system, but you should be aware of the practice. Should someone mention that your system seems to be generating a large number of odd or controversial postings that can't be attributed to anyone, you should take notice.

Installing the NNTP Server

The NNTP server is called `nntpd`, for `nntp daemon`. `Nntpd` can be configured as either a stand-alone server that is started at system boot time from the `/etc/rc.inet2` file or a `daemon` managed by `inetd`. If you plan to run `nntpd` via `inetd`, make sure that the following entry in `/etc/inetd.conf` is available:

```
nntp      stream   tcp nowait      news      /usr/etc/in.nntpd
          nntpd
```

Given `nntp`'s availability, you'll most likely have to just uncomment this line instead of typing it in. In addition, make sure you have the following line uncommented in `/etc/services`:

```
nntp    119/tcp    readnews untp     # Network News Transfer
          Protocol
```

You also need a `.tmp` directory in your news spool to temporarily store any incoming articles that `nntpd` also needs. You can create this using the `mkdir` command; then change the file's ownership to news so it can handle the news daemon. The following commands will set this up for you.

```
# mkdir /var/spool/news/.tmp
# chown news.news /var/spool/news/.tmp
```

If you decide to configure `nntpd` as a stand-alone daemon, your first step is to make sure that you've got the following line in `/etc/inetd.conf` commented _out_.

```
# nntp     stream   tcp nowait      news
             /usr/etc/in.nntpd   nntpd
```

Of course, you'll still have to create a `.tmp` directory and **chown** it to news for the rest of the system to fall into place.

Chapter 22

Setting Up Your Users' Newsreaders

● ●

In This Chapter

▶ The .newsrc file

▶ The Big Three Newsreaders

▶ Setting up tin

▶ Setting up trn

▶ Setting up nn

▶ Setting up pine mail to use news

▶ Setting up Netscape Communicator to use news

▶ Which newsreader for your users?

● ●

*I*f you've followed Chapters 20 and 21 to set up the back end processes of your news server, you're ready to select a newsreader process to sort, queue, and display the news from the groups the users select. You'll be learning about the big three news processes which, until pine and Netscape came along, were the big thing in news communication. And of course, you'll also be learning how to configure a user's Netscape Communicator to handle news.

Read All about It! Newsgroup Postings!

Newsgroups are postings on a particular subject from people located around the world who share an interest in that subject. At last count, there were more than 35,000 groups on various topics, trading the latest information on their professions, studies, and hobbies.

Newsgroup names are specific as to the content of what's being talked about. For example, you can find discussions on the following:

✔ Advancing Linux issues in the tech world: `comp.os.linux.advocacy`

✔ Restaurants located in the San Francisco Bay Area: `sfba.food`

✔ Everyone's favorite purple dinosaur — and no, I did *not* make this newsgroup up: `alt.barney.die.die.die`

Newsreader Configuration

Newsreader programs are intended to enable users to function (post articles, or skim the contents comfortably) within the news system easily. The quality of this interface is subject of endless flame wars.

A *flame* is techie talk for a remark that ranges from sarcasm to an outright insult. A *flame war* is a slang term for an argument that has rapidly degenerated into name-calling. They're quite fun to engage in, if you're under the age of 12, but otherwise steer clear.

Configuring the .newsrc file

Whatever program you use to get news, both utilities read your list of newsgroups from your `.newsrc` file. You can create this in your home directory using the `vi` editor, as follows:

1. **Using your `vi` editor or the `touch` command, create the `.newsrc` file.**

   ```
   Linuxbox% touch .newsrc
   ```

   Remember, to list the file, you have to use `ls  -a`, which displays all the hidden dot files in Linux.

2. **Type the list of newsgroups you'd like to read about (called *subscribing*). For example:**

   ```
   comp.os.linux.advocacy
   sfba.food
   alt.photography
   rec.music.classical
   ```

   If you don't know the exact name of a newsgroup you'd like to subscribe to, you can search for the name on the Internet using any search engine (such as Yahoo! or Excite) on your Netscape Communicator Web browser.

3. **If you're using the `vi` editor to create this file, make sure you write and save the entries you've made with the `:wq` commands.**

   From now on, to add or delete a newsgroup, just edit your `.newsrc` file with the `vi` editor.

The Big Three in the Linux Newsreader World

While you have multiple options when it comes to running newsreaders in Linux, the most basic three that can be found on most any Linux box are trn, tin, and nn. What distinguishes these programs mostly is the way they generate and handle threads.

While many of the functions of these processes have been taken over by the newer, GUI-based Windows applications such as Outlook, there's still nothing more efficient or lightweight to run on a Linux box. And no matter how antiquated your Linux box may be, you can count on at least one of these programs being installed on the machine.

Turning to trn

Trn stands for Threaded Read News because it uses threads prepared by a program called mthreads. Upon startup, trn will do the following:

1. **It will look for your** .newsrc **file, which is your list of subscribed-to newsgroups. If** trn **doesn't find a** .newsrc, **it will automatically create one.**

2. Trn **next inputs the** .newsrc **file, listing the first several newsgroups with unread news.**

3. Trn **then performs consistency checks on your** .newsrc. **If your** .newsrc **is out of date,** trn **posts a warning to the screen and then updates your** .newsrc.

4. Trn **checks for new newsgroups that have been created since you last used the newsreader and asks you if you want it to add them to your** .newsrc.

5. **Finally,** trn **goes to its top prompt level — the newsgroup-selection level.**

Keep in mind that mthreads has to be invoked regularly from cron to update the index files that store the threads of discussion. Mthreads is a very useful utility that is the real core of the trn setup. The -a option makes mthread automatically turn on threading for new groups as they are created; -v enables verbose log messages to mthreads' log file (mt.log in the directory where you have trn installed).

You can start up mthreads from the command line. However, make sure that when you start it up the first time, it's followed by the list of newsgroups that you've specified in your .newsrc file.

```
Linuxbox% mthreads comp.os.linux.advocacy, sfba.food,
            alt.barney.die.die.die
```

After that, you simply invoke it without any option at all to make it thread any newly arrived articles. As a habit, it's good to run this once or twice a day to ensure that the news threads are properly updated. (Of course, you can increase this amount if you get complaints from users who are news junkies.) To save yourself the bother, automate this process with the `cron` process that you read about in Chapter 6.

Another option for networks with a lot of heavy traffic (or hordes of the aforementioned news junkies) is to run the `mthreads` program in `daemon` mode. When the `mthreads` program is started at boot time using the `-d` option, it puts itself in the background. `Mthreads` then checks every ten minutes for newly arrived articles and threads them. To run `mthreads` in `daemon` mode, put the following line in your `/etc/rc.news` file:

```
/usr/local/bin/rn/mthreads -deav
```

A newsreader made out of tin

To begin with, the `tin` newsreader isn't really made out of tin or any related metal. In fact, some people think that because of its old-sounding name, it's one of the oldest programs out in the Linux world. That's not quite true, because `tin` is surprisingly more flexible in its threading scheme than `trn`. `Tin` does its threading when a user enters a selected newsgroup, which is a more complex but also more efficient way of doing threading.

Which reminds me — you should always change the permissioning of the `tin` binary to the following:

```
-rwsr-r- tin
```

This setting, called *setuid*, ensures that `tin` will place its thread databases in the `/var/spool/news/.index`.

Without this setting, `tin` will copy its threading databases in the user's home directory below `.tin/index`. This doesn't affect anything, until you have enough users accessing enough news to fill up the entire user's disk partition, which generally makes the entire machine crash. Not pretty.

Configuring nn for news

The most widely used of the Big Three newsreaders is nn, which jokingly stands for No News (as in No News is Good News). nn is more advanced in that it allows thread generation combined with database consistency checks, and access restrictions and usage statistics.

The `nn` threads database daemon is `nnmaster`. It's normally started from the `/etc/rc.news` or `/etc/rc.inet2` startup scripts during boot time. You can also manually invoke it in its default setting, which is as follows:

```
Linuxbox% /usr/local/lib/nn/nnmaster -l -r -C
```

You can also set up the `cron` daemon to start `nnmaster` periodically. A sample invocation is

```
# /usr/local/lib/nn/nnmaster comp.os.linux.advocacy,
         sfba.food, alt.barney.die.die.die
```

The `nn` program allows two methods for you to expunge expired articles from the news databases. The first is to update the database by scanning the newsgroup directories and discarding the entries whose corresponding article is no longer available. This is the default operation, or you can specify it from `nnmaster` with the `-E` option as I show here:

```
Linuxbox% /usr/local/lib/nn/nnmaster -l -r -C -E
```

Alternatively, you can specify `nn` to discard the entire database and to start collecting all new news articles. This may be done by giving `-E3` to `nnmaster` as follows:

```
Linuxbox% /usr/local/lib/nn/nnmaster -l -r -C -E3
```

The `nnmaster` reads the groups file, located in the `/usr/local/lib/nn` directory. If this file does not exist, it's automatically created. Each line in the file contains a line with the group's name, followed by time stamps and/or option flags. You can edit these flags to enable certain behavior for the group in question, but you shouldn't change the order in which the groups appear. The flags allowed and their effects are detailed in the `nnmaster` manual page, too.

Configuring Pine Mail to Handle News

One of the major reasons I recommend the pine e-mail utility in the last chapter is that pine enables you to read Internet newsgroup postings. Using either pine or your Web browser (such as Netscape Communicator, which is described in Chapter 18) is the easiest, simplest way to read newsgroup postings.

I like pine because it's the Linux equivalent of the Swiss Army knife. Not only can it send and receive e-mail, handle attachments, and create aliases, but it makes reading newsgroups as easy as checking e-mail. With only a little extra configuration, you won't even have to switch between your e-mail and your news programs. Not bad for a utility that's automatically installed for you, whether off the Net or from a Linux CD-ROM.

Here's how you can configure pine to handle news.

1. **Type** pine **at the command line.**

2. **Press S, and then press C.**

   The configuration screen appears.

3. **Move the cursor down to** nntp-server **and press C to change the configuration.**

4. **Type the name of your ISP's news server and press Enter.**

   Just like with mail, each organization has a machine dedicated to handling news. Often it's the same machine.

5. **Exit pine by typing** q.

6. **When pine asks whether you want to save the changes, press Y for yes.**

   From now on, when you start pine and look at your mail folders, you'll also have the option to look at your listed newsgroups.

Configuring Netscape Communicator to Handle News

Like pine, Netscape is a program that has multiple functions. While it's great for surfing the Web, it can also help read your news. A major advantage of reading news from your Web browser is that if you see a Web site mentioned in a news posting, you're only a few clicks away from checking out the information for yourself.

Here's how you can configure Netscape to handle news:

1. **Start Netscape Communicator.**

2. **Choose Edit⇨Preferences.**

   You'll see a list of Categories on the left-hand side of the Preference screen. Midway down the list of choices is Mail & Groups.

3. **Click on the small arrow just to the left of Mail & Groups.**

   The arrow flips down and you get a menu of different categories under the Mail & Groups listing.

4. **Click on Groups Server.**

   The screen to the right will list the settings, which will probably be blank, since you haven't set anything yet.

5. **Click in the allotted space below the Discussion Groups (News) Server field. Type in the name of your ISP's news server.**

   If asked, you don't have to select a News Directory — Netscape will set one up for you automatically.

6. **Type the name of your ISP's news server.**

   Communicator automatically reads the `.newsrc` file.

7. **Now that Netscape knows which news server to connect to, click on the Window pull-down menu. Click on Netscape News to select it.**

   Netscape reads your `.newsrc` file. You are now able to read all the news-groups you specified when you edited the `.newsrc` file.

Which Newsreader Is Best for Your Users?

As with electronic mail readers, you can't necessarily block your users from using one form of the news program over another; you should implement a policy where you encourage the use of one or two newsreaders. In the long run, this saves time for you since you won't have to master the administration intricacies of five or six different systems.

A good way to gently prod your user community toward some kind of standard is to set out an ironclad rule of your own, that rule being: If it's not on your list of items to support, you simply won't perform administration tasks on the program if it breaks. True, this can be tough, but if the policy is well known in advance, users won't be able to give you much grief about it by claiming "ignorance of the law."

As to which program you should encourage on your system, it depends on your personal preferences and the Linux machines you've inherited. Older programs such as the Big Three are extremely lightweight. For example, on a 50 Mhz 486 (a rather antiquated machine from the early 90s), the `tin` news-reader takes just under a minute to sort out a thread of 1,000 articles. This estimated time would triple or quadruple on a heavily loaded and active news server at peak times.

However, older versions of newsreaders may lack NNTP support. Additionally, being that they are older UNIX-based processes, they'll be a little harder to administer due to their terse error messaging. On the balance then, if you have reasonably powerful machines, you'll find your job a lot easier when using the semiautomated news systems of Netscape and pine mail.

Part VII
Network Security

The 5th Wave By Rich Tennant

"I can never remember — are the bubble lights VESA or PCI?"

In this part . . .

*P*art VII looks at the networking issues that fall somewhere between law-and-order and cloak-and-dagger.
You get a briefing on what you need to know about secur-
ing your Linux network against hackers, crackers, and just
plain thievery. You learn how to — and how not to — set
passwords in Linux, and you take to heart (well, we can
hope) some sage advice on how to set up strong, hard-to-
crack passwords. You learn some ways of preventing
interlopers from stealing your network passwords (and
you may be surprised at how low-tech the theft can be).

Back in the nonvirtual world, you learn how to protect your
machines from theft and physical damage — including how
smart storage practices both enhance security and can
limit damage in the event of a flood, air-conditioning
outage, or building fire. (If you know how to protect against
asteroid strikes, you *are* a wizard.)

Finally, you learn some handy techniques to help you
secure your network on the software side, with an eye
toward eliminating temptation for those people who are
less than honest. And for the Sherlock Holmes in all of us,
Part VII offers some ways to track a cyber-burglary and
catch the crooks.

Chapter 23

Password Protection and Cryptography

The most important — and basic — of your security needs are user and root passwords. Having secure passwords that are hard to guess or "crack" (such as using your username, nickname, or birthday) is vitally important for you and all your users.

Although some of the more recent Linux distributions include password (sometimes named *passwd*) programs that do not allow you to set an easily guessed password, you don't have to count on this feature alone. You discover in this chapter that it's critical to the security of your system that you establish some kind of password policy to prevent users from granting a cracker easy access to your system.

Hackers versus crackers

Time for a little terminology. To many people, a hacker is the same thing as a cracker, but the reality is very different. The term *hacker* is used for anyone who likes to program, tinker, or just bang on a computer keyboard a heck of a lot (hence the term *hacking*).

The *cracker* is a subspecies of hacker, and it's a term used to describe those (thankfully few) hackers who like to "crack" security and break into systems. So, a hacker won't crack into your system, but a cracker will certainly hack into yours.

How Passwords Are Automatically Encrypted in Linux

Linux uses a one-way encryption algorithm called DES (Data Encryption Standard) to encrypt passwords. This encrypted password is normally stored in the /etc/passwd file (which you saw in Chapter 3) and occasionally in the /etc/shadow file, which you can read about in more detail a little farther into this chapter.

When any user attempts to log in, the password entered from the Passwd: prompt is then encrypted again and compared with the encryption pattern stored your /etc/passwd or shadow file. If the patterns match, access is allowed.

Although DES is a two-way encryption algorithm, the variant that Linux uses is specifically made one-way only. Using a one-way encrypter prevents someone from cracking your password by reversing the encrypter to get the password from the contents of /etc/passwd (or /etc/shadow).

What Evil Lurks in the Hearts of Men? The /etc/shadow File Knows!

At first glance, it seems like an odd idea to have a shadow file just for the encrypted field of the /etc/passwd file. After all, although users can change directories and even use the vi editor on the /etc/passwd file, they can't make any changes without root permission. What's more, even if they were able to, how could they crack a one-way encryption program?

Well, times do change quickly in the Linux world. New guesser programs are available to those on the Internet who are equally adventurous and unscrupulous. All a user has to do is take advantage of a little-known gap in the UNIX-based permissioning system. For example, say that the /etc/passwd file is set as it should be, with the following permissions:

```
-rw-r—r— passwd
```

These permissions are set correctly: No one except root has the w, or write permissions, to change this file. But that doesn't stop the diabolically clever user from *copying* the file into his or her home directory, where they now have full permissions over the file.

To use a real-world analogy, this is like a bank robber who knows he can't break the bank's safe. So the criminal brings the safe to his home, where he has all of his lockpicks and blowtorches to work with. Now, it's only a matter of time before he can figure out the way to break in.

Once in their home directory — or better yet, a locally mounted directory so that you can't see what's going on without logging in — they can do whatever they want. If they have a guesser program to crack the encryption, they can use the resulting password in the original copy of the /etc/passwd file and start coming and going as they please.

Because it's very difficult to prevent file copying — it's a basic utility in Linux in any case — shadow passwords have been developed. Shadow passwords are a means of keeping your encrypted password field from being seen by any users (with the exception of root).

Shadow passwords are saved in a special file called /etc/shadow, which only privileged users (again, usually only root) can read. In order to use shadow passwords, you need to do the following:

1. **Su to root:**

```
Linuxbox% su
Passwd: *****
#
```

2. **Cd to the /etc directory and run the following command:**

```
pwconv
```

Pwconv, or Password Converter, does just what it sounds like: It converts your password system over to use shadow passwords. The encrypted fields in /etc/password are copied into the /etc/shadow file, hidden, and re-encrypted from all prying eyes except root's.

Crack and John the Ripper

Password cracking programs are a kind of brute force method of cracking your system. Instead of going after the encrypted entries in your `passwd` or `shadow` file, the password cracking programs focus on the unencrypted `passwd` entry itself. They try every word in the dictionary, and then try variations on those words, encrypting each one and checking it against your encrypted password. If they get a match, they know what your password is.

The two most widespread cracking programs are the self-explanatory Crack and John the Ripper. These programs are available on the Web from personal Web sites, which tend to change frequently, but if you do a Web search, you should be able to find them.

You may consider doing this as a good security technique — steal, or rather borrow, a page from the cracker's own books and try running them on your system to detect weak spots! For example, if your `passwd` program is not enforcing hard-to-guess passwords, you could run Crack to make sure your users' passwords are secure.

Run Crack or John the Ripper after hours because each of these programs can be very resource-intensive. (It just doesn't sound like a good excuse if you explain that the reason you crashed the server was that you were trying to break in.) However, at the end of the Crack or John the Ripper session, you should be able to tell if an attacker could get in using them.

Afterwards, you can take the next step and notify the users with weak passwords to get their act in gear and put together a stronger one. I recommend that you periodically run Crack against your own password database to prevent any weak passwords from ruining your network's security.

Good and Bad Passwords

The trouble with good passwords is that what defines a password as good or bad is completely different to the user than to the administrator. A case in point: One user I had adamantly refused to change his password, which was his first name. "It's an excellent password," he explained, "because I can always remember it."

Arguing with logic like that is hard — and truth be told, he was right, from his point of view. But as an administrator, you must keep in mind that your top priority, even if people bother you because they forgot their password, is to keep the system secure.

On the other hand, demanding that people use random, meaningless strings of numbers and/or letters is equally useless because any user who knows how to change passwords will do so on their own out of frustration. Where can the dividing line be drawn?

Bad to good compromises

A good way to find a good level of password protection is to look at examples of bad passwords and learn — without the harsh sting of a cracker pilfering your system — how to select good ones.

Some of the worst passwords in the world are the easy ones. For example, say that I have the following users on my system, each with the following passwords shown in Table 23-1:

Table 23-1:	Really, Really Bad Password Examples
User Name	*Password*
dsmith	danny
kclark	clarkk
kiko	030770
loki	LoKi
stever	rsteve
wally	wally

Which of these passwords are the bad ones? Trick question — they're all bad enough to give any Linux administrator a screaming nightmare. The absolute first thing that a human cracker — let alone a sophisticated program like Crack — is going to do is check on all kinds of variances of the user's name, birthdate, or other readily available information. If you have passwords like this on your system, you owe it to yourself to establish a password policy immediately.

The first basic rule is that a password should have no direct connection to a user. Again, that includes

- ✔ First names
- ✔ Last names
- ✔ Birthdates
- ✔ Usernames
- ✔ Nicknames

Mirror, mirror, on the wall, what's the worst password of them all?

Although there can never be one best password, there can be a worst one! Without further ado, I give you the worst password of all:

Awful, isn't it? Yes, I know you didn't see anything. That's the point. For convenience's sake, some administrators actually allow a user account (usually a system maintenance account) to log in without a password! Never, ever let this happen. To be doubly sure, check your /etc/passwd file. Here's an example of a passwd file that contains a ticking time bomb:

```
root:EIUiuh654DSA:0:0:Root
    User:/:/bin/csh

averagejoe:128939JY:100:101:A.
    Joe:/usr/home/averagejoe:/b
    in/csh
```

```
kiko:654KLQWER:105:108: Kara
    'Kiko'
    Karlson:/usr/home/kiko:/bin
    /csh

nobody::122:Dummy
    Account:/usr/home/nobody:/b
    in/sh

wally:TROI8761111:105:161:
    Wally the Wonder
    User:/usr/home/wally:/bin/
    sh
```

You notice that the second line from the bottom, the nobody administration account, has nothing between the two colons delineating the encrypted password! This way, if you or anyone else logs in as that account, no password will be required to get in and complete some system mayhem.

In addition, although capital letters — even oddly interspersed — don't cause programs much of a problem, it's better to intersperse some numbers in with the letters to make things more secretive.

Encryption Protocols: S-HTTP and SSL

Encryption protocols are a tricky, black box kind of subject, which requires another whole book to explain and do any justice. For now, you just need to be aware of the different types of protocols you have at your disposal. Should you want to work more directly with these protocols, pick up an encryption guidebook or search for information off the Internet.

S-HTTP

S-HTTP is an Internet-specific protocol. It was designed to provide authentication security while supporting the mathematical cryptographic algorithms. This is actually done during the connection requests between the client and the outside server(s) involved in each transaction. S-HTTP is limited to any specific software that supports implementing it.

SSL

SSL, or Secure Sockets Layer, was developed by Netscape to provide encryption security between the Netscape web browser and the Internet. SSL is useful in that it provides both client and server authentication.

Currently, SSL is most commonly used when going to a secure site to view a secure online document with Communicator. It creates a secure communication environment between Communicator and the Web. All in all, considering that SSL comes with the newer versions of Netscape, it's quite a handy freebie.

Sticky Passwords? Try Cooking Your Data with PAM

Newer versions of the Red Hat Linux distribution come with another great free utility, the Pluggable Authentication Module, otherwise known as PAM. PAM allows you to change your authentication methods and requirements on the fly. It also enables shadow passwords. And as an extra bonus, PAM lets you set permissions to allow specific users to log in only at specific times from specific places.

Best of all, the newer versions of PAM actually force a user to select a password that is recognized by a dictionary checker (for example, PAM forces users to stop making the worst of the password errors).

If you have Red Hat Linux, look to your documentation on how to configure PAM. You can also surf over to the PAM Web site for more information:

```
www.kernel.org/pub/linux/libs/pam/index.html
```

CFS and TCFS

Two more encryption utilities you may find useful are CFS and TCFS. CFS, which stands for Cryptographic File System, is a utility that enables you to encrypt entire directories.

CFS also enables you to give permission specific users to store encrypted files on these encrypted directories, adding an additional layer of security. CFS is available on some distributions of Red Hat Linux; if you don't have a copy and want more information, it is available at www.replay.com/redhat.

TCFS, the Transparent Cryptographic File System, is a newer version of CFS with greater capabilities. Its chief advantage is that TCFS is user transparent, which is the same attribute that makes CFS so easy to use and administer. You can find more information about this new utility at the Red Hat site or at `edu-gw.dia.unisa.it/tcfs`.

PGP and Public-Key Cryptography

PGP stands for Pretty Good Privacy, and to answer the question everybody asks when I tell them this, no, I didn't make that up. PGP uses a technology called public-key cryptography, which uses one key for encryption and a different key for a message's decryption. Therefore, in order to use PGP, both parties need to have this key.

Because of this limitation, PGP is most commonly used between two or more users who have agreed to send private e-mails to each other. Overall, PGP works well with Linux. Because describing how to use this one utility can easily take another two or three chapters, I recommend that you look at the best PGP primer on the Web that I've found:

```
www.pgp.com/service/export/faq/55faq.cgi
```

If you don't currently have PGP on your system, you can also get a copy through this site.

Keep in mind that due to export restrictions by the U.S. Government, `ftp`ing or otherwise exporting encryption technology of most any kind is prohibited. So unless you want Mulder and Scully from the *X-Files* going through your house trying to determine where you disappeared to last week, just don't do it.

The Future of Security — Features to Watch For

S/MIME

S/MIME, or Secure Multipurpose Internet Mail Extension, is an encryption standard used to encrypt electronic mail and other types of messages on the Internet. It is an open standard developed by RSA, so probably we will see it on Linux one day soon. More information on S/MIME can be found at:

```
home.netscape.com/assist/security/smime/overview.html
```

Secure Telnet Sessions

The Secure Telnet Session utility, or stelnet, is a program that allows users to log in to remote systems with an automatically encrypted connection. Stelnet uses SSL, the Secure Sockets Layer protocol developed by Netscape. The newer versions of Netscape offer this option for you automatically. If you want to upgrade to ensure that your version of Netscape comes so equipped, go to the Netscape home site and download the latest freeware version.

The Linux IPSEC implementation

Another kind of cryptographic implementation in the works is the Linux IPSEC. IPSEC is an effort to create cryptographically secure communications right at the IP network level. Its further goals are to provide authentication, integrity, access control, and confidentiality. Information on IPSEC and their anticipated releases can be found at:

```
www.ietf.org/html.charters/ipsec-charter.html
```

Generic Graphics Interface project

The Linux GGI project's goal, or Generic Graphics Interface, is to move video code into the Linux kernel, which would in turn control access to the video system. This improves console restoration in case of down time and also provides an extra layer of security against crackers pulling passwords or other information from your graphics interface.

Creating and Enforcing a Good Password Policy

Creating a standardized, regularly enforced password policy is in everyone's best interest. Brute force attacks, such as the Crack program, can often guess passwords unless your password is sufficiently obscure. But worse, over time, the security of your system naturally degrades.

Password degradation happens naturally over time because without a strict password policy, people will:

✔ Lend out passwords to friends.

✔ Forget that they're still logged in and allow someone to view their password.

✔ Walk by someone just as they're typing in their password.

To combat this, you must have a good system in place to continually revamp your password system. Having seen many, many Linux sites where security ranged from bad to nonexistent, I can give you a sliding scale as to how good your password changing policy may be. See where yours fits in on this list:

✔ **Worst:** Asking users to change their password whenever they happen to come into your office and ask you for help on an unrelated problem.

✔ **Just plain bad:** Requesting users to change their passwords in a memo that's circulated around the office. (Circulated right into the recycle bin, that is.)

✔ **Better:** Requesting users to change their passwords via the Message of the Day File, which they see every time they log in to the system.

Here's how you can do this the better way:

When the time starts to run short (usually within a week of having to change the password), a warning will pop up whenever users log in, reminding them to change their password. Should users foolishly ignore the warnings, they'll have to come to you for a new password after the password does actually expire.

To prevent your being bothered too much with this sort of thing, you can set your password time-outs for every four to six months — again, only if your system has security problems and/or you've got extremely valuable data to protect, which brings me to the final, important topic that you need to consider.

Your Last, Best (Sort of) Defense

To begin with, I have to share with you an awful truth: None of these password security techniques will stop a cracker who's insanely bent on getting on to your system. A truly determined cracker can get into any Linux system, given enough time. This isn't a result of any deficiency on Linux's part. The fact is, anything designed by humans can also be taken apart by other humans.

Your last, best defense for defending your system should be to examine every part of the so-called sensitive files on your system and ask: Is this *really* that valuable?

Your answer should be: If it's really so invaluable, then don't put it on an open computer system such as Linux. Consider this: One of the most guarded secrets on the planet is the formula for *Coca-Cola*. Is the formula kept on a Linux network? Absolutely not — it's in a vault at Coke Headquarters. No matter how skilled a thief is, chances are that he or she can't sneak into a well-guarded building and make off with the vault without being detected.

Note that I'm not saying that the thief wouldn't succeed. But when you're dealing with a system like Linux, which was designed to be open and to share information freely by default, you're stacking the odds against yourself by not keeping files locally or on floppy disk.

Don't go to the other extreme, either. You also have to ask whether the data you're protecting is truly that valuable. If you're an administrator at a Fortune 500 company, then probably so. But if you're just taking care of user accounts, office forms, and tons of user mail between pen pals, then probably not.

That's not to knock the importance of anyone's correspondence. And regardless of how monetarily important your network's information is, you need to always make a prudent effort to secure it.

Chapter 24

Visible and Invisible Locks

● ●

In This Chapter

▶ Creating physical security on your Linux network

▶ Maintaining file and filesystem security

▶ Implementing network security

▶ Avoiding flooding attacks

▶ Detecting security breaches

▶ Understanding security through obscurity

● ●

*I*n this chapter, you discover the ways you can make your Linux network more secure in areas that go beyond user passwords. You may be surprised to learn that more than half your security is low-tech. You'll see that half your security tasks will actually revolve around making your computer lab safe from physical threats.

The other part of your responsibility is to secure your user accounts, your data, and the network as a whole. Most of the user account safeguards are covered in Chapter 23, so you'll be getting into more detail on the latter two in this one. You'll see how you can safeguard your network with properly editing files and permissions. And finally, you'll figure out how you can use system logs to start tracking an intruder if you suspect a network break-in.

Lock, Stock, and Barrel — Your Linux Network's Physical Security

The first layer in your security plan should always be the control of physical access to your machines. I can hear people now: "But this is a Linux book! If I wanted to learn about chains, locks, and anti-theft devices, I would have bought *The Club™ For Dummies!*"

Incidentally, there is no book called *The Club™ For Dummies*. Rumor has it that the book was on the drawing board but somebody stole it.

Believe it or not, about half of your problems come from physical security issues. No, you probably won't have to worry about someone changing a user's passwords if a machine is stolen. Your bigger concern is more mundane; that theft, the good old fashioned kind of physical theft, is just as costly to you as it is to the car lot or corner candy store. (To make matters worse, it's a lot easier to steal a computer than an entire car lot or a whole candy store.)

Your physical security methods should be tailored to the environment you administer. Think common sense with a dash of good-natured paranoia. For example, if your network is at home, you probably don't need more than a sturdy door lock, to which you hold the key. If you run a university computer lab, consider locks on CPUs, keyboards, and cabling. If you're in a corporate environment, you may consider magnetic key card readers, locked cabinets, and a video surveillance system.

Your Two Kinds of Locks (Physical and Screen)

Physical locks need little explanation. My only advice is that you lock the object you don't want moved to another object that can't be sawed through with a hacksaw. Screen locks are the beginning of network security, in that it prevents casual dropping of passwords to those who shouldn't be looking at unattended screens.

If you have trouble distinguishing these two kinds of locks, remember: The ones that you can loosen with a spray of WD-40 are the physical ones.

Physical computer locks

Most computer vendors, when selling machines to a lab-like setup, include a kind of case lock system. Depending on the design, case locks can prevent your computer from being stolen (unless the thieves decide to saw through your table). Other designs make it difficult for thieves to open the computer, and some designs even prevent a new (illegal) user from adding a new keyboard.

Cable locks are another item you need to be familiar with. While I haven't seen much in the way of mouse locks, a cable lock is a flexible, plastic-covered steel cord, which normally attaches to your keyboards. It can also loop around the case locks on a monitor or CPU.

These locks can be useful features, but keep in mind that mass-manufactured locks of this sort are usually low quality and can easily be defeated by a determined burglar with a lot of time or a diamond coated hacksaw. However, the deterrence value is such that even an old style padlock can prevent problems from happening.

The screen lock: Xlock

Locking your console is highly recommended so that if you leave your machine unattended, no one tampers with or looks at your work. Your best bet in this area is xlock. Xlock is a display locker that is included in Linux distributions that support X Windows.

Xlock locks the X server until the user enters the password at the keyboard (but not remotely). While xlock is running, all new server connections are refused. The screen is blanked and a changing pattern is put on the screen. If a key or a mouse button is pressed, then the user is prompted for the password of the user who started xlock. When the correct password is typed, the screen is unlocked.

Keep in mind that locking your console only prevents initial tampering. A truly vindictive cracker can disrupt you by switching the machine off, or simply move to another machine that does not have xlock running. While you can't get paranoid to the point of locking your power switch in the on position, you can at least make sure that xlock is running properly on all of your user platforms.

Red Hat Linux contains vlock, a simple little program that allows you to lock some or all of the virtual consoles on your Linux box.

Files and Filesystem Security

File and filesystem security policies are designed to protect the next level of your Linux setup: the protection of your system's data. Linux data covers all of the files in Linux that can be edited with the vi editor. Basically this covers over 90 percent of what you find on any given Linux network. About the only things you can't directly vi are binaries.

Smart file permissions

File permissioning, which you learned about in detail in Chapter 3, is the biggest determinant of how stable and secure your syetm is once someone logs in to it. As a basic rule, when in doubt, cut it out of the loop and don't let users write or execute it. Consider, the /etc/passwd file is just fine as follows:

```
-rw-r--r-- passwd
```

But the same file with the following permissions is a disaster waiting to happen:

```
-rw-r--rw- passwd
```

What's the difference? Well, start letting users reconfigure anyone's user passwords and you'll learn in a hurry. Never, ever allow system critical files to be left in a state where anyone can edit them.

Some other suggestions:

- ✔ Use the nosuid option in /etc/fstab for partitions that are writable by others than root. You may also wish to use nodev and noexec on users' home partitions, as well as /var.

  SUID stands for set-user-id permissions. If the set user ID access mode is set in the owner permissions, and the file is executable, processes that run it are granted access to system resources based on the user who owns the file, as opposed to the user who created the process. Because of this, SUID is a serious security risk. SUID processes can be exploited to give the cracker a root shell.

- ✔ If using NFS to export filesystems, configure /etc/exports with the most restrictive access possible. Use the chmod command to do this if necessary.

- ✔ Never let anyone besides root read, write, or execute the /var/log/wtmp and /var/run/utmp files. These files contain the login records for all users on your system, so that any knowledgeable cracker will try to get in and disable these files.

  If you suspect an unauthorized login and the the /var/log/wtmp and /var/run/utmp files have been deleted or compromised, you can use the following option to take the trail up:

```
last | more
```

The last command shows a list of who's logged into your system, including from where and when the login was done. I suggest you pipe this to the more command because you may get a lot of data, and this way you can scroll down through the list with a tap of the space bar. Of course, you can also direct it to a text file if you want to use the vi editor to view the results. Redirect the output of last, as in the following example where the output is sent to the file gotcha.

```
last > gotcha
```

Searching out the trouble spots

You should determine which of your files are writable by any user, particularly your sensitive system files. Directories that are writable by everyone are even more dangerous, because it allows a cracker to add or delete files at will. To locate all world-writable files on your system, use the following command as root:

```
# find / -perm -2 ! -type 1 -ls
```

Once you get the results, determine why the files listed are writable by all users. If you see a file that definitely should not be writable by all, make sure to check the date. If it's been modified recently without your knowledge, a cracker may have already zapped you!

You should also do a search for .rhosts files. A .rhost file on a separate machine allows that machine to become a trusted host, allowing access to multiple machines on your network. You can locate all .rhosts files on your system with the following command, again from the root account:

```
# find /home -name .rhosts -print
```

Integrity Checking with Tripwire

An integrity checking piece of software like Tripwire should always be one of the network tools you acquire with your Linux installation. Tripwire works by running checksums on all your important binaries and configuration files. It then compares the results against a database of former values. Any changes are flagged and brought to your attention.

As soon as you have Tripwire setup, it's a good idea to run it as part of your normal security administration duties to see if anything has changed. Make sure to keep a backup copy of Tripwire, *off* your network. If it's on a floppy disk in your safe-deposit box, even the best cracker in the world won't be able to touch it.

I recommend that you run Tripwire every night via a cron job. The entry in your cron table should look something like what follows:

```
Run Tripwire at 1am and re-direct results to file
        /etc/trip the wire
01 00 * * * root /usr/local/adm/tcheck/tripwire >
        /etc/trip_the_wire
```

You can find Tripwire at `www.tripwiresecurity.com`. It's also included on this book's accompanying CD-ROM.

Network Security

Network security is a bit trickier than the other levels of security administration. This is because at this level, Linux by its very nature is designed to be open to share data freely. Always keep in mind that Linux's default of being a sharing system works to your disadvantage here.

NFS security

Exporting filesystems by its very nature is creating a potential security risk. Because individual users have access to their own NFS-mounted files, the remote root user can log in or `su` to their account and have total access to the user's files.

Therefore, always make sure that you export to only those machines that you really need to. Reduce potential security holes by exporting only directories you really, truly need to export.

Never export your entire root directory.

NIS security

If a cracker knows your domain name, they can persuade `ypserv` to hand over a copy of your site's NIS maps. To prevent this from happening, `ypserv` supports the securenets utility. This utility can be used to restrict access to a given set of hosts. At startup, `ypserv` attempts to load the securenets information from a file called `/var/yp/securenets`. A sample securenets file may look like this:

```
# allow connections from local host
host 127.0.0.1
# netmask same as 255.255.255.255 127.0.0.1
#
# allow connections from any host
# on the 160.101.80.58 network
255.255.255.0   160.101.80.58
# allow connections from any host
# between 160.101.80.58 and 255.255.252.0
255.255.252.0   160.101.80.58
```

If `ypserv` receives a request from an address that doesn't match the securenets entries, the request is ignored and a warning message is logged. Keep in mind that the creation of the securenets file is not automatic. If the `/var/yp/securenets` file does not exist, `ypserv` allows connections from any host.

Verify your DNS information

Always keep your DNS information current. Knowing the hosts on your network increases the level of your security. If a given host lacks a DNS entry, then an unauthorized, or bogus host may have attached itself to your network. Many services can be configured to not accept connections from hosts that do not have valid DNS entries.

Flooding Attacks

In college, I knew a fellow who had a dispute with the local pizza company. To extract a form of payback, he kept on speed-dialing them during their dinner rush, tying up their phone lines and interfering with the company's ability to handle incoming orders.

Oddly enough, this childish form of prank is exactly what a flooding or denial of service attack is. A cracker, or vengeful user, can try to make some resource too busy to answer legitimate requests. Here are a few of these kinds of attacks you should be aware of:

✔ **The Pentium "F00F" Bug:** It was recently discovered that a series of assembly codes sent to a genuine Intel Pentium processor can reboot the machine. (Note that this isn't a Linux problem — it happens with MSDOS, OS/2, and Windows!)

This bug is the least serious of your worries, because Pentiums are being replaced with higher-speed chips today. For example, this problem only seems to affect Pentium chips. If you have a Pentium Pro or higher, you should be in the clear.

✔ **Spray Flooding:** Spray flooding is a variant of what you learned not to do in Chapter 8. The attacker sends a "flood" of TCP packets to your machine by rapidly repeating `spray` commands. If the attacker is doing this from a host with better bandwidth than yours, your machine will be so busy handling packets that it's unable to send anything on the network.

✔ **The Fabled Ping o' Death:** Although it sounds like a combat move for Mortal Kombat or any violent video game, the Ping O' Death is a real threat. A Ping o' Death attack sends `ICMP ECHO REQUEST` packets that are too large to fit in the kernel data structures intended to store them.

Large packets of this sort cause many systems to hang or even crash. This problem is supposed to be fixed, but one continues to hear rumors about it on the Internet.

Detecting Security Compromises

Often, the sign of a security compromise is easy to spot, because the cracker wants to leave a calling card for you. This can be in the form of a virus, deleted files, or a truly bizarre Message of the day. All are equally unpleasant to walk in on early in the morning.

However, be on the lookout for signs that you may have a breach.

✔ On the physical side, check regularly for signs of tampering with your case or cable locks.

✔ On the network side of things, it's a good idea to check through your system logs and note any discrepancies. The first thing to always note is when your machine was rebooted. Unlike certain Microsoft-centric operating systems, it is very rare for a Linux system to need rebooting on a regular basis. You can look in log files, or use the `last | more` command discussed earlier in this chapter.

Some items or conditions to check for in your logs include:

✔ Records of multiple reboots or restarting of services.

✔ Short or incomplete logs.

✔ Logs that are just plain missing!

✔ Logs with incorrect permissions or ownership.

✔ Multiple `su` entries; or multiple attempts and failures to log in as root.

✔ Logins from machines you don't recognize on your network.

✔ Logins from strange places, like Kalamazoo, Tazmania, or someplace claiming to be "off planet."

Take these steps to keep your logs secure:

✔ Always start by changing the permissions on the files in `/var/log` to make them readable and writable by only a limited number of users.

A limited number of *one* (root) is a good place to start.

✔ You can find out where your distribution is logging to by looking at your `/etc/syslog.conf` file. This file tells `syslogd`, the system logging daemon (which runs on every version of Linux), where to log various messages. Other log files you want to check include `/var/log` and `/var/mail.log`.

✔ If your log files have been tampered with, check the date and time stamps on the entries. Even the most thorough crackers won't bother to change an entire date stamp series in a log file. If you can spot when the strange entries seem to be taking place, you can determine when the tampering started.

Security through Obscurity

The intruder typically modifies log files in order to cover their tracks, but the log files should still be checked for strange happenings. If you've been savvy enough to save some of the older log files, you may be able to check out any date or time discrepancies.

"Security through obscurity" is a hotly debated topic at times in the Linux newsgroups. Making your network obscure can mean one of two things: that you're relying on increased security by keeping your system small and relatively low-profile. Or it could mean that you're configuring your services such as telnet through nonstandard ports, to discourage one-shot crackers from trying to get in.

These are both of limited use. Just because your site is small, or you don't have *TIME* magazine do a write-up on your site, doesn't mean a cracker won't take a swing at your network. Keep in mind that crackers are usually very intelligent people in a very smart field, and they like a challenge.

The second mode of operation with nonstandard ports is equally so-so. First, getting everything on your system to use your custom ports is a bit more work, because you're not accepting system defaults. (Of course if you're lucky enough to be running your system from scratch, then you can do what you want from ground zero.)

This just isn't that effective against an experienced cracker. Using a network sniffer, a cracker can usually locate nonstandard ports by following the network traffic. In fact, on Solaris (another form of UNIX, this time by Sun Microsystems), there's even a packet sniffing utility called Snoop.

On the plus side, both of these methods are dirt cheap. (Dirt cheap meaning free, in this case.) On the whole then, your best bet if you go this route is to use the advice given before: If you truly have something that is invaluable (and isn't shared, vi'ed, or complied on a daily basis), you're better off getting it out of your system. Step back for a moment and ask what you're really spending money to protect. Is it worth it?

That's for you to decide, as there can be no objective guidelines for a subjective area. But if someone does break in, you can take a stab at tracking him or her down.

Chapter 25

Elementary, My Dear Watson: Tracking Security Breaches

· ·

In This Chapter

▶ Keeping calm when the chips are down

▶ What to do when you spot a break-in actually in progress

▶ What to do after a break-in is reported

▶ Backups and recovery

▶ Turning the show over to the pros

· ·

*N*o matter how insignificant your network, no matter how well you protect your network, there may very well come a time when you come into work to find your passwords changed, files deleted, or a playful message inserted into your .motd file. You've been the victim of a cyber-burglary! Prior to this chapter, you've been focusing on prevention and protection. In this one, you'll be learning what to do in the aftermath of a cyber-crime.

Above all, don't panic. Think of your network as a crime scene where the criminal's footprints are clearly imprinted in the snow. Act too slowly and the snow will melt, removing the tracks. But acting rashly is even worse; it's the equivalent of stepping all over the place, muddying and confusing the evidence imprinted in the snow. What to do (after you take a deep breath and notify your users, if needed) depends on whether you're there for the heinous deed or whether you're just looking at the aftermath.

What to Do If the Security Compromise Is Still in Progress

If the security breach is still in progress when you've discovered it, what you do varies greatly with the type of breach. By and large, purposeful security breaches fall into three main categories.

The local user gone bad

Luckily, this will be the most common of your security problems if you catch the breach in "real-time." I say "luckily" because it's an easy breach to deal with, and it's also relatively easy to change the behavior of a member of your user community. The majority of the time, the user isn't really out to destroy anything, they're either just curious or trying to test their knowledge against yours.

First, confirm that they are in fact who you think they are. Call the user's office if you have their extension, or locate the host that the person is logging in from. If you can locate them, ask them what they think they are up to — always assume that it's an honest mistake. If something still sounds fishy to you, then try to take them aside and explain the rules to them gently but firmly.

If the pattern persists, you can either call in management, or you can deal with the problem yourself. The best way to deal with continued internal problems is the following:

1. **Su to root and change directories to the /etc area.**

```
Linuxbox% su
Passwd: *****
# cd /etc
```

2. **Vi the password file to include an asterisk in the encrypted password field. For example, let's say that your /etc/passwd file looks as follows:**

```
root:EIUiuh654DSA:0:0:Root User:/:/bin/csh
loki:ZXCE302822:100:132:Loki, God of
        Mischief:/usr/home/loki:/bin/csh
nobody:OOWAJHQL2:105:122:Dummy
        Account:/usr/home/nobody:/bin/sh
wally:TROI8761111:105:161: Wally the Wonder
        User:/usr/home/wally:/bin/sh
```

3. **If user account "loki" is causing all the mischief and refuses to stop, edit the file so it looks as follows:**

```
root:EIUiuh654DSA:0:0:Root User:/:/bin/csh
loki:*:100:132:Loki, God of
        Mischief:/usr/home/loki:/bin/csh
nobody:OOWAJHQL2:105:122:Dummy
        Account:/usr/home/nobody:/bin/sh
wally:TROI8761111:105:161: Wally the Wonder
        User:/usr/home/wally:/bin/sh
```

You may be wondering, "But the asterisk is a wildcard! Aren't you opening his account up to more security problems?" That's not the case here. Annoying as it may seem, this is one of Linux's quirks — in the /etc/passwd file, an asterisk means that the account is "locked."

When a user's account is locked, no password will work for that user until you decide to reactivate the account. You can do that by removing the asterisk and running "passwd" to reset the password on the user's account.

Why not just delete the user's passwd entry? Because we always want to assume the best in people — if this person honestly reforms, it's a good deal easier to unlock an account rather than construct a whole new account from scratch.

A more serious situation arises when you have an internal user problem and the user isn't even on the network. For example, they're in their office when the account says that they're logged in from an off-site host! Right away, you need to investigate further. This person's user account has been compromised in some way, and you have a "network cracker" situation to deal with.

The network cracker

Network crackers, if they're worth their salt, are very difficult, if not impossible to trace. If you detect a breach in progress, you should be spending your time not on locating them but on isolating them before they do any (or more) damage to your system. Your top priority is to disconnect them from your network.

While this may inconvenience your users, you have to be ruthless about this. Unplug your modem cable if they're coming in from outside. Unplug the Ethernet connection if they're connected that way. Although you're sure to annoy some of your users if it's normal work hours, but an interrupted print job is a real good deal compared with the possibility of someone erasing all your user's files.

After you've disconnected the network, run a process search for any programs or scripts they may have activated on site and kill them. For example, let's say you find network cracker "loki" on your system and disconnect it. Do the following:

1. **Su to root and search for processes started by user account "loki."**

```
Linuxbox% su
Passwd: *****
# ps -aef |grep loki
```

2. **Let's say you find that loki is running two scripts:**

```
loki   754  1707  5 14:12:02 pts/0      0:00 trash_the_place
loki   755  1707  5 14:12:02 pts/0      0:00
       delete_all_passwds
```

3. **Drop these processes in their tracks with a "kill–9" command:**

```
# kill -9 754 755
```

Monitor your site well for the next few minutes. If you're lucky, your cracker might think he had a momentary network glitch and will try to get back in.

A physical compromise

Although I've never experienced it, I have heard of one case where someone actually spotted an intruder breaking into their computer lab. This should be where your responsibility ends. Call your company or university security, or the local police if the lab is in your private residence.

Don't attract attention to yourself if you've been spotted. Make use of your time while you're waiting for the authorities to arrive. If you're in a safe area, log into a machine and start killing scripts that look suspicious, or disconnect the main server's network connections if you can do it from where you are. Your goal at this point is not to bring the suspect in — that's for other people — but to reduce or eliminate the damage that may be occurring at that very minute.

What to Do If the Security Compromise Has Already Taken Place

More often than not, you'll find out that your network has been compromised "after the fact." This will either come from you spotting a suspicious looking log, a process running that you nor any of your users set into motion, or users coming up and complaining that their mail file has been edited. What's a good Linux system administrator to do?

Assessing damage

Your first task is to asses the damage to the system. What exactly has been compromised? If you're running the Tripwire program, you can use it to perform an integrity check. If you don't run Tripwire, you may have to settle for cd'ing into different directories to see what's gone, or (worse yet) wait for users to complain that they can't get file X, Y, or Z.

Tripwire, being such a useful utility, is included on the CD-ROM that accompanies this book.

In the case of significant breaches, you might consider saving your Linux configuration files (/etc/passwd, /etc/inet.d and the like) to another machine or to a floppy disk. You could then reinstall Linux on your server fresh.

Reinstallation is essential if the intruder has compromised the *root* account. If you have time, you can make a backup of the current state of the system if you feel there may be evidence that helps you track down the cracker.

Reinstallation also has one big advantage to simply restoring the system from an old backup. Since you can never be exactly sure when the system was compromised, your backup may contain the same elements of your network (like a compromised /etc/passwd file) that allowed the cracker to slip through in the first place.

Finally, you have to be cautious of any binaries that you restore, as the cracker may have placed a couple "Trojan horses" to further compromise your system.

Worms, viruses, and trojans, oh my!

You've probably heard about viruses, which are programs that "infect" your computer system and cause it to crash or go into some kind of odd behavior. The other two kinds of cracker programs are less well known.

Worms, for example, are a kind of subset of the virus programs. Their sole purpose in life is to fill up and eat away at the memory on your machine until it grinds to a halt or crashes. Trojan Horses are another kind of "gotcha" program cooked up by crackers.

A "Trojan" is a program that is solely designed to get you to type in some crucial bit of information (such as your root password), send it to the cracker, then delete itself. Sometimes it's hard to know for sure if you've been stung by one of these kamikaze programs. When in doubt though, change your passwords!

Patching up the fence

Once you determine how your system was compromised, try to close that gap. For example, let's say that you determine that multiple telnet sessions from an unknown host appeared during the break-in. Disable the telnet service on your network.

Check your software documentation or your Linux vendor's web site for an updated version or security patch that deals with the problem. Often, simply changing the version of your compromised process is enough to stop a cracker from coming back for seconds.

Reporting It In to the Pros

Always report a network security breach to your superiors and to the professionals if you're dealing with a network cracker. To be sure, the chance of catching a reasonably proficient cracker is quite slim. This is, ironically, due to the increasingly high level of network connectivity we have today.

A cracker won't hack into your system from his or her own workstation; instead they'll break into an intermediate system, and then come in through it. More sophisticated crackers will break into multiple networks, to ensure that the entire trail will be lost or wiped out by the time they're being followed.

If you're the victim of this kind of crime and you want to pursue it, here's who you should notify:

- First, notify any security organizations you are a part of.

- Notify your Linux system vendor. Network break-ins make people more worried about using Linux — particularly their brand of it — so they have a motive to help you find the cracker.

- Notify the system administrator at the site where the attacker attacked your system. If the cracker went through several systems to get to yours, then each of these sites should know their security has also been compromised.

- Notify the Internic and send them an email with all log entries, dates and times that relate to the breach.

- For truly big stuff like industrial espionage, notify the FBI, which actually has a "cybercrimes" division.

Part VIII

Linux Disasters and Recovery Techniques

The 5th Wave
By Rich Tennant

"You the guy having trouble staying connected to the network?"

In this part . . .

Hurricanes? Earthquakes? Forest fires? Mere annoy-ances compared to what can happen if somebody pulls the wrong plug on your Linux system at a crucial time. Whether you've suffered a blackout from a blown fuse, a scorching power surge, or a magnetic pulse from a nearby nuclear explosion, you know the first thing you have to do:

Get the Linux system back on line!

(See how this work clarifies your priorities?) Help is at hand: Part VIII shows you how to reduce your system's vulnerability to power changes, dips, and surges. With its wizardly guidance, you undertake the quest to protect your system from universal chaos, random strangeness, and even program faults like the dreaded Y2K bug.

You also see how to recover quickly from a major problem — including the proper procedure for bringing your system back up from a power outage or surge. (Sorry, but you're on your own with that nuclear-explosion thing.) For problems a bit less severe than a meltdown, a whole chapter on Linux troubleshooting issues gives you a jump-start on effective solutions.

On the far side of Part VIII, you may catch yourself start-ing to enjoy a new perspective on things — up to and including network snarl-ups. As a former manager once told me, "Be thankful for some problems. Without them, you might not have a job!" Of course, no one book (or set of books, for that matter) can ever cover *all* the obscure, bizarre issues you may encounter in your tenure as a Linux system administrator — hey, it's a job *and* an adven-ture — but you'll have a good handle on some common problems. It's a better place to start from.

Chapter 26

Minimizing System Crashes

●●●

In This Chapter

▶ Preventing the worst from happening

▶ Your backup policy

▶ BRU

▶ PerfectBACKUP

▶ The "Tar" Command

●●●

*W*hile Linux has a deserved reputation for stability, you can never be too sure about getting all of your data back in the event of a system crash. In this chapter, you'll learn how to determine if your system needs backups, and if so, how to determine what kind of backup policy you need. You'll also see how you can spot warning signs of a machine crash.

You'll also learn about the backup utilities that are available for Linux. You have a lot to choose from, whether it's a commercial backup utility or a standard Linux one. Of the Linux utilities, you'll be learning how to use both tar and cpio.

Spotting Potential Trouble Spots

Linux is such a well-behaved system, that spotting potential trouble coming down the road is easy. That isn't to say that Linux doesn't have its share of quirks! However, a consistent pattern of certain kinds of errors is a sure sign that something is broken on your system.

Once you spot the trouble — or at least its symptom — your first move should not be to solve the problem. Instead, move to make backups of the system in case anything goes haywire, so at least you have some rubble to pick up after the explosion. Next, determine the cause of the continued problem and fix it. If you don't know the fix offhand, do some research first (the troubleshooting chapter in this book is a good place to start), roll up your sleeves, and prepare to get your hands dirty.

You're most likely to be heading for a system crash if you start seeing any of the following signs cropping up on a consistent basis:

✔ You receive error messages when trying to save files on either a networked drive or a drive that's local to one of your main servers.

When you see these errors, use the following command:

```
df -k .
```

This will show the amount of free space left on a drive's partition. If you're below 5 percent, you're filling up the entire disk slice. There's no surer way to crash a machine than to overload it with data. Immediately look for large files that can be safely deleted.

✔ Your NFS server is not responding to system requests.

If you get the messages "Stale NFS file handle" or "NFS server not responding," then you have an NFS problem. This can be due to problems with the NFS daemon, or a hardware problem with the NFS server itself. Either way, you need to check this out ASAP.

✔ A network packet collision rate of more than five percent.

Running the netstat utility will often tell you if you simply have too much network traffic. A high collision rate means that you need to upgrade your network, or your network daemons may simply give up the ghost and crash the system.

One problem that definitely won't lead to a system-wide crash is where you have monitor problems. If you boot up and you get a blank screen, check your monitor cables and the graphics card in your Linux box. Since the monitor is a purely nonnetworked interface, it will be annoying to you, but hardly fatal for the user community at large.

Your Backup Policy

Your backup policy should reflect the state, need, and budget of your system. While many people say that regardless of the size of your system, you need a backup policy, I disagree. I feel you should make backups, for nothing else than to help restore your system settings in the event of a crash. But let's face it, if you run a network where people save material only to floppy disks and social e-mail is the main use of the system, you'll find a backup policy to be more of a pain than a panacea.

You should set a cron job to do perform the "tar" or "cpio" command at certain intervals to save the most valuable information from your site. You can save your data on several kinds of medium, including tape drives, external hard drives, or CD-ROMs. You can even use floppy disks, but your network had better be small. The only mistake you want to avoid here is to not save the information locally (that is, on a portion of the disk which may crash and be unrecoverable). How you set up and run your backup device should be determined by your device's vendor or user guide.

You should plan on doing a *quarterly* backup if your situation approximates the following:

- ✔ You have one or two servers distributing data.
- ✔ Your users store minimal amounts of data.
- ✔ Most of the data is personal e-mail.
- ✔ Your network is mostly "flat," that is, very little use of NFS.

You should plan on doing a *monthly* backup if your situation approximates the following:

- ✔ You have a couple of servers running at all times.
- ✔ Your users need the network to store departmental files which change on a weekly basis.
- ✔ Most of the data is word processing or spreadsheets.
- ✔ Your user community uses the machines for full business days at a time.

You should plan on doing a *weekly* backup if your situation approximates the following:

- ✔ You run a bank of servers.
- ✔ Your users store most of their information on the servers.
- ✔ The data is valuable financial or technical information.
- ✔ Your user community needs this network as the company's backbone.

You should plan on doing a *daily* backup if your situation approximates the following:

- ✔ You have more users and/or servers than the smaller member nations of NATO.
- ✔ Your data is valuable and irreplaceable.
- ✔ Your users do heavy software development or anything else that requires daily change.
- ✔ Your user community will be after you with pitchforks and torches if the network goes down.

When the Going Gets Tough, the Tough Start Backing Up

Linux has several commercial software products to smooth out and automate your backup procedures.

BRU

BRU, the "Backup and Restore" program, is based on the older, "tar" program that you can still find on Linux by default. Where BRU really shines is that it supports and works with NFS, NIS, and Netware. BRU also has reasonably good data recovery systems, so if someone waved the electromagnet too close to your backup tapes, you're not completely out of luck.

BRU is also very user friendly in that it has a menu driven interface, so long as you run X Windows. You can find out more about this product from www.estline.com.

PerfectBACKUP+

PerfectBACKUP is more flexible and more user friendly than BRU. It's more flexible in that it allows file compression, support for all file types, and it's intelligent enough to switch to a different backup system if one is full or damaged. It's more user friendly in that it has a menu-driven system that works with ASCII text and also Motif interfaces.

You can find out more about PerfectBACKUP at www.home.xl.ca/ perfectBackup. Bring your checkbook!

In the noncommercial world, you can easily complete your backup tasks with the standard utilities of tar and cpio. Your criteria should fall into the quarterly or monthly backup schedule, however, because tar and cpio aren't as fast as the commercial products.

Also, unlike commercial products, you'll have to make sure that the backup media you're using (tapes, CDs, etc) is in good working order. Tar and cpio won't complain to you if they can't do their jobs completely. With that caveat in mind, tar and cpio are some of the finest and most useful tools you'll find in Linux.

Tar

Tar is one of the oldest, most reliable Linux utilities in existence. It's called tar not because it sticks to anything, but because it's shorthand for "Tape ARchive." The tar command options you'll find most useful are:

Table 26-1	Tar Command Options
Command Option	*What It Does*
-c	Create a new tar file.
-f	Use archive file or device F (default /dev/rmt0).
-r	Append the new tar files to the end of an archive.
-t	List the contents of a tar archive.
-x	Extract a tar file.
-v	Reply verbosely when processing files.

As an example, let's say that you want to tar up the file /tmp/superfile. So long as you own the file, you don't have to become root to use tar. Perform the following command on the file "superfile."

```
Linuxbox% tar -cvf superfile
```

The tar command does its thing, perhaps even scrolling a list by you of the files inside the "superfile" to remind you of what the contents are. When finished, you can do an "ls" on the file, and you'll see it's still there, but reduced in size:

```
Linuxbox% superfile.tar
```

The ".tar" suffice at the end is a flag to notify you that this file is no longer readable unless you run "tar" to extract it. And speaking of running tar again, here's the simplest way to do just that:

```
Linuxbox% tar -xvf superfile.tar
```

Note that the setting is for verbose extraction this time, and the name you're specifying is the .tar file, not the original file name, "superfile."

Chapter 27

Linux Troubleshooting

● ●

In This Chapter

▶ Avoiding startup problems

▶ Covering basic administration issues

▶ Tackling password problems

▶ Dealing with hung or crashed programs

▶ Accessing external disk drives

▶ Troubleshooting NFS problems

▶ Can't find the answer?

● ●

*I*n this chapter, I offer solutions to some of the most common problems you'll encounter with your Linux system. Of course, other chapters in the book highlight many solutions to common problems through the sections marked with Tip, Warning, or Technical Stuff icons. You won't find those solutions repeated in this chapter.

To be fair, you may not find the solution to every problem you'll encounter here, either. But when you have a true Linux problem that stymies every attempt you or your administrators make to fix it, check this chapter first. And if you don't find the solution here, you'll no doubt find suggestions on where to go next.

Warding Off Startup Problems

By default, the Linux operating system performs a series of system integrity checks before it comes on line. The extensive checking that Linux does before making its resources available is one of the reasons Linux is such a stable system. By and large, the only startup problems you encounter revolve around the overzealous nature of the checking process.

Checking your kernel on every reboot (NOT!)

When you make additions to your system that affect the Linux kernel, Linux checks the file systems on each reboot. If your system runs `fsck` (the structure-checking utility) each time, chances are it thinks that you're making more changes than you actually are. To fix this situation, `su` to root and run the following:

```
Linuxbox% su
Passwd: *****
# rdev -R /zImage 1
```

The preceding command resets the program flags to keep the `fsck` startup script from thinking that you modified the kernel.

Avoiding busy devices on reboot

If your Linux shutdown command fails to kill all processes and `umount` the disks, then you can get the *device busy* error as the system tries to compensate for the mistake during reboot. You can correct things by adding the following line to `/etc/rc.d/init.d/halt` or `/etc/rc.d/rc.0` for all your mounted file systems except / (the root directory):

```
mount -o remount,ro /mount.dir
```

If you continue to have `fsck` processes running automatically after the fixes discussed in this section, you definitely have a problem with the hard disk on your system. Back up all your files onto another machine and spring for a new hard drive — immediately.

Basic Administration Issues: Directories and Processes

Over 75 percent of your daily troubleshooting problems that aren't immediately apparent relate to the amount of space on your system. Actually, that's not quite true — the problems revolve around not having enough space! Therefore, make sure that you're familiar with how to track down problems. After you determine a problem's source, you can resolve a lack-of-space issue with a carefully placed `mv`, `cp`, or `rm` command.

Finding out which directories are the largest

When you're suddenly running short on space, your first step is checking for the largest directories. Doing this helps you narrow down the location of the largest file you need to delete. Run the following du, or *disk usage,* command. You don't have to be at root to run this.

```
Linuxbox% du -S | sort -n
```

Identifying the biggest files on your hard-drive

Your next step is to locate the biggest files, as follows.

```
ls -l | sort +4n
```

Most of the time, huge files that appear out of thin air are the result of either:

- ✔ A user's log file running out of control, usually when said user is on vacation.
- ✔ A user who's downloading something truly huge from the Internet via ftp.

Luckily, both situations are easily dealt with from the root account. Fire up the rm command and remove those overgrown files!

Finding out what process is eating up your memory

Another problem you may encounter happens when a runaway process begins stealing so many CPU cycles that your whole machine slows down. Run the following command to locate the offending process.

```
ps -aux | sort +4n
```

After you locate the hoggish process, get the PID (process ID number) from this command and kill it. If the process is out of control, you'll likely have to use the kill -9 command.

Password Problems

Most administrators face the two problems that I describe in the following sections at some point in their careers.

Users forget their login passwords

A forgotten user password is the easiest problem to solve in this whole chapter. In fact, instead of restoring the user's password, make it policy to create a new password for a user who forgets one. Not only does this approach increase security, it also encourages your users to remember their old passwords!

To fix the forgotten-password problem, su to root and run the passwd command. For example, say that user Loki forgot his password. His old password is not relevant at this point because we're going to give him a brand new one!

```
Linuxbox% su
Passwd: *****
# passwd Loki
```

Linux prompts you for a new password for user Loki. You have to type it twice to ensure that no typos get in the way.

You, the root user, forget the root password

While not fatal in and of itself, forgetting the root password is extremely humiliating — and potentially catastrophic — if you have a system problem while you're struggling with password issues for root. Follow these steps to take care of a forgotten root password:

1. **Boot your computer from your Linux boot diskette and get to your Linux root partition on the hard drive.**

2. **Open the /etc/passwd file with the vi editor.**

3. **Find the root entry and prepare to edit it.**

   The root entry in /etc/passwd may look like the following:

   ```
   root:EIUiuh654DSA:0:0:Root User:/:/bin/csh
   ```

4. **Delete the encrypted password section of the root entry.**

   The second field is the one you want to delete. In the example, remove the `EIUiuh654DSA`, and the result looks like:

   ```
   root::0:0:Root User:/:/bin/csh
   ```

   The root account now has no password.

5. **Reboot the computer. At the login prompt, type root, press enter for the password, and you'll be logged in.**

6. **Set the password for root with the** `passwd` **command (as detailed in Chapter 6) for setting a user password.**

Dealing with Programs that Go Crash in the Night

Believe it or not, you may run across some buggy programs under Linux. A crashed or hung application doesn't generally lead to a reboot. However, any operating system that has processes continually malfunctioning can be a sign of hardware or configuration problems.

If you see programs hanging on a consistent basis, start checking for adequate space on your system and reviewing network and host parameters for misconfigurations or corrupt data files.

Killing a program that's already hung

A program that *hangs* is one that simply sits there and does nothing; to make matters worse, it normally locks up your whole screen.

You can kill any hung program with the `kill` or `kill -9` command.

Before taking that drastic step, however, try to kill a program more gently. You can often kill any program running from the command line in the foreground (such as vi) by pressing Ctrl+C.

If Ctrl+C has no effect, start with a `ps` command to get the process ID number and run the `kill` command. One feature that may come in handy is a `kill` command with a shortcut — `killall` — that lets you kill programs by name. You're best off running this at root. For example, the following command kills any program with *telnet* in its name.

```
# killall telnet
```

To hang or not hang, that is the question. . .

Keep in mind that some programs that look like they're not doing anything may in fact be hard at work. For example, when you run `ftp` to get or put files on your system, always switch on the hash markings. The scrolling hash marks are a healthy indicator that all is well with an otherwise silent program.

X-windows-based programs have no control terminals. To kill one of these programs, do the following:

1. **Type the following in an X-terminal.**

   ```
   # xkill
   ```

2. **Point your cursor into the window of the program you want to kill and press the left mouse button.**

   The program terminates, and the program's window disappears for good measure as well!

Note that if your X-windows system crashes so that it cannot recover, you're best off to put the X-server itself out of its misery by pressing Ctrl+Alt+Backspace.

Getting to the core of the matter

When a program crashes (that is, it exits unexpectedly rather than hanging around), it often dumps a *core* into the directory where you started it. This action is accompanied by an error message, such as `bus error`, which, contrary to rumors, has nothing to do with your local mass transit company.

A *core file* is a memory image that is meant to be a debugging tool. If you don't plan to debug the program, delete the core as follows:

```
Linuxbox% rm core
```

Don't keep core files around unless your vendor requests to see them. Core files, by nature, are huge and take up valuable disk space.

Accessing Your External Disk Drives

In this case, *external drives* means any piece of computer hardware that isn't your CPU itself. To further confuse matters, *external* doesn't mean that the device can't share the same case! External devices can include internally mounted CD-ROM drives and even the standard floppy drive that comes with some UNIX boxes.

Getting to your CD-ROM

If you can't automatically access your CD-ROM, you have to mount it manually. As root, mount the CD-ROM with the following command:

```
Linuxbox% su
Passwd: ****
# mount -t auto /dev/cdrom /mnt/cdrom
```

The contents of the CD appear in the directory /mnt/cdrom. If you're using X-windows or CDE, you can call up a File Manager program that displays the contents of the newly mounted file system. You shouldn't encounter this problem on PCs that run Linux.

To unmount a mounted CD, follow these steps:

1. **Exit the** /mnt/cdrom **directory.**

2. **Become root.**

3. **Use the umount command as follows:**

   ```
   # umount /dev/cdrom
   ```

If you cannot unmount because the device is busy, make sure that you're not in the /mnt directory. Use the pwd command to determine your directory location and then cd out of the directory if you are in /mnt. If you still get a busy device error message, determine whether any other users on your system are in this directory and ask them to move out.

Accessing your floppy disk

Mounting a floppy disk in Linux is similar to mounting a CD-ROM drive or any other kind of file system. It's all the same thing to Linux, and you'll use similar syntax. Mount the floppy as follows:

```
Linuxbox% su
Passwd: ****
# mount -t auto /dev/fd0 /mnt/floppy
```

After a successful mount, the files from the floppy appear in the directory /mnt/floppy. Again, if you run CDE or X-windows, you can see the contents graphically if you start the File Manager. You won't be able to eject the disk until you unmount the floppy. To do this, use the following command:

```
# umount /mnt/floppy
```

Next, eject the disk with this command:

```
# eject floppy
```

Sometimes, you don't need to type **eject floppy** — only **eject**. The exact pattern depends on the version of Linux you use.

Mounting your zip drive

Mount the parallel port external zip drive to emulate a SCSI connection with the following commands:

```
Linuxbox% su
Passwd: ****
# mount -t vfat /dev/sda4 /mnt/zipdrive
```

To umount, follow the same model procedure as listed above for floppies and CD-ROM drives.

Printing pages with a margin for hole punching

I take an entire chapter (Chapter 7) to cover printers, and the vast majority of Linux systems sold today come with automated setup programs. However, one question comes up time and again from people with *really* antiquated systems: "How do I print pages with a margin for punching holes?"

The following is an invaluable script for those who need to print and punch on a regular basis. Mike Dickey, mdickey@thorplus.lib.purdue.edu, wrote this script:

```
#!/bin/sh
# /usr/local/bin/print
# a simple formatted printout, to enable someone to
# 3-hole punch the output and put it in a binder
cat $1 | pr -t -o 5 -w 85 | lpr
```

Mounting and NFS Troubleshooting

A fair number of your troubleshooting issues may revolve around mounting. Whether you mount file systems manually or rely on NFS, you can resolve most of your troubles by running the mount command, checking for the mount daemon, or editing the NFS critical host files. However, you may find that some of the following solutions also come in handy.

Getting stale nfs handle errors during normal use

A known bug from older versions of Linux can cause `stale nfs handle` error message during periods of normal use. While the message doesn't cause your system to crash or freeze, it's annoying. You can fix this bug by replacing your NFS server software with versions 2beta16 and later.

Finding that you can't register with portmap

Another known bug, found in the startup scripts on older versions of the Caldera brand of Linux, may cause your system to display `Can't register with portmap: system error on send` when mounting a file system. Contact Caldera to obtain a fix or check for the fix on their Web site. You can probably download the appropriate patch.

The NFS name resolution doesn't jibe with the exports list

You may be denied access to your external drives if the NFS name resolution doesn't quite match the exports list. For example, mount permission may be denied to machine `Loki` because the list says export to `Loki` when the machine's name is resolved as `Loki.Asgard.com`.

Fix this error by exporting to both forms of the name. Add `Loki.Asgard.com` to the `/export` directory.

Having to limit user group participation

You may find that the server won't accept a mount from a user account that is listed in more than eight user groups. This is another known bug with only one known fix. Determine which group you can remove the user from and change the entries in the `/etc/group` file. I know of no reason that users have to be in more than eight groups simultaneously — they're probably drowning in e-mail!

Unmounting, rebooting, and hanging, oh my!

When rebooting, a machine sometimes hangs when trying to unmount a hung NFS server. This quirk really has no fix. Just don't try to unmount NFS servers when rebooting or halting. It doesn't hurt anything if you don't unmount the NFS servers at that time.

Where to Go If You Can't Find the Answer Here

To keep abreast of the latest Linux troubleshooting tips and bug fixes, do some of the following on a regular basis:

- ✔ **Read Linux newsgroups.** I recommend `comp.os.linux.announce`, `comp.security.announce`, or any new newsgroup that crops up with Linux in the name.

- ✔ **Read publications dedicated to the Linux world.** For example, John Fisk, the creator of the *Linux Gazette,* puts out an excellent e-zine on the Web. Check it out at `www.linuxgazette.com`.

- ✔ **Keep a good set of Linux Reference material around.** This book, of course, falls into that category (plug, plug, plug), but you can also find more technical reference manuals, which may be dry as dust, but can still be good as encyclopedic reference material.

✔ **Make friends with senior network administrators.** This is probably the most important thing you can do to increase your Linux knowledge. Linux has a quirky, band-of-brothers mentality about it. A lot of material that you won't find in your technical reference guides gets passed on via oral tradition. (I tried to pass on some of these same secret things via the Tips and Warnings in this book, but I'm only scratching the surface.) Your best bet is to spring for a pizza on an evening when your senior network administrator is especially craving pepperoni and sausage.

✔ **Look for Linux administration groups.** If you don't have a senior administrator to bribe (um, butter up), then search the Web for Linux administration organizations in your area. Try to attend a few functions; you may make some new friends, and you'll certainly meet people who have seen problems that can make your head spin!

Chapter 28

Fumigating the Year 2000 Bug

. . . .

In This Chapter

▶ Defining the Y2K problem

▶ Counting down to a different Linux date

▶ Testing and date problems

▶ Checking out C programs

▶ Backing up to stay covered

. . . .

*I*n this chapter, you can read about the origins of the famous (or infamous) Y2K bug and how it relates to your Linux system and its operation after January 1, 2000 AD rolls around. You can see what trouble spots you have in your system and how to solve them before the Year 2000 fireworks kick off.

Why Y2K?

In a sense, the whole Y2K problem is a modern-day parable of why you shouldn't cut corners when it comes to your work. Essentially, when computers were first being used for something more than complex arithmetic, the decision was made to save space by counting the year with the last two digits of the date. Though a good choice in the short term, it's come back to haunt us a couple of decades further down the line.

Therefore, come the year 2000, some programs will be unable to tell the difference between the years 2000 and 1900. This confusion could mean phone bills lasting 100 years or your bank account lasting less than a second. The effects depend on how programs actually run, as opposed to what so-called experts guess will happen.

Most of the experts who aren't predicting that civilization will regress to the Stone Age agree that between five and ten percent of computer networks in the United States alone will be drastically affected by the Y2K bug. This number may not seem statistically significant to you — missing five percent of the questions on a test still gets you an A, for example. But with the way networks are hooked together today, a cascading effect could cause outages far out of proportion to the number of systems that actually go down.

Where Y2K hits below the belt in the Linux world

Now for some good news: If you run Linux, you'll face very few problems come the turn of the millennium. Unlike some of the rumors that you may have heard about on the Internet or from millennium doomsday prophets, Linux is going to remain the king of operating system stability come the year 2000. Why? Well, because of this Y2038 bug that everyone's talking about.

Linux, like the UNIX operating system, uses libraries that store its system dates as 32-bit integers. These libraries contain a counter that tracks the seconds since 1970. Since there are 32 bits in the integer, the counter isn't scheduled to overflow until the year 2038!

Okay, so what to do about the Y2038 bug?

Well, if you really think you'll be taking care of the same Linux system 38 years after the millennium, I think you deserve to get your company gold watch early! But Y2K serves as a parable about how you shouldn't cut corners, so I suggest you keep an eye on Linux development. Unless you're a developer yourself, your best use of your time is spent watching Linux news. Given the devotion that Linux inspires in its user community, it's a practical certainty that a development team somewhere in the Linux-using world will have the system software upgraded to store dates as 64-bit integers by 2038.

Does this mean that you can ignore the Y2K bug and party like it's 1999? Well, not yet. Just because Linux isn't set up to bomb out in 2000 doesn't mean that its applications are not susceptible to the millennium bug. It also doesn't mean that your system resources are completely safe come the turn of the century, either. But at least this latter problem is easy to test by using the `date` parameter on your Linux system.

It's a Date! An Expiration Date, Actually

The date parameter in Linux refers to the system date set in your local Linux box. Be aware of two items of note: First, the date is set locally, so each machine on your network may be set to a different time or date. Unfortunately, no mechanism is available that lets you set the date across an entire network from a central server, NFS-style. Say that you run date on your NFS server, Linuxbox:

```
Linuxbox% date
Jul 13 07:15 1999
```

Next, you run date on the machine pinto.

```
Pinto% date
Jul 23 10:11 1987
```

Which is correct? Since Linux time is purely subjective (that is, what you told the machine), then you're better off looking at your watch.

The second item to note is that date is an incredibly easy thing to set, allowing you to test out Y2K-ish conditions on your machine without too many problems.

Testing. . . testing. . . anyone home?

Your best bet for starting your Y2K testing is to let your system run during the off hours — a quiet evening when nobody is logged on — and change the date on one of your machines. I advise that you set it to a few minutes before midnight on that crucial night, December 31, 1999. Then, sit back, let the clock roll over, and start running through Linux commands, visit all the local file connections, and check to see that none of your daemons have died or cannot be restarted. Here's a set of step-by-step instructions.

1. **Become** Root.

```
Linuxbox% su
#
```

2. **Run the** date **command with a date to** Input: **In this case, use** December 31, 1999 **at** 11:55 p.m.

```
# date 1231115599
```

3. **Check the results of this command on the system time by running** date **with no additional extensions.**

You should get:

```
# date
# Dec 31 11:55 1999
```

4. **Give it five minutes or so. When midnight (system time) rolls around, start testing. If you're really ambitious, and it won't affect others on the system, try rebooting your machine to make sure all processes start back up properly.**

Note that although this procedure is a good way to test out basic system functionality, it still won't give you an idea about how bad your other, more difficult problem, will be. This problem is actually outside of Linux itself — the vendors' programs that run on your Linux system may cause you the most grief.

From C to shining C programs: The Linux bane

Linux, and most programs written for Linux, are written in a programming language called C. Depending on the software programming libraries used in building your software, you may have serious problems on Y2K day. You could end up with a malfunctioning database, a speechless word processor, or a sputtering screen saver. You have a couple different options to take when faced with this problem.

Option 1: Do nothing

Of course there's a possibility that you'll have problems. But then, is it worth your time and effort? Be realistic. It's one thing if you manage a Linux system that runs a stock trading floor. But if you're the administrator for a Linux card cataloging system in the library of Podunk, East Nowheresville, how is a little down time going to hurt you? Many programs with a Y2K bug will simply need to be restarted. More to the point, if you run the library system in Podunk, will anyone notice if your system thinks it's the year 1900?

Option 2: Cheat a little

Yes, I know this Y2K bug is a parable about not cutting corners, but then, I'm not in your shoes. Again, if you don't have a pressing need to correct all Y2K problems, who's to say that you can't play with the system dates to your heart's content? If you have a Y2K problem with a piece of software that isn't compliant and exists in one location only, then fix the problem by changing the system date on that one machine!

Ever want to visit the Fabulous Fifties? The Roaring Twenties? Fire up the date command and turn your Linux box into a time machine!

Option 3: Fix the problem, but not on your own time

Your best bet is to fix the problem — but not by turning into a Y2K guru. Instead, think more like a project manager than a programmer. It's unlikely you'll have the time or the inclination to debug the code in every program. Instead, make a quick inventory of all the programs you use.

Say you come up with

- ✔ StarOffice
- ✔ Applix
- ✔ Oracle
- ✔ Netscape

Determine the versions you're using for each application. Then, make a chart to plot out the actions you take on each application. Locate the user documentation and call, write, or e-mail the vendor from the company's Web site or corporate headquarters. You must determine whether you're running Y2K-compliant software.

If you're not, then your next step is to find out which, if any, of their versions are compliant. Make the upgrade if you can justify the cost. Usually you'll be able to, as the majority of companies providing Linux software would like to keep you as customers, so ensuring that you have a Y2K-compliant piece of their work is in their best interest.

If they don't have any plans for making the software compliant at all, then evaluate how important the program is. Will it truly shut your office down if it crashes in January? Is it worth switching to another brand? Just remember that in the worst case scenario, where you can't replace the software and it's set to go up in flames like the Hindenberg on the night of Y2K, then don't hide that fact from the users in your community. Make sure they know to save their work or prepare to transfer it to another program. You never, ever want to be caught making promises that a vendor can't keep!

Did I Mention Backups?

I preach about the value of backup systems in Chapter 26. I wasn't joking then, and I'm not joking now. If you skipped to this chapter, go to Chapter 26 and save that data before you do anything else. If you already read Chapter 26, then go back and reread it. Nothing is as good as reinforcement on that point. Backups are your way of making sure you don't have to face an angry world of users and managers when you come back from your New Year's party on January 1, 2000.

Part IX
The Part of Tens

The 5th Wave   By Rich Tennant

CUSTOMER PHONE SERVICE AT DISNEY CORP.

In this part . . .

*P*art *Nine* is The Part of *Tens?* Yep. (You *have* been
paying attention. Cool.) If you're a veteran *...For
Dummies* reader, you already know that the Part of Tens is
all about summing up valuable information. If you're new
to the *...For Dummies* fold, you're in for a treat.

The Part of Tens gives you lists of — you guessed it — ten
things which will enrich your experience as a Linux
administrator, or just plain make your job a lot easier.

In this particular instance, you get my personal ratings
and recommendations on these strategic matters:

- The top 10 utilities a Linux administrator should have
  available for ready use.

- The top 10 tools your user community should have
  available.

- The top 10 Web sites where you can get even more
  Linux information to slake your insatiable thirst for
  Linux knowledge. (And if you've got one of those,
  you're definitely in the right field!)

Chapter 29

Ten Types of Linux Utilities You Should Know

*T*his chapter serves, in a way, as a recap of this book and a notice about how much more there is in the Linux world. In this section, I list many types of Linux tools that you may be familiar with, such as text editors and news processors.

I also include here new topics that you should try to get familiar with, depending on the work that your Linux network does. For example, if your site does a lot of software development, be sure to refer to the Development Tools section to see what you should be picking up next.

Linux is a huge operating system in the sense that it does so much with so little. Whether you want text processing, graphic design, or database management, you can find a program that runs on Linux. And chances are, it runs more quickly, takes less money to implement, and stays running with more stability than any comparable application.

Ten Types of Tools that Run under Linux

Running from the simple to the hideously complex, Linux covers the entire spectrum of tools and utilities. Listed here by category are the types of tools that you should make yourself familiar with, if for no other purpose than to make your life as a Linux administrator easier.

Shells

The most basic functionality from your Linux system consists of shell commands and utilities. The type of shell you use drastically affects how you code your programs and handle all aspects of your Linux world. So consider yourself fortunate that Linux handles so many kinds of shells and shell utilities with little problem. These shells include (but are not limited to):

- The Bourne shell (sh): The most basic of the shells.
- The Bourne-Again shell (bash): The successor to sh, it has a funnier name.
- The C shell (csh): Has the most user features.
- The Korn shell (ksh): The best all-around programming shell.

Graphical interfaces

Despite having little in the way of graphic interface on its own, Linux supports a surprising number of GUI interfaces. This boom just reflects the changing times — processing power isn't quite as scarce as it was ten years ago — but Linux GUIs are still stripped down compared to Windows systems. They have fewer services for users, but they're still lightweight enough to speed Linux along. These interfaces include (but are not limited to):

- The GNOME Desktop
- The KDE Desktop
- The X11R6 (XFree86 3.*x*) Environment
- CDE (The Common Desktop Environment)

UNIX commands and utilities

Linux is a member of the UNIX SVR4 family. The SVR4 clan, which includes Solaris, HPUX, and most other UNIX brands, descends from the old AT&T workings with UNIX. The split in the UNIX family between SVR4 and BSD (the

Berkeley side of doing things) is cause for endless debate and flame wars between the more passionate in the Linux community.

What this acronym-fest comes down to is: If you know a member of the UNIX SVR4 family, you can work very well with Linux. Some of the basic UNIX utilities you should know are ones that you may have already encountered in this book, such as:

- ✔ ls
- ✔ cd
- ✔ ping
- ✔ rlogin
- ✔ shutdown

If you want an even more basic introduction to the basic Linux/UNIX commands, check out *Linux For Dummies*, 2nd Edition, by Jon "Maddog" Hall.

Computer languages

Linux is able to handle many different kinds of computer languages — in fact, the kernel is built with C. You should have no problems running any of the following programming languages on a Linux system:

- ✔ C
- ✔ C++
- ✔ Common Lisp
- ✔ Fortran
- ✔ Java
- ✔ Modula-3
- ✔ Pascal
- ✔ Perl
- ✔ Python
- ✔ Tcl/tk

Development tools

Linux is a very popular development platform for many programmers, simply because it's so stable. On the other hand, the reason could simply be that Linux takes less time to reboot if a program crashes, taking the whole system with it. Linux will run the following development utilities and more:

- cvs
- gcc
- gdb
- make
- perl
- prof
- rcs

Networking

Linux offers you a wealth of networking options — perhaps too many to choose from intelligently. Don't try to learn everything at once — it's a good way to end up overwhelmed. Pick and choose what your network uses from the following list, which is by no means complete!

- PPP
- UUCP
- SLIP
- The TCP/IP communication toolset
- kermit
- pcomm
- xcomm

News and mail programs

You should be able to make use of the following products:

- C-news
- elm
- mail
- nn
- pine
- tin
- trn

Games

Linux isn't known for cutting-edge graphics or great fanfare of any sort, but you can find a host of Linux-native games on the Web, particularly at the FTP sites put out by Sun Microsystems. You'll find such timeless, job-wasting programs as:

- Nethack
- MUDS — Multiuser Dungeon Systems, which is an interactive, role-playing adventure sort of thing. Don't leave your sword at home!
- X games (named for the X Windows system), including an old favorite, Xpong.

Editors

Linux editors are not designed to produce printer product as much as to edit files within the Linux system. Since Linux inherited most of the UNIX editors, you can find a myriad of editors, including:

- awk
- ez
- GNU Emacs
- MicroEmacs
- jove
- Pico
- sed
- vi
- vim
- XEmacs

Text processing

Straightforward text processors are also abundant in Linux. These include:

- ✔ Applixware
- ✔ Ex
- ✔ groff
- ✔ StarOffice
- ✔ TeX
- ✔ vi

You can find more details on text editors for Linux in Chapter 30.

Chapter 30

Ten Applications Every Linux User Needs on Their Virtual Desktop

In This Chapter

▶ Text editors
▶ Spreadsheets
▶ Image processors
▶ Databases
▶ Web browsing

*Y*ou can find literally dozens of user applications for the benefit of your Linux user community, but you should always have certain ones available. The following ten programs are the most popular to work with in Linux due to their stability, ease of use, and wide availability. Another advantage to using these programs is that you have the option of purchasing maintenance contracts from the vendors.

Text Editors

Several text editors are available for Linux; the ones I list here are the most widely available. Which editor you choose should depend on the volume of text processing that goes on at your site, the needs of your user community (text versus graphics), and your site's budget.

Of course, if you run Windows machines which also use the Linux operating system, you can simply run Microsoft Word or WordPerfect for Windows. You can easily port documents from these programs into Linux ASCII text by saving the work as a Text Only document.

WordPerfect 8.0 for Linux

WordPerfect is often considered the best overall word processor in the world, though that doesn't sit well with a certain man in Seattle. But the fact remains that on Linux, WordPerfect is lightweight enough to really move, and on top of all that, you can even get a sample copy at `http://linux.corel.com/linux8/download.htm`.

This freeware version of WordPerfect is a full copy of the original, lacking only the following functions:

- ✔ Equation Editor
- ✔ Chart Editor
- ✔ Graphics Placement

WP8 is normally launched through an icon if you run Linux with a graphical environment (such as X Windows). Otherwise, you can execute the binary with the following command: **/usr/local/wp8/wpbin/xwp**

StarOffice Suite

StarOffice looks a lot like Microsoft Office for Windows. Like Microsoft Office, it's a complete office suite: word processor, spreadsheet, and presentation program. You can get the entire version for free at the following site: `www.stardivision.com/freeoffice`.

Of course, if you need certain goodies like vendor support or a networkable copy that multiple users can type away at to their hearts' content, you'll have to pay. But the complete "try before you buy" philosophy makes this utility an excellent buy.

My only caveat about StarOffice is that you need a fair amount of computer muscle to run the entire suite of product. Much like Microsoft Office, which it's often compared to, you'll probably find it too much of a hassle to run without at least 32 MB of physical memory for it to play with. However, if you have the equipment, this can be the best buy for you, particularly if you have a lot of users who have been weaned to the Microsoft look of applications.

Applixware

Like StarOffice, Applixware is another entire suite of programs. Applixware contains a word processor and spreadsheet, graphics, presentation, mail, and

HTML tools. Overall, I like the look and feel of Applixware better than any of the other application suite programs. It's also incredibly stable, and it's less memory intensive (usually) than StarOffice.

The down side? Unlike StarOffice, Applix doesn't provide a freeware version. Also, after you purchase the set of license keys for the application, you may find that updating the keys once per year is a real hassle, as it's neither simple nor straightforward. However, you should at the very least check out what Applix has available. See the site at `www.applix.com/appware/linux/index.htm` for more information.

Spreadsheets

While Linux spreadsheets won't have the designers of Microsoft Excel losing sleep at night, they're still pretty good and, on the average, more stable than the typical new software release from that big company up in Washington State.

Xess

Xess (pronounced, as you might guess, "excess") is overall the best spreadsheet available for Linux. You can purchase Xess from `www.ais.com/linux_corner.html`, or you can try out the free shareware version of Xess, called Xess-lite. This version can also be downloaded from their site.

Xess is a one-shot product; that is, it focuses on doing spreadsheets and nothing else. The tradeoff is that the product is extremely lightweight and fast, which can be a plus if you're behind the 8 ball in putting your Gantt charts or financial reports for your company together at the last minute.

Applixware (again)

Yes, it's Applixware again. Although it's the opposite of Xess in that it's not a one-shot (it's a complete suite of utilities, like Microsoft Office), Applixware is actually a very good spreadsheet program.

Again, I'm not aware of any freeware versions of this program, but you can check out the details at the Applixware Web site at `www.applix.com/appware/linux/index.htm`.

Image Processing

As unbelievable as it may sound, Linux, the operating system without a GUI, actually has some respectable computer-assisted design programs. What makes Linux shine in this department is the fact that so little of the processing power goes to the operating system (a GUI is, after all, a big drag) that a lot is left over for CAD processing.

Microstation

By its reputation, Microstation makes a CAD system which is as good as the industry standard, AutoCAD. It's not strictly a Linux product, but you can get the Linux version from the academic edition of the product, which is located at www.microstation.com/academic/products/linux.htm. I haven't heard of this as freeware, so be prepared to make out a vendor's agreement.

VariCAD

Another piece of proprietary software you should check out in the CAD market is VariCAD. VariCAD is a slightly older product, but you can get full details and determine whether it is the product for you by visiting the company's Web site: www.varicad.com.

Databases

DBAs (database administrators) are well represented in the Linux world. As with other flavors of UNIX, Linux is a hot choice for data warehousing due to its lightweight processes and, more importantly, the inherent stability of Linux over Windows.

Sybase for Linux

Sybase, which has made strong inroads into certain industry niches like e-commerce and finance, is a popular choice for Linux systems. Though thoroughly proprietary (I doubt you'll find a freeware version of Sybase floating around on the Web), it's well worth your while to check out what's available for your site at Sybase's home page: www.sybase.com.

Oracle for Linux

Everything I've said about Sybase goes double for Oracle: It's a popular choice for UNIX/Linux systems, it's great in certain industry niches, and sure as anything, it's hard to find a freeware copy of Oracle sitting around! Still, go to the `www.oracle.com` Web site and you can start wending your way through the vendor mazes to get your favorite DBA a copy.

Web Browser: Netscape

Although I've already covered this topic in the book, let me again say that the Red Hat decision to incorporate Netscape on their install CD-ROM is hands down the best freebie in Linux. True, you can get Netscape free off the Web without Linux, but I appreciate the small convenience factor.

Netscape in Linux has the same look and feel as Netscape for Windows.

Chapter 31

Ten Web Sites Every Linux Administrator Should Know

*B*ecause Linux has such strong roots in the freeware area, the World Wide Web is fertile ground to find the latest and greatest improvements in the Linux world. This chapter is organized around four areas of Linux information on the Internet: new Linux software, Linux information, Linux administration, and Linux security.

Also, keep in mind that both Linux and the Web are evolving at an ever-increasing rate. Don't restrict yourself to just these sites! Make use of your favorite Internet search engine (Yahoo!, Excite, and so on) and search out the newest and most useful Linux pages for your own network.

Where to Get Linux Software

Here are several excellent online resources for Linux software.

www.linux.org/aps/index.html

This site contains an excellent list of Linux applications that you can locate and download for use on your system. Keep in mind that since most of these products are freeware and come from organizations which may not support the code, the term YMMV definitely applies!

For the acronym challenged: YMMV stands for Your Mileage May Vary. It's a nifty term for suggesting caution when installing Linux (or any software) product.

ftp://sunsite.unc.edu/pub/Linux

The Sunsite contains oodles of Linux software from Sun Microsystems. Though download times can be slow during business hours, your benefit is that most of the items from this site have at least gone through a basic QA process.

Okay, one more acronym: QA stands for Quality Assurance and will at the very least mean that your computer won't burst into flames when you install a given product.

www.freshmeat.org

This site is useful as a sort of action update on the ever-evolving state of Linux software creation. Very good updates on releases of Linux software.

General Linux Information

Okay, you've got every Linux book ever published. But you want to chat directly with other Linux types and get the latest scoop. Here's where to get even more Linux info.

www.slashdot.org/

A good connection to true Linux wizards. This is a discussion forum for Linux issues. If you have a question on Linux that you can't find the answer to through books, intuitive deduction, or reading tea leaves, post it here.

As with any discussion group, be polite. Exhaust other avenues first; massive posting of questions will only annoy other readers and may cause people to avoid your posts.

http://linuxtoday.com/

If you become a serious Linux administrator, make this site part of your daily reading. Breaking news on the Linux scene, with reasonable update times.

Linux Administration

Online resources can also provide a little bit of everything.

www.linuxberg.com/

Linuxberg is a sort of Wal-Mart of Linux information. They quite literally have a bit of everything on this site. Highly recommended. And no, I don't know where the Linuxberg name comes from.

www.redhat.com/

The Red Hat site should already be on your Bookmark list if you use any version of Red Hat Linux. In my opinion, the most useful page on this site is `www.redhat.com/support/docs/hardware.html`. This is a Linux hardware compatibility list, which is info that I haven't been able to locate elsewhere with as much up-to-date information.

www.replay.com

This site is a good archive of security programs and features. They're located outside the United States, so they don't need to obey cryptography restrictions on the export of "crypto programs."

Note that this freedom from restricted exports does NOT transfer to you, however.

Part X
Appendixes

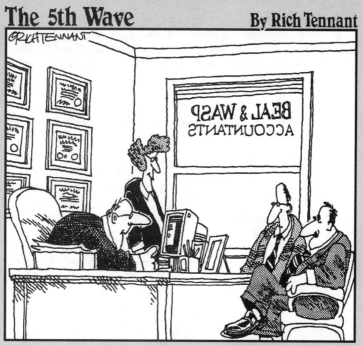

The 5th Wave   By Rich Tennant

BEAL & WASP ACCOUNTANTS

"OUR GOAL IS TO MAXIMIZE YOUR UPSIDE AND MINIMIZE YOUR DOWNSIDE WHILE WE PROTECT OUR OWN BACKSIDE."

In this part . . .

*P*art X offers you some resources for the future —
compilations of information that you'll find useful in
your daily job as a Linux system administrator. Specifically,
the included information gives you an edge on some immediately handy topics:

- ✔ The `vi` editor. Because `vi` is the mainstay of your
  Linux apprenticeship, you'll find this section a vital
  resource whenever you edit your files.

- ✔ A list of what you'll find on the included CD-ROM.
  We've packed the disc with hand-picked utilities
  to aid and abet your quest for ever-more-efficient
  administration. Better yet, you won't need to surf
  the Web to find them — just install them off the
  CD-ROM.

Appendix A

Vi Editor Commands: A Quick Summary

In This Appendix

▶ Moving around in vi

▶ Appending text

▶ Deleting text

▶ Text changes

▶ Copying

▶ Undo Last

▶ Writing and editing commands

The vi editor in Linux can be tricky. It's also amazingly complex — so much so that entire books have been written on it. For your basic administration needs, you'll rarely have to go beyond the command sets in this appendix.

TIP

Many people (mostly new users) complain that vi isn't very user friendly. Now that you have this guide, you can confidently reply the same way an old system administrator friend of mine does: "Vi isn't unfriendly to users . . . it's just very selective about who it likes!"

Table A-1	Vi Move Commands
Command Option	*What It Does*
h	Moves the cursor one character to the left.
j	Moves the cursor one line downward.
l	Moves the cursor one character to the right.
K	Moves the cursor one line upward.

(continued)

Table A-1 *(continued)*

Command Option	What It Does
$	Moves the cursor to the end of the current line.
^	Moves the cursor to the first CHAR of the line.
f<char>	Moves the cursor <char>s to the right (find).
F<char>	Moves the cursor <char>s to the left.
w	Moves the cursor words forward.
b	Moves the cursor words backward.
e	Moves the cursor forward to the end of the next word.
M	Moves the cursor to the middle line of the screen.
}	Moves the cursor a paragraph forward.
{	Moves the cursor a paragraph backward.
n	Repeats the last action.

Getting 100 percent from the percent sign

The % command in vi is one of the handiest tools when you're writing scripts or debugging someone else's code. The % sign finds the next curly bracket ({})and goes to its match when you press it again. This tool is useful because many programs use curly brackets to specify sections of code. A missing curly bracket (also called a French brace for no reason I can think of) can cause a whole script or program to go awry.

Table A-2   **Appending Commands**

Command Option	What It Does
a	Appends text after the cursor.
A	Appends text at the end of the line.
i	Inserts text before the cursor.
o	Opens a new line below the current one.
O	Opens a new line above the current one.

Table A-3	Deleting Commands
Command Option	*What It Does*
x	Deletes chars under and after the cursor.
X	Deletes chars before the cursor.
dd	Deletes an entire line.
D	Deletes the rest of the line after the cursor.
:[x,y]d	Deletes lines x through y.

Table A-4	Text Change Commands
Command Option	*What It Does*
r<char>	Replaces one character with another.
R	Overwrites the rest of the line.
s	Substitutes < > chars.
S	Substitutes < > lines.
c<move>	Changes from beginning to endpoint of < >.
C	Changes the rest of the line and < > - 1 next lines.

Table A-5	Copy Text Commands
Command Option	*What It Does*
y<move>	Yanks (Linux-speak for copying from beginning to endpoint of < >.
yy	Yanks < > lines.
m<a-z>	Marks the cursor position with a letter.

Table A-6	Undo Commands
Command Option	**What It Does**
u	Undoes the latest change.
U	Undoes all changes on a line.
:u	Undoes the last substitution on the line.
:q!	Quits vi without writing (Linux-speak for saving).
:e!	Reedits file. Useful if you've accidentally added or deleted lines from a file.

Note that U only works if you *haven't moved off the line yet!*

Table A-7	Writing & Editing Commands
Command Option	**What It Does**
:q	Quits vi.
:q!	Quits vi without writing.
:w	Writes to the file.
:w <name>	Writes to the file with a different filename.
:w >> <name>	Appends your changes to the file <name>.
:w! <name>	Overwrites the file <name>.
:x,y w <name>	Writes lines x through y to the file <name>.
:wq	Writes to the file and quits vi.

Appendix B

About the CD

On the CD-ROM:

▶ Tripwire, the standard in Linux network security today

▶ ACUA, an alternate interface program for Linux

▶ Diskcheck, a useful utility to protect and warn you about disk errors

▶ Logwatch, which automatically monitors your various system logs for errors or security breaches

▶ Mon, a program that monitors your system's performance

▶ Linuxconf, a program that makes configuring your Linux box easier

▶ WebMin, a Webmaster utility to run a Web server from your Linux box

To use the CD that accompanies this book, make sure your computer meets the minimum system requirements listed below.

System Requirements

✔ A PC with a 486 or faster processor, or a Mac OS computer with a 68030 or faster processor.

✔ Microsoft Windows 3.1 or later, or Mac OS system software 7.5 or later.

✔ At least 8MB of total RAM installed on your computer.

For best performance, we recommend that Windows 95-equipped PCs and Mac OS computers with PowerPC processors have at least 16MB of RAM installed.

✔ At least 150 MB of hard drive space available to install all the software from this CD. (You'll need less hard drive space if you don't install every program.)

✔ A CD-ROM drive — double-speed (2x) or faster.

✔ A sound card for PCs. (Mac OS computers have built-in sound support.)

✔ A monitor capable of displaying at least 256 colors or grayscale.

✔ A modem with a speed of at least 14,400 bps.

If you need more information on the basics, check out *PCs For Dummies,* 6th Edition, by Dan Gookin; *Macs For Dummies,* 6th Edition, by David Pogue; *Windows 98 For Dummies, Windows 95 For Dummies,* or *Windows 3.11 For Dummies,* 4th Edition, all by Andy Rathbone (all above books published by IDG Books Worldwide, Inc.).

For more basic Linux information, you can also check out *Linux For Dummies,* 2nd Edition, by Jon "Maddog" Hall.

If your computer doesn't match up to most of these requirements, you may have problems using the contents of the CD.

Accessing the CD

This CD is designed to be accessed with either a Windows system or a Linux system.

Linux

1. **Insert the CD into your computer's CD-ROM drive.**

   Give your computer a moment to take a look at the CD.

2. **When the light on your CD-ROM drive goes out, go to the command prompt and type** `mount -t iso9660 /dev/cdrom /mnt/cdrom`, **then press Enter.**

3. **Type** `cd /mnt/cdrom`, **then press Enter.**

4. **Type** `ls`.

   This step lists the files from the CD.

Windows 95 or 98

1. **Insert the CD into your computer's CD-ROM drive.**

   Give your computer a moment to take a look at the CD.

2. **When the light on your CD-ROM drive goes out, double click on the**

My Computer icon (It's probably in the top left corner of your desk-top.)

This action opens the My Computer window, which shows you all the drives attached to your computer, the Control Panel, and a couple other handy things.

3. Double click on the icon for your CD-ROM drive.

Another window opens, showing you all the folders and files on the CD.

Using the CD

This CD is designed to be accessed with either a Windows system or a Linux system.

Linux

1. To view the licenses in their respective directories, type vi **and the file name of the license (either gpl.txt or IDG_EULA.txt).**

This file contains the end-user license that you agree to by using the CD. In Linux, the most convenient way to read this file is to use the vi editor. When you are done reading the license, exit the program by pressing Esc, then typing :q!.

2. Use the cp **command to copy the program you want to run from the** /cdrom **directory to where you want to store it.**

For example, if you want to copy mon from /cdrom to your /etc directory, enter cp mon /etc

3. Use the cd **command to change directories to the directory you placed the program.**

For example, if mon is in the /etc directory, you should type the following to get to the /etc directory: cd /etc

4. Type the name of the program you want to run, then press Enter.

On some systems, Linux may claim that it can't find the program. If it acts this way, it's just being fussy. Type a period and a slash in front of the program you want to start, then press Enter. This tells Linux that you want this specific program, right in the current directory.

Windows 95 or 98

In each of the folders you will find a file that contains the license agreement for that particular software. The file names are either gpl.txt (General Public License) or IDG_Eula.txt. These files contain the licenses that you agree to by using the CD. When you are done reading each license, close the program (most likely NotePad) that displayed the file.

1. **Double-click the file called Readme.txt.**

   This file contains instructions about installing the software from this CD. It can be helpful to leave this text file open while you are using the CD.

2. **Double click the folder for the software you are interested in.**

   Be sure to read the descriptions of the programs in the next section of this appendix (much of this information also shows up in the Readme file). These descriptions will give you more precise information about the programs' folder names, and about finding and running the installer program.

What You'll Find

Here's a summary of the software on this CD arranged by category.

Note that all of these products are either freeware (after all, this is Linux), or on certain extended releases of the Red Hat CD-ROM. In cases where a vendor is either not available or the product is too limited for a vendor to maintain it with regular updates, no Web site information will be listed. In this case, you can either track the product down from the Red Hat Web site, do a Web search/newsgroup request to get the product, extract it from a Red Hat CD-ROM, or pull it from the CD-ROM accompanying this book.

Linux security

Tripwire

For Linux Systems and Windows Machines Running Linux. Tripwire is an excellent add-on to your Linux system due to its good security coverage and lightweight processes. Most Red Hat and other recent releases of Linux have this utility bundled in.

Logwatch

For Linux Systems and Windows Machines Running Linux. Logwatch, which automatically monitors your various systems logs for errors or security breaches. An excellent add-on to your Linux system due to its good security coverage and lightweight processes.

Linux networking

Webmin

For Linux Systems and Windows Machines Running Linux. Webmin is a Webmaster utility to run a Web server from your Linux box. You can get more information on how to use the product from `http://www.webmin.com/webmin` and download updated versions of this application from `ftp://ftp.webmin.com/webmin-0.71.tar.gz`.

Linuxconf

For Linux Systems and Windows Machines Running Linux. Linuxconf is a program that makes configuring your Linux box easier for network and printer connections. You can get more information on how to use the product and download updated versions of this application from `www.solucorp.qc.ca/linuxconf`.

Linux administration

ACUA

For Linux Systems and Windows Machines Running Linux. ACUA is an administration tool that focuses on user administration and automates many of the user-related administration tasks such as account creation and freezing. It also will increase your level of security by enforcing a changing password system (detailed in Chapter 23).

You can get more information on how to use the product at and download updated versions of this application at the following Web site: `http://acua.gist.net.au/2.0/index.html`.

Diskcheck

For Linux Systems and Windows Machines Running Linux. Diskcheck runs hourly (unless you configure it otherwise) in the background and warns you if you're running low on disk space or are prone to other developing problems.

Mon

For Linux Systems and Windows Machines Running Linux. Mon is a program that monitors your system's network and application performance. You can get more information on how to use the product at and get updated versions of this application from: `ftp://ftp.kernel.org/pub/software/admin/mon`.

If You've Got Problems (Of the CD Kind)

I tried my best to compile programs that work on most computers with the minimum system requirements. Alas, your computer may differ, and some programs may not work properly for some reason.

The two likeliest problems are:

- ✔ You don't have enough memory (RAM) for the programs you want to use.
- ✔ You have other programs running that are affecting installation or running of a program.

If you get error messages like Not enough memory or Setup cannot continue, try one or more of these methods and then try using the software again:

- ✔ Turn off any antivirus software that you have on your computer. Installers sometimes mimic virus activity and may make your computer incorrectly believe that it is being infected by a virus.

- ✔ Close all running programs. The more programs you're running, the less memory is available to other programs. Installers also typically update files and programs. So if you keep other programs running, installation may not work properly.

- ✔ Have your local computer store add more RAM to your computer.

  This is, admittedly, a drastic and somewhat expensive step. However, if you have a Windows 95 PC or a Mac OS computer with a PowerPC chip, adding more memory can really help the speed of your computer and allow more programs to run at the same time. This may include closing the CD interface and running a product's installation program from Windows Explorer.

If you still have trouble with installing the items from the CD, please call the IDG Books Worldwide Customer Service phone number: 800-762-2974 (outside the U.S.: 317-596-5430).

Index

(continued)

• S •

(continued)

Notes

Notes

GNU GENERAL PUBLIC LICENSE

TERMS AND CONDITIONS FOR COPYING, DISTRIBUTION AND MODIFICATION

0. This License applies to any program or other work which contains a notice placed by the copyright holder saying it may be distributed under the terms of this General Public License. The "Program", below, refers to any such program or work, and a "work based on the Program" means either the Program or any derivative work under copyright law: that is to say, a work containing the Program or a portion of it, either verbatim or with modifications and/or translated into another language. (Hereinafter, translation is included without limitation in the term "modification".) Each licensee is addressed as "you". Activities other than copying, distribution and modification are not covered by this License; they are outside its scope. The act of running the Program is not restricted, and the output from the Program is covered only if its contents constitute a work based on the Program (independent of having been made by running the Program). Whether that is true depends on what the Program does.

1. You may copy and distribute verbatim copies of the Program's source code as you receive it, in any medium, provided that you conspicuously and appropriately publish on each copy an appropriate copyright notice and disclaimer of warranty; keep intact all the notices that refer to this License and to the absence of any warranty; and give any other recipients of the Program a copy of this License along with the Program. You may charge a fee for the physical act of transferring a copy, and you may at your option offer warranty protection in exchange for a fee.

2. You may modify your copy or copies of the Program or any portion of it, thus forming a work based on the Program, and copy and distribute such modifications or work under the terms of Section 1 above, provided that you also meet all of these conditions:

a) You must cause the modified files to carry prominent notices stating that you changed the files and the date of any change.

b) You must cause any work that you distribute or publish, that in whole or in part contains or is derived from the Program or any part thereof, to be licensed as a whole at no charge to all third parties under the terms of this License.

c) If the modified program normally reads commands interactively when run, you must cause it, when started running for such interactive use in the most ordinary way, to print or display an announcement including an appropriate copyright notice and a notice that there is no warranty (or else, saying that you provide a warranty) and that users may redistribute the program under these conditions, and telling the user how to view a copy of this License. (Exception: if the Program itself is interactive but does not normally print such an announcement, your work based on the Program is not required to print an announcement.)

These requirements apply to the modified work as a whole. If identifiable sections of that work are not derived from the Program, and can be reasonably considered independent and separate works in themselves, then this License, and its terms, do not apply to those sections when you distribute them as separate works. But when you distribute the same sections as part of a whole which is a work based on the Program, the distribution of the whole must be on the terms of this License, whose permissions for other licensees extend to the entire whole, and thus to each and every part regardless of who wrote it. Thus, it is not the intent of this section to claim rights or contest your rights to work written entirely by you; rather, the intent is to exercise the right to control the distribution of derivative or collective works based on the Program. In addition, mere aggregation of another work not based on the Program with the Program (or with a work based on the Program) on a volume of a storage or distribution medium does not bring the other work under the scope of this License.

3. You may copy and distribute the Program (or a work based on it, under Section 2) in object code or executable form under the terms of Sections 1 and 2 above provided that you also do one of the following: a) Accompany it with the complete corresponding machine-readable source code, which must be distributed under the terms of Sections 1 and 2 above on a medium customarily used for software interchange; or, b) Accompany it with a written offer, valid for at least three years, to give any third party, for a charge no more than your cost of physically performing source distribution, a complete machine-readable copy of the corresponding source code, to be distributed under the terms of Sections 1 and 2 above on a medium customarily used for software interchange; or, c) Accompany it with the information you received as to the offer to distribute corresponding source code. (This alternative is allowed only for noncommercial distribution and only if you received the program in object code or executable form with such an offer, in accord with Subsection b above.) The source code for a work means the preferred form of the work for making modifications to it. For an executable work, complete source code means all the source code for all modules it contains, plus any associated interface definition files, plus the scripts used to control compilation and installation of the executable. However, as a special exception, the source code distributed need not include anything that is normally distributed (in either source or binary form) with the major components (compiler, kernel, and so on) of the operating system on which the executable runs, unless that component itself accompanies the executable. If distribution of executable or object code is made by offering access to copy from a designated place, then offering equivalent access to copy the source code from the same place counts as distribution of the source code, even though third parties are not compelled to copy the source along with the object code.

4. You may not copy, modify, sublicense, or distribute the Program except as expressly provided under this License. Any attempt otherwise to copy, modify, sublicense or distribute the Program is void, and will automatically terminate your rights under this License. However, parties who have received copies, or rights, from you under this License will not have their licenses terminated so long as such parties remain in full compliance.

5. You are not required to accept this License, since you have not signed it. However, nothing else grants you permission to modify or distribute the Program or its derivative works. These actions are prohibited by law if you do not accept this License. Therefore, by modifying or distributing the Program (or any work based on the Program), you indicate your acceptance of this License to do so, and all its terms and conditions for copying, distributing or modifying the Program or works based on it.

6. Each time you redistribute the Program (or any work based on the Program), the recipient automatically receives a license from the original licensor to copy, distribute or modify the Program subject to these terms and conditions. You may not impose any further restrictions on the recipients' exercise of the rights granted herein. You are not responsible for enforcing compliance by third parties to this License.

7. If, as a consequence of a court judgment or allegation of patent infringement or for any other reason (not limited to patent issues), conditions are imposed on you (whether by court order, agreement or otherwise) that contradict the conditions of this License, they do not excuse you from the conditions of this License. If you cannot distribute so as to satisfy simultaneously your obligations under this License and any other pertinent obligations, then as a consequence you may not distribute the Program at all. For example, if a patent license would not permit royalty-free redistribution of the Program by all those who receive copies directly or indirectly through you, then the only way you could satisfy both it and this License would be to refrain entirely from distribution of the Program. If any portion of this section is held invalid or unenforceable under any particular circumstance, the balance of the section is intended to apply and the section as a whole is intended to apply in other circumstances. It is not the purpose of this section to induce you to infringe any patents or other property right claims or to contest validity of any such claims; this section has the sole purpose of protecting the integrity of the free software distribution system, which is implemented by public license practices. Many people have made generous contributions to the wide range of software distributed through that system in reliance on consistent application of that system; it is up to the author/donor to decide if he or she is willing to distribute software through any other system and a licensee cannot impose that choice. This section is intended to make thoroughly clear what is believed to be a consequence of the rest of this License.

8. If the distribution and/or use of the Program is restricted in certain countries either by patents or by copyrighted interfaces, the original copyright holder who places the Program under this License may add an explicit geographical distribution limitation excluding those countries, so that distribution is permitted only in or among countries not thus excluded. In such case, this License incorporates the limitation as if written in the body of this License.

9. The Free Software Foundation may publish revised and/or new versions of the General Public License from time to time. Such new versions will be similar in spirit to the present version, but may differ in detail to address new problems or concerns. Each version is given a distinguishing version number. If the Program specifies a version number of this License which applies to it and "any later version", you have the option of following the terms and conditions either of that version or of any later version published by the Free Software Foundation. If the Program does not specify a version number of this License, you may choose any version ever published by the Free Software Foundation.

10. If you wish to incorporate parts of the Program into other free programs whose distribution conditions are different, write to the author to ask for permission. For software which is copyrighted by the Free Software Foundation, write to the Free Software Foundation; we sometimes make exceptions for this. Our decision will be guided by the two goals of preserving the free status of all derivatives of our free software and of promoting the sharing and reuse of software generally.

NO WARRANTY

11. BECAUSE THE PROGRAM IS LICENSED FREE OF CHARGE, THERE IS NO WARRANTY FOR THE PROGRAM, TO THE EXTENT PERMITTED BY APPLICABLE LAW. EXCEPT WHEN OTHERWISE STATED IN WRITING THE COPYRIGHT HOLDERS AND/OR OTHER PARTIES PROVIDE THE PROGRAM "AS IS" WITHOUT WARRANTY OF ANY KIND, EITHER EXPRESSED OR IMPLIED, INCLUDING, BUT NOT LIMITED TO, THE IMPLIED WARRANTIES OF MERCHANTABILITY AND FITNESS FOR A PARTICULAR PURPOSE. THE ENTIRE RISK AS TO THE QUALITY AND PERFORMANCE OF THE PROGRAM IS WITH YOU. SHOULD THE PROGRAM PROVE DEFECTIVE, YOU ASSUME THE COST OF ALL NECESSARY SERVICING, REPAIR OR CORRECTION.

12. IN NO EVENT UNLESS REQUIRED BY APPLICABLE LAW OR AGREED TO IN WRITING WILL ANY COPYRIGHT HOLDER, OR ANY OTHER PARTY WHO MAY MODIFY AND/OR REDISTRIBUTE THE PROGRAM AS PERMITTED ABOVE, BE LIABLE TO YOU FOR DAMAGES, INCLUDING ANY GENERAL, SPECIAL, INCIDENTAL OR CONSEQUENTIAL DAMAGES ARISING OUT OF THE USE OR INABILITY TO USE THE PROGRAM (INCLUDING BUT NOT LIMITED TO LOSS OF DATA OR DATA BEING RENDERED INACCURATE OR LOSSES SUSTAINED BY YOU OR THIRD PARTIES OR A FAILURE OF THE PROGRAM TO OPERATE WITH ANY OTHER PROGRAMS), EVEN IF SUCH HOLDER OR OTHER PARTY HAS BEEN ADVISED OF THE POSSIBILITY OF SUCH DAMAGES.

IDG Books Worldwide, Inc., End-User License Agreement

READ THIS. You should carefully read these terms and conditions before opening the software packet(s) included with this book ("Book"). This is a license agreement ("Agreement") between you and IDG Books Worldwide, Inc. ("IDGB"). By opening the accompanying software packet(s), you acknowledge that you have read and accept the following terms and conditions. If you do not agree and do not want to be bound by such terms and conditions, promptly return the Book and the unopened software packet(s) to the place you obtained them for a full refund.

1. **License Grant.** IDGB grants to you (either an individual or entity) a nonexclusive license to use one copy of the enclosed software program(s) (collectively, the "Software") solely for your own personal or business purposes on a single computer (whether a standard computer or a workstation component of a multiuser network). The Software is in use on a computer when it is loaded into temporary memory (RAM) or installed into permanent memory (hard disk, CD-ROM, or other storage device). IDGB reserves all rights not expressly granted herein.

2. **Ownership.** IDGB is the owner of all right, title, and interest, including copyright, in and to the compilation of the Software recorded on the disk(s) or CD-ROM ("Software Media"). Copyright to the individual programs recorded on the Software Media is owned by the author or other authorized copyright owner of each program. Ownership of the Software and all proprietary rights relating thereto remain with IDGB and its licensers.

3. **Restrictions on Use and Transfer.**

   (a) You may only (i) make one copy of the Software for backup or archival purposes, or (ii) transfer the Software to a single hard disk, provided that you keep the original for backup or archival purposes. You may not (i) rent or lease the Software, (ii) copy or reproduce the Software through a LAN or other network system or through any computer subscriber system or bulletin-board system, or (iii) modify, adapt, or create derivative works based on the Software.

   (b) You may not reverse engineer, decompile, or disassemble the Software. You may transfer the Software and user documentation on a permanent basis, provided that the transferee agrees to accept the terms and conditions of this Agreement and you retain no copies. If the Software is an update or has been updated, any transfer must include the most recent update and all prior versions.

4. **Restrictions on Use of Individual Programs.** You must follow the individual requirements and restrictions detailed for each individual program in the "About the CD" section of this Book. These limitations are also contained in the individual license agreements recorded on the Software Media. These limitations may include a requirement that after using the program for a specified period of time, the user must pay a registration fee or discontinue use. By opening the Software packet(s), you will be agreeing to abide by the licenses and restrictions for these individual programs that are detailed in the "About the CD" section and on the Software Media. None of the material on this Software Media or listed in this Book may ever be redistributed, in original or modified form, for commercial purposes.

5. **Limited Warranty.**

   (a) IDGB warrants that the Software and Software Media are free from defects in materials and workmanship under normal use for a period of sixty (60) days from the date of purchase of this Book. If IDGB receives notification within the warranty period of defects in materials or workmanship, IDGB will replace the defective Software Media.

   (b) IDGB AND THE AUTHOR OF THE BOOK DISCLAIM ALL OTHER WARRANTIES, EXPRESS OR IMPLIED, INCLUDING WITHOUT LIMITATION IMPLIED WARRANTIES OF MERCHANTABILITY AND FITNESS FOR A PARTICULAR PURPOSE, WITH RESPECT TO THE SOFTWARE, THE PROGRAMS, THE SOURCE CODE CONTAINED THEREIN, AND/OR THE TECHNIQUES DESCRIBED IN THIS BOOK. IDGB DOES NOT WARRANT THAT THE FUNCTIONS CONTAINED IN THE SOFTWARE WILL MEET YOUR REQUIREMENTS OR THAT THE OPERATION OF THE SOFTWARE WILL BE ERROR FREE.

   (c) This limited warranty gives you specific legal rights, and you may have other rights that vary from jurisdiction to jurisdiction.

6. **Remedies.**

   (a) IDGB's entire liability and your exclusive remedy for defects in materials and workmanship shall be limited to replacement of the Software Media, which may be returned to IDGB with a copy of your receipt at the following address: Software Media Fulfillment Department, Attn.: *Linux Administration For Dummies*, IDG Books Worldwide, Inc., 7260 Shadeland Station, Ste. 100, Indianapolis, IN 46256, or call 800-762-2974. Please allow three to four weeks for delivery. This Limited Warranty is void if failure of the Software Media has resulted from accident, abuse, or misapplication. Any replacement Software Media will be warranted for the remainder of the original warranty period or thirty (30) days, whichever is longer.

   (b) In no event shall IDGB or the author be liable for any damages whatsoever (including without limitation damages for loss of business profits, business interruption, loss of business information, or any other pecuniary loss) arising from the use of or inability to use the Book or the Software, even if IDGB has been advised of the possibility of such damages.

   (c) Because some jurisdictions do not allow the exclusion or limitation of liability for consequential or incidental damages, the above limitation or exclusion may not apply to you.

7. **U.S. Government Restricted Rights.** Use, duplication, or disclosure of the Software by the U.S. Government is subject to restrictions stated in paragraph (c)(1)(ii) of the Rights in Technical Data and Computer Software clause of DFARS 252.227-7013, and in subparagraphs (a) through (d) of the Commercial Computer–Restricted Rights clause at FAR 52.227-19, and in similar clauses in the NASA FAR supplement, when applicable.

8. **General.** This Agreement constitutes the entire understanding of the parties and revokes and supersedes all prior agreements, oral or written, between them and may not be modified or amended except in a writing signed by both parties hereto that specifically refers to this Agreement. This Agreement shall take precedence over any other documents that may be in conflict herewith. If any one or more provisions contained in this Agreement are held by any court or tribunal to be invalid, illegal, or otherwise unenforceable, each and every other provision shall remain in full force and effect.

Installation Instructions

This CD is designed to be accessed with either a Windows system or a Linux system.

Linux

1. **To view the licenses in their respective directories, type vi and the file name of the license (either gpl.txt or IDG_EULA.txt).**

   This file contains the end-user license that you agree to by using the CD. In Linux, the most convenient way to read this file is to use the vi editor. When you are done reading the license, exit the program by pressing Esc, then typing `:q!`.

2. **Use the `cp` command to copy the program you want to run from the `/cdrom` directory to where you want to store it.**

3. **Use the `cd` command to change directories to the directory you placed the program.**

4. **Type the name of the program you want to run, then press Enter.**

   On some systems, you neet to type a period and a slash in front of the program you want to start, then press Enter. This tells Linux that you want this specific program, right in the current directory.

Windows

In each of the folders you will find a file that contains the license agreement for that particular software. The file names are either gpl.txt (General Public License) or IDG_Eula.txt. These files contain the licenses that you agree to by using the CD. When you are done reading each license, close the program (most likely NotePad) that displayed the file.

1. **Double-click the file called Readme.txt.**

   This file contains instructions about installing the software from this CD. It can be helpful to leave this text file open while you are using the CD.

2. **Double click the folder for the software you are interested in.**

3. **Copy the software to your hard drive; follow its Readme instructions.**

WWW.DUMMIES.COM

YOUR ONLINE RESOURCE

Discover Dummies Online!

The Dummies Web Site is your fun and friendly online resource for the latest information about ...*For Dummies*® books and your favorite topics. The Web site is the place to communicate with us, exchange ideas with other ...*For Dummies* readers, chat with authors, and have fun!

Ten Fun and Useful Things You Can Do at www.dummies.com

1. Win free ...*For Dummies* books and more!
2. Register your book and be entered in a prize drawing.
3. Meet your favorite authors through the IDG Books Author Chat Series.
4. Exchange helpful information with other ...*For Dummies* readers.
5. Discover other great ...*For Dummies* books you must have!
6. Purchase Dummieswear™ exclusively from our Web site.
7. Buy ...*For Dummies* books online.
8. Talk to us. Make comments, ask questions, get answers!
9. Download free software.
10. Find additional useful resources from authors.

Link directly to these ten fun and useful things at
http://www.dummies.com/10useful

SURF THE NET

WWW.DUMMIES.COM

For other technology titles from IDG Books Worldwide, go to
www.idgbooks.com

Not on the Web yet? It's easy to get started with *Dummies 101*®: *The Internet For Windows*®*98* or *The Internet For Dummies*®, 6th Edition, at local retailers everywhere.

IDG BOOKS WORLDWIDE

Find other ...*For Dummies* books on these topics:
Business • Career • Databases • Food & Beverage • Games • Gardening • Graphics • Hardware
Health & Fitness • Internet and the World Wide Web • Networking • Office Suites
Operating Systems • Personal Finance • Pets • Programming • Recreation • Sports
Spreadsheets • Teacher Resources • Test Prep • Word Processing

IDG BOOKS WORLDWIDE BOOK REGISTRATION

We want to hear from you!

Visit **http://my2cents.dummies.com** to register this book and tell us how you liked it!

- Get entered in our monthly prize giveaway.

- Give us feedback about this book — tell us what you like best, what you like least, or maybe what you'd like to ask the author and us to change!

- Let us know any other *...For Dummies*® topics that interest you.

Your feedback helps us determine what books to publish, tells us what coverage to add as we revise our books, and lets us know whether we're meeting your needs as a *...For Dummies* reader. You're our most valuable resource, and what you have to say is important to us!

Not on the Web yet? It's easy to get started with *Dummies 101*®*: The Internet For Windows*® *98* or *The Internet For Dummies*®, 6th Edition, at local retailers everywhere.

Or let us know what you think by sending us a letter at the following address:

...For Dummies Book Registration
Dummies Press
7260 Shadeland Station, Suite 100
Indianapolis, IN 46256-3917
Fax 317-596-5498

BESTSELLING
BOOK SERIES